African Theatre for Development

Art for self-determination

Edited by
Kamal Salhi

intellect™

ExETER, ENGLAND

First Published in 1998 by
Intellect Books
School of Art and Design, Earl Richards Road North, Exeter EX2 6AS

Copy Editor:	Lucy Kind
Cover Design:	Amanda Brown
Production:	Valerie Massicot
	Sophia Dartzali

A catalogue record for this book is available from the British Library

ISBN 1-871516-77-3

Printed and bound in Great Britain by 4edge Ltd, Hockley. www.4edge.co.uk

Contents

Acknowledgements   iv

Introduction   1

1. Neither 'Fixed Masterpiece' nor 'Popular Distraction':
   voice, transformation and encounter
   in Theatre for Development   5
   Frances Harding

2. Product or Process: Theatre for Development
   in Africa   23
   Osita Okagbu

3. Didactic Showmen: Theatre for Development in
   Contemporary South Africa   43
   Page Laws

4. Post-Colonial Theatre for Development in Algeria:
   Kateb Yacine's early experience   69
   Kamal Salhi

5. Uses and Abuses of Theatre for Development:
   political struggle and development theatre
   in the Ethiopia – Eritrea war   97
   Jane Plastow

6. Satires in Theatre for Development Practice
   in Tanzania   115
   Juma Adamu Bakari

7. **Popular Theatre and Development Communication in West Africa: paradigms, processes and prospects**   **135**
Bala A. Musa

8. **Werewere Liking and the Development of Ritual Theatre in Cameroon: towards a new feminine theatre for Africa**   **155**
Valerie Orlando

9. **Women Playwrights and Performers respond to the project of development**   **175**
Laura Box

Acknowledgements

My thanks go to Professor Martin Banham and Dr Jane Plastow, both from the University of Leeds, and Professor Peter Thomson and Leslie du S. Read, both from the University of Exeter. They graciously offered unstinting encouragement throughout the period of the preparation of this book.

I should also like to thank the Department of Drama at Exeter University for offering me a long stay as a research fellow and the British Academy for the three-year scholarship without which my research would have not been possible.

I moved to the University of Leeds as a lecturer in the school of Modern Languages and Cultures where, among other projects, I have been able to finalise this publication thanks to the understanding of the French Department.

My thanks go to all those who sent their contributions but, because of time constraints, could not have been included in this particular project. This book has been made possible thanks to the following unfailing colleagues: Frances Harding, Osita Okagbu, Page Laws, Juma Adamu Bakari, Bala A. Musa, Valerie Orlando and Laura Box, all scholars developing expertise in the areas they discuss in the respective chapters of this book.

This book is in memory of those African artists, writers and dramatists who strived to contribute to their peoples' liberation and Independence. They died while hoping for more or were assassinated because they possessed the key to their nation's future.

Introduction

Kamal Salhi

This is not a history of African Theatre for Development. My concern is to indicate the scope of this theatre, to discuss its purpose and indeed to indicate the directions in which this particular type of theatre is moving.

While writing the chapters of this book, I appreciated the common concern and mutual understanding of my co-authors and their attempts to supply a set of perspectives that I intend to develop here. A general study does not necessarily preclude more specialised studies. However, I wanted to design this book as a cohesive force to help the reader understand what Theatre for Development might be and how it works within the framework of post-Independence Africa. Even if I loaded an entire encyclopaedia onto Theatre for Development, I would first have to determine what to include and what was not relevant to my primary interest and inquiry. Here I deal with the Theatre for Development as an art form consisting of works written for the stage – indoors or outdoors – intended to be performed, and which correspond to the fundamental needs of social groups. Because, in the final analysis, Theatre for Development should be alive to the needs of people in advance, it should suggest the framework for the society of the future. African artists and theatre practitioners understand these needs and respond to them.

There are two reasons why this study is needed. First is the general ignorance about African Theatre for Development, in University circles and even among theatre scholars. Second, since Africa has passed through the colonial experience, since a pattern of euphoria and disillusionment has been common to the independent nations, and since all African countries share the same stresses between the traditional and the modern ways of life, generalisations are still possible.

This study covers different regions of Africa. North Africa may be said to have quite different customs and traditional beliefs from those of most of the rest of Africa. There has been a good deal of influence from the Arab countries across the Sahara and down the East coast of Africa but, since Islam is antagonistic to drama, this has not led to the same intensity of theatrical developments as in the rest of the continent. Chapter Four is, in a way, an attempt to question this thesis. The absence of a strong theatre tradition in some parts of North Africa cannot be explained by the fact that Islam does not allow it. Nor can the prohibition of the image as representation be a convincing argument as it is not the Quran which forbids it, but the Islamic tradition or the *Hadith*. This distinction is important because it strengthens the hypothesis that it is a social/historical reality rather than a dogma. The prohibition of pictoral representation was a way to affirm the new religion in relation to the pre-Islamic era. God had to be imposed as a Spirit. This prohibition does not have a dogmatic character but rather an ideological or 'pedagogical' one. An impulse behind Chapter Four and Chapter Nine is the conviction that North African dramatic practice from 1970 to the present, is a significant response to this critical debate. Both chapters argue how the 'official' national theatre failed to address the nation in any way that could be seen genuinely as an art for self-determination especially in the light of the post-colonial theatre of Kateb Yacine and the more recent performance of Fadela Assous. Their theatre has played a vital role in all social, political and national concerns. It has also served as a fertile work place for prominent dramatists. Chapters Four and Nine discuss the theatre as a potential art for development and analyse those dramatists' theatrical endeavours in post-colonial North Africa.

Within Sub-Saharan Africa, Ethiopia and the Republic of South Africa may not have shared the typical experience of the succession of colonialism and Independence. In South Africa, European settlement was earlier and heavier than elsewhere and the disruption of traditional African culture was greater. Chapter Three considers the recent history and current status of Theatre for Development in South Africa. In five sections, this chapter discusses a variety of aspects ranging from the didactic nature of Theatre for Development through the extended definitions of the terms often associated with and applied to performance practices, to the perspectives on the future of South African theatre. Chapter Five offers an example of the differences that have resulted in the Ethiopia-Eritrea war, while elsewhere on the continent nationalist movements have championed traditional values, as an assertion of the African's right to a greater role in society. In that, governments often justify their domination in the modern society. This chapter draws upon Ethiopia-Eritrea where theatrical experience matches that of the rest of Africa. It is about theatre as a means of empowering and the 'relationships between propaganda imperatives and popular theatre initiatives'. It also investigates the relationship between 'political freedoms and the development of theatres of empowerment'.

An understanding of the traditions in East African theatre and dramatic literature are fundamental in providing a context where the developing art can envision new possibilities, and perhaps new theatres. Chapter Six explains how Theatre for Development in Tanzania can be seen not only as an effective, but also as an appropriate medium of communication in community development. The problem of how to practise this theatre is argued in the light of the opinion that 'the people [are] being robbed of the opportunity to voice their own concerns and do their own thinking'. Viewed and analysed through specific examples, the theatre in Tanzania records, signals and effects changes in the culture. It fosters an understanding in the community which accommodates the theatre's artistic, educational, social, moral, spiritual and political aspects. While entertainment value is a significant portion of the theatrical event in Tanzania and cannot be overlooked, Chapter Six brings in an understanding that the theatre should be utilised to encourage constructive changes in the society. Examples in this chapter show the extent to which the dominant authorities can be offended and how artists directly confront the ruling authorities.

In Central Africa, dramatic experiences have affected the people of Cameroon and new theatrical trends include women dramatists who have not been merely transient and who reflect African consciousness on stage. Chapter Eight explores the theatre work of Werewere Liking and her post-modern agenda. It argues that the francophone dramatist 'has fought an uphill battle both because of her gender and her un-orthodox dramatic style to tackle post-modern questions'. In her theatre practice there is preference to adopt a product as the main objective of theatre and which looks to the future. The theatrical process necessarily implies an interaction between the different means of expression in traditional rituals, that is body, voice, space and objects, and images of character in fictional situations. The chapter concludes that Werewere 'seeks to bring to the dramatic world the beauty of what she describes as both the spirituality and the physical plenitude of life that are inherent in every culture'. As such she forces her audience to review preconceived ideas of postcolonialism and promotes a new African theatre practice.

Due to geographical factors and the influence of trading with more technologically advanced societies, West Africa becomes more complex and social role more diversified than where there was perhaps only a struggle to subsist. Artistic invention seems to be pre-eminent in both traditional and literary drama. It is worth noting that West Africa has had an initial advantage in the development of drama based on European models, since this region was the first part of Africa to be colonised. Chapter Seven explores the intersect between dramatic arts and development communication theories. Chapter Two examines the different programmes and practices of Theatre for Development. Both sections undertake a critique of the traditional role of popular theatre as a means of expression, conscientisation, empowerment and mobilisation of the largely silent majority in West Africa. Examples of how theatre has functioned as a tool for social change in Ghana, Togo, Burkina Faso, Mali, Nigeria and other West African countries are discussed. By keeping the focus on trends in West African theatre and communication, and by analysing the gradual shifts in structure, themes, roles and even audiences of that popular theatre, Chapter Seven argues that basic assumptions about the intuitive relationship between popular theatre and participatory development at grassroots level need to be re-examined in the light of changes that are transforming the communication industry in the region, including theatre. The argument also takes from the influences and political patronage, the various constraints of new world and the compelling urge to reach a global audience. While folk artists, especially those who perform in native languages, try to keep in touch with world view and address local problems such as illiteracy, injustice, hygiene and poverty, those who write or perform for national audiences often succumb to the temptation to borrow foreign styles and themes. Chapter Two discusses an experimental programme and shows whether 'the various theories, methodologies and practices have succeeded or failed in achieving the basic objective of Theatre for Development'.

Chapter One provides the necessary background focusing specifically on the definitions of and approaches to Theatre for Development and its 'identities'. In fact, it elaborates the theoretical ramifications of the book's focus. Indeed, it is also an attempt to provide a framework in which the subsequent discussions are formulated. It deals with such questions as the nature of African theatre: whether or not Theatre for Development is a 'foreign' concept, and finally the characteristic features of this theatre as it is understood and conceived in most of Africa today. References and examples have been drawn from different places in Africa as a whole where it was felt that this was appropriate and in order to clarify the issues.

Neither 'Fixed Masterpiece' nor 'Popular Distraction': voice, transformation and encounter in Theatre for Development

Frances Harding

I. Harnessing 'deeply combative inventions'

The content and personnel of Theatre for Development derive from 'on-the-ground' situations and embrace the logic of a Freireian-Boalian paradigm of direct fictionalising and dramatising which lead ideally to action in real life. In practice, Theatre for Development has found itself frequently and perhaps increasingly blocked by this direct cause-analysis-action paradigm into a role as a theatre of social information and social education. However, as well as recognising in itself these processes of communication, Theatre for Development may need to exploit more fully its identity as 'theatre' since much of its strength and attractiveness is the very fact that it is creative, 'theatrical', 'dramatic' and 'spectacular'.

Among these unique and exhilarating qualities is the discovery of the right to speak, the ability to articulate a point of view and through performing, the freedom to reveal another 'self'. By selecting events and characters from real life, a fictional narrative is constructed, giving form to imagination. Out of this - voice, action, imagination - a performance is created which in turn creates a performer-audience encounter that is simultaneously 'real and not-real'. In performance, the performers within the drama encounter others outside of it, who, through engaging directly in the drama either by words or by action can, at any point, become performers. It is this encounter facilitated through fiction which enables the 'real' encounter to take place, either simultaneously (within the fiction) or subsequent to it. The exhilaration inherent in each of these discoveries and experiences distinguishes Theatre for Development from other processes of analysis and representation.

'Development' refers as much to 'consciousness-raising' as to material development and essentially encompasses the kinds of inner experiences or *realisations* that I have been referring to and which I call 'transformations'. At a later stage it is this experience of transformation, not necessarily a resolution to clear a well or establish a fund to build a clinic, which can make a significant difference in the life of the individual or group from the 'host' community. It is such a transformation in one's own self-perception that may eventually lead to development of a material sort. The practical benefits that can be achieved by a community arise out of the confidence and understanding inherent in the transformation.

Abah describes such a transformation within a drama about 'two political aspirants . . .

canvassing for votes'[1] which took place through the intervention of Etta, a woman farmer and well-known singer in Onyuwei village, Nigeria, in 1989:

> She . . . opens the firing shot in song. She articulates the point of view of the community . . . She sums up the community's resignation. She nips in and out of character, one time she is a pregnant woman who cannot have medical attention because of the remoteness of her village from the nearest medical centre, another moment she is something else. She illustrates one issue dramatically, the other she enhances with her songs . . . Another lady takes a . . . stick to indicate that she is playing the role of an elderly lady. The audience has taken over the process and the facilitators can only look on. The magic of the theatre is beginning.[2]

On a much later visit, Abah saw a village meeting at which there was a heated discussion about which crop to plant. The men stated that they were planting one thing and the women said no they should plant a different one. The men refused, so the women said that if the men went ahead and planted that crop, they would not weed it for the men. The women's choice of crop was planted! Abah is certain that such confidence shown by the women would not have been possible prior to the Workshop.[3]

Artaud and Theatre for Development

Artaud disdained the 'fixed masterpiece' unresponsive to contemporary needs, but at the same time, he was not a populist and abhorred what he saw as the theatre's debasement into 'a means of popular distraction'. He rejected the idea that *whatever* theatre was produced by the populace, was edifying. These two phrases suggest two poles on a continuum rather than two opposing possibilities and offer a useful framework for placing Theatre for Development into a spectrum of engaged drama.

Artaud passionately believed that theatre was about much more than taking people's minds off the struggles of life and ascribes to Shakespeare responsibility for the: 'aberration and decline, this disinterested idea of theatre which wishes a theatrical performance to leave the public intact, without setting off one image that will shake the organism to its foundations and leave an ineffable scar.'[4]

Theatre for Development in providing a fictional framework within which people explore their own real lives is designed to leave an 'ineffable scar'. Artaud wanted theatre to be a deeply affecting encounter between its participant-audience and its participant-performers, so that each individual should take with them a changed perception of reality and a changed mode of interacting with reality. He deplored a theatre detached from realities and proposed a 'theatre of cruelty' wherein the spectator is compelled to understand that, 'we are not free. And the sky can still fall on our heads. And the theatre has been created to teach us that first of all.'[5]

This 'cruelty' was to be achieved not by directly confronting situations of exploitation, injustice and inequality but through exploring the aesthetics, skills and forms of theatre which would so affect the senses of the participant-audience that they would be transformed by the encounter. Exoticising and 'othering', Artaud envisioned a perfect theatre based on performance forms and content distant from his own. Nevertheless, this skewed historicity should not blind us to making use of Artaud's central precept of the transformative power of performance. Artaud was concerned with a professional theatre, not one arising out of the abilities of untrained non-specialists, but it is his perception of the potential power of theatre rather than his social analysis that is of interest here.

Soyinka too described this transformative quality of 'acting', at once elemental and affecting: 'Acting is therefore a contradiction of the tragic spirit, yet it is also its natural complement. To act, the Promethian instinct of rebellion, channels anguish into a creative purpose which releases man from a totally destructive despair, releasing from within him the most energetic, deeply combative inventions which without usurping the territory of the infernal gulf, bridges it with visionary hopes.'[6]

David Kerr quotes Derrida's vision of performance where 'the spectator presenting himself as spectator will . . . efface within himself the difference between the actor and the spectator, the represented and representor...' and goes on to say: 'I believe that utopian vision has in no way been achieved in the theatre experiments of Artaud, Brook or Grotowski, but that something approaching it was inherent in some African indigenous performing arts.'[7]

Within all theatre, the particular relationship between spectator and actor is a variable one, so that sometimes the spectator is a participant-spectator and sometimes an audience-spectator. The former connotes a more interactive, contributive role than that of the latter which suggests an observer role, attending a performance in order to be entertained and acted upon, wooed. Boal has made the experiential transfer between a spectator role and actor role a central pivot of his later writings devising the word 'spectactor' to encompass his ideal. Theatre for Development relies at every stage of the process on the contribution of participant-spectators to *create* the drama. In other words, their interactions and reactions are not optional extras without which the drama will go ahead anyway, but the *sine qua non*, the very basis of the drama, without which there will be no drama. In Theatre for Development, everyone who is present at rehearsal or performance is a participant-performer *and* a participant-spectator. The opportunity to shift more than once between the two positions is the mechanism which gives Theatre for Development its power. As David Kerr suggests, many African performances do require participation and initially it seems that the two positions parallel a passive recipient role and an active executive one. However, I will suggest that within local performances, the 'fixed masterpiece' is still firmly in place and that 'popular distraction' thrives. Theatre for Development through transferring responsibility for the *creation* of a performance to non-specialists and a combination of *analysis* and *performing* offers new sets of relationships, as well as new forms and new content. In its shifting, non-literate, analytical approach, Theatre for Development is a committed, open-ended theatre that is neither the 'fixed masterpiece' nor the 'popular distraction' that Antonin Artaud deplored.

Change world-wide in the sixties and onwards

During the liberating period of the sixties and into the seventies, a world-wide resistance to the dominance of text-based, professional theatre grew and this provided creative space for the growth of a wide range of alternative theatres. The 'fixed masterpiece' both as text and as performance reflected an ideology of superiority, so the search for alternatives took place on several fronts, embracing form, aesthetics and political awareness. Some theatre companies and individual actors prioritised the expression of direct political commitment, retaining the written script as an eventual outcome of any project such as in the performances of John Mc Grath and the 7:84[8] theatre company in Scotland, that of the actor-writer-director Robert Serumaga in Uganda and of Dario Fo in Italy. These professionally initiated dramas which were researched and scripted by the writer-director, were performed in pubs and clubs and village halls as well as in small local theatres. They largely retained the basic audience-performer relationship, albeit with opportunities for varying degrees of audience response throughout the performance.

For other companies such as Bread and Puppet Theatre Company in the United States and Welfare State Company in England, the Travelling Theatres of Makerere, Zambia and Malawi and the Guerilla Theatre of western Nigeria, the primary ways in which they challenged existing forms was through devising an alternative to the three-act play and then performing it in locations other than that of formal theatre. Involvement with the local community at the preparatory stage was not a priority. Some of these companies devised spectacles - often using local legend and myth as well as contemporary local issues - and placed great emphasis on immediate audience participation during the performance, initiating comic chases and encouraging dialogue interactions.

Alongside these two broad categories, both of whom retained the professional performer-actor as central to their performances, was the growth of a myriad of street theatre and community theatre approaches which were distinguished by a concern to engage a specific community in a particular work, and in which the professional performer played a lesser role. Whilst the work of Augusto Boal in Latin America, Sistren Theatre Company in Jamaica and Ngugi wa Thiongo and Ngugi wa Mirii in Kenya are amongst the best known examples of this approach, everywhere there were hundreds of locally initiated performances in which people drew for the content of their performance on local legend, knowledge or issues and for their personnel on local people and then played to audiences drawn from the local community. In this loosely defined third category, there was usually a mix of professionals and local people organising the event, as at Kamariithu, but responsibility for the construction and production of the play was deliberately shared with a specific, geographically defined community. This emphasised the participatory aspect at all stages of the preparation and is distinct from what David Kerr has called the 'heroic *auteur*' approach which offered a ready-made, albeit relevant, performance by professionals for the entertainment and response of the community.[9] It is the participatory style of community theatre that is most closely linked in its practice and ideology to Theatre for Development.

It is almost impossible to overstate the impact of these world-wide moves, at once diverse and concerted, away from the earlier reverence for the published playtext and the proscenium arch. This really was the overthrow of the dominance of the 'fixed masterpiece', though not happily of all fixed masterpieces. With this overthrow, perhaps more slowly, came the questioning of established forms of actor-training and acting styles. Stanislavski's 'naturalism', was no longer seen as the harbinger of truth onstage, and in many instances within Africa was being replaced by greater attention to indigenous forms of representation. Simultaneously, from Europe, an alternative professional influence on acting styles - Grotowski's 'poor' theatre - began to be evidenced in the urban theatre of South Africa[10] and in Robert Serumaga's work in Kampala, Uganda[11]. 'Improvisation', previously mainly known as a means of covering up errors and fluffed lines on stage, became the buzzword for creative performing. The difference between its old and new meaning lay in the fact that it did not imply 'unrehearsed' but rather a technique of building up a performance in an interactive mode of sharing moves, lines, dance, words, stillness, touch, narrative and dialogue. Whole performances were advertised as 'improvised', not 'scripted'; 'devised', not 'directed'. It was this shift away from the glorifying of the scripted word that freed up the latent creativity in many people, enabling them to move directly from imagination to movement and to take charge of their own performances.

One other crucial factor in the rise of the new performances, was the disappearance of the cluttered, 'realist' stage. Pavements, village squares, market places were the new sets for the new theatre, for 'here-and-now theatricality'[12] or 'rough theatre'[13]. Everywhere people were reinstating performance into their lives and extending old forms to incorporate new approaches. Most importantly of all, however, was the fact that performance had moved away from being the prerogative of a few highly trained specialists towards once again being the right of everyone to make and to do. Local performance was re-jigged, re-formed and displayed in new and barely recognisable settings and forms.

In Nigeria, one of the most outstanding examples was the form of performance by the Tiv people called *kwagh-hir*, meaning 'a wonderful or marvellous thing', in which puppet-sized figures performed on mobile wooden stages about the size of a table. Hidden from view by the decorated sides of these stages, young men manipulated the figures from underneath to articulate in imagery, sound and narrative, their social and political resistance to the threats of a neighbouring political giant. From its inception, aesthetics were always as important as content and context in the new *kwagh-hir*. This vibrant form of performance derived its content from storytelling traditions and from the world of humans and a world of non-human beings, the *adzov*. The new form of theatre was so effective that within Tiv society, power moved temporarily from those elders aligning with the external political force to those identified with the opposition.

A directly politicised form of performance, *kwagh-hir* was also used in commenting on or directly supporting development, *where this served an internal political purpose*. In one well-known piece, for example, which was popular during the seventies and eighties, a puppet doctor operates on a woman who is about to have Caesarian operation. Carefully the puppet doctor lifts the puppet baby from the puppet woman's stomach. The baby is 'alive and well'. The message here is that miscarriages are not inevitable. Women - and their husbands - can take control of a difficult birth and get to hospital where she can be safely delivered of her baby. Thus the supernatural forces manipulated destructively by those men with access to supernatural power and believed to be harming the baby, can, through personal action, be resisted. This kind of theatre seems to simply be promoting a health message, yet at another, deeper level, it is challenging established forms of authority, where they are perceived as negative or even destructive.

Such a multi-layered message can only be conveyed to a local audience, because of their sophisticated knowledge about local relationships of power and how these are articulated in the society through something as seemingly unrelated as a difficult birth. To the outsider, in its content, this is overtly about a matter concerning women's health, yet to the insider, it is also, and perhaps primarily, an in-group challenge to the relationships of power among men.

Within the belief system from which *kwagh-hir* stems, the central characters, the supernatural *adzov*, are implicitly in opposition to the most powerful form of negative supernatural power, *tsav*, held by the elders in the society. Today, most *kwagh-hir* groups publicly play down this connection but their formation, structure and location as well as the individual skits are a response to this supernatural underpinning. It is men who have access in both instances to supernatural power, (*tsav* and *adzov*). Thus whilst many of the topics taken up by the *kwagh-hir* groups are pertinent to the whole community, they often emphasise the concerns of men in the community rather than all sectors of it, and rarely those of women, even as in the instance given, when the skit is overtly focused on an issue of grave concern to women. This must draw our attention to the nuances of meaning in the use of local performance where it is tightly linked to existing forms of social organisation and to the difficulties inherent in using them.

Because most of the significant forms of performance are linked to relationships of power - however diffuse or obscure these are to the outsider's eye - and although Theatre for Development wants to use local performance, it may not be able to go beyond the use of general or popular forms of music, song and dance which are available to everyone. Abah gives several examples of the effective use of popular dances and songs[14], but it is his description of the performance of Etta, a 'well-known performer'[15] that we understand the full potential for meaning in the use of local performances.

As can be seen from the example of *kwagh-hir*, the use of local forms of performance runs the risk of confirming the social stratification implicit in them, because it is often in them that the most important religious, political and economic relationships are articulated. The right to perform key roles, transforms the individual performer, confirming him, as well as his character, as powerful in his society. Thus not only is the message powerful, but the messenger accrues power. As it is most often the young men of the society who fulfil the more physically demanding roles in performances and the older men the more intellectually demanding roles of public storyteller and poet, underlying inequalities may remain unchallenged, since beneficiaries are not likely to undermine their own privileges. A simple riposte of using generation- or gender-specific forms of performance only serves to further confirm the status quo because it leaves intact the most powerful forms, unchallenged and unreformed. The 'fixed masterpiece' remains in place.

New forms of theatre arise in response to new social conditions. For greater freedom of inclusivity, in many instances one has to look for new organisations.

Uganda and the changing theatres

Uganda has had a range of theatre activities which have responded to different political and social situations over the decades. I consider firstly, the work of Robert Serumaga, the actor-director who was such a powerful figure in theatre in Uganda. Although his work was primarily political in its focus, he chose to work through form especially language, movement and aesthetics. He acknowledged the influence on his work of theatre styles and movements beyond the national boundaries, but increasingly found the most important core in the movement and styles of performances within Uganda. His work enables us to consider the response to development from within the professional theatre.

A range of urban theatre forms arose out of local initiatives and are appreciated by large numbers of people and reflect their concerns. Usually performed in local, often makeshift venues, they identify some of the concerns of the urban people. Like Serumaga, albeit from an entirely different spectrum of performance, these performers use influences from outside Uganda - international 'pop' music, clothes, language, as well as from within. Whilst these performances show another response to development, as Marion Frank[16] notes, these amalgams of foreign and national entertainments can create conflicting messages within a single performance.

Finally, I consider Theatre for Development in some of its many local forms.

Robert Serumaga - a man for all seasons

Robert Serumaga sought to express and explore his ideas on the relationship of indigenous Ugandan performance to contemporary Ugandan society. He worked outwards from his art through form, sound and movement, raising the consciousness of the performers and audience through an increase in knowledge and confidence in local forms at the same time as he accommodated international influences.

Serumaga was driven both by aesthetics and politics. Working closely with a group of performers, he sought to devise a form of theatre relevant to his country and arising out of its many traditions of performance. Like many people working in alternative theatre, however, he also derived continual and substantial stimulus from international influences as diverse as the theatre of Japan, South Africa (particularly Grotowski), Latin-America (particularly Boal) and the Black Theatre of Harlem. His work exemplifies the struggle of an individual artist experimenting with form, aesthetics and content in an effort to formulate a theatre which would both express political concern and communicate with ordinary people and which was informed by the need to bring the real and the theatrical into a direct relationship.

In 1971, having experimented with the 'obscure form of the absurd'[17], he moved on in his play *Majjangwa and Nakirigya*, to a style that was more accessible to ordinary people and which drew on already existing familiar elements. In retrospect, it is significant to note that he introduced a *representation* of open-air market and street theatre as the central trope of his play, *Majjangwa*, although at this stage he stopped short of actually taking the play outdoors. For his central characters, he chose the two eponymous beggars, husband and wife, who were real figures, well-known local Kampala characters who earned a meagre daily living by moving from one market to another. The husband, Majjangwa, played his drum whilst his wife, Nakirigya, danced, a dance which each time was soon 'to degenerate later to actions like kissing and sex play on the pavement for five shillings.'[18] From a starting point in their real-life story of a downward spiral from respected performers to their present situation, Serumaga was to weave a commentary on current Ugandan life, juxtaposing the crude form of entertainment re-presented in the play with 'beautiful elevated poetry' so as to draw out the 'social and political criticism in the subtext.'[19] Serumaga's engagement with the 'real' in this work meant that prior to the beginning of rehearsals of *Majjangwa*, he did not have an ending worked out. This came in the form of a real political murder which took place under Amin's regime and which provided an apt - and dangerous - metaphor for the conclusion to the play. Reality for the audience in this case meant that during the performance, they were drawn into a very real danger through their complicity in the drama and felt 'tense with fear.'[20].

In his next play, *Renga Moi*, he used the Acholi legend of the Warrior who was ritually barred from engaging in battle following the birth of his twins. Faced with the dilemma of seeing his people overrun without his help, *Renga Moi* nevertheless opts to fight. His people then extract a penalty for this by demanding the death of his twin children as ritual purification for his contravention of their laws. In this play, Serumaga confronts the dilemma of the price to be paid for helping one's own people. More and more during rehearsal he began to ask his performers to share their skills drawn from their own cultures and to incorporate these in the performance. Serumaga developed the relationship of his actors to his changing perspectives on theatre and most of the young actors in the production of *Renga Moi* were to become the actors in his company, Abafumi Co. Importantly too, in *Renga Moi*, he began his experiments with the use of several of the languages of Uganda onstage, sometimes intertwining them in a single dialogue.

Following this experiment in language, in his next play, *Amayirikiti*, he took things further and sought to demonstrate that the use of words and language was not itself the only way to make oneself heard. He moved towards giving people a voice that did not rely on a language so that language could not become a barrier to understanding a performance. Sound and movement became increasingly important. At the same time, he had begun to put into practice many of the theatrical approaches that he devised from his ever-closer relationship to the performances of Uganda and took his performance outdoors into the theatre car park and used the theatre building as a backdrop to it.

Serumaga sought to find a form that did not rely for its 'alternativeness' on its difference from a dominant Euro-American tradition, but one which whilst accommodating international influences, relied primarily on bringing together many different conventions and practices in Ugandan performance.

Eventually Serumaga gave up representations of struggle and entered the struggle directly until his death in exile in Kenya in 1980.

The urban genres of theatre

In the seventies, under the Amin regime, a local and very popular, *genre* of theatre took over in Kampala. Fearful of retribution if they produced anything critical, performers produced a diet of bland farces which dealt in stereotypical characters and situations. Audiences flocked to them and their participation and applause throughout was so vociferous in the indoor theatres where they were performed, that it overwhelmed and 'disorganised actors and weakened further the hurriedly written and poorly structured and poorly produced plays.'[21] Theatre had become a commercial venture, a 'means of popular distraction' for an 'audience for whom anything that provoked laughter was good theatre'[22] and provided some relief from the horrors of the time. So successful however was theatre work as a commercial venture that the number of companies rose from 20 in 1970 to 250 in 1985. The content and skill of the popular theatre practice was to reach new lows before signalling an upturn in focus and ability. Mbowa chronicles the re-introduction of a critical element in the occasional play of Kanyike and Mubike[23] in 1977 and by the 1980s, the 'chains of fear'[24] inhibiting the artist in Ugandan theatre, were removed and some social criticism again became possible.

If, as I suggested earlier, we must look to new organisations for a greater degree of inclusivity in performance forms, it is in the burgeoning urban theatre that they should be found. However, even recent forms of performance arising out of specific urban migratory processes,[25] follow established organisational practice and, for example, perpetuate a gender division and stratification. Breitenger refers to a particular *genre* which he names very aptly as 'neighbourhood theatre in the suburbs'26 or 'suburban theatre'[27] for short, in which even although the content of the play challenges all sorts of other inequalities, the composition of these companies continues to favour young men in the leading organisational role and the leading performance role:

> The founding and running of a theatrical group usually by a gifted person who is author, director and leading actor all in one, is financially, organisationally and structurally easily manageable. The division of labour and responsibility within the groups is also easily controllable, since no elaborate and complex hierarchical management structures need to be built up, although the title of 'managing director' will be awarded to the group leader. The internal structure is that of a self-help co-operative.[28]

Yet there is not a sense of the role of 'managing director' being one that in practice, a young woman would occupy.

Marion Frank[29] describes the work of JK Ebonita who uses electronic media, and a 'pop' style of performance along with 'traditional' dances and clothes to convey the message which in the end, is contradictory. 'A contradiction develops between the cognitive, rational system of the audience that understands the demand for monogamy and faithfulness in order to avoid the infection with AIDS, and its affective subconscious system. On that level, an appeal is made to traditional moral norms with visual elements belonging to western culture. The communication may thus work only on a superficial level, which may not result in a change of behaviour.'[30]

Breitenger records the further development of this freewheeling, open-air, income-generating theatre that was responding to a need for light entertainment. In spite of its light-heartedness, Breitenger suggests, it successfully focuses on the insecurities experienced by the migrant population in the cities of Uganda:

> The immediate cash-nexus emphasises the quality of the income-generating activity. In the suburban context, theatre provides a supplementary income, which makes survival possible or at least easier, through self-initiative and autonomous activity. As such, what appeared to be pure entertainment theatre has, for the performers, an important developmental quality beyond the merely financial; it also entails a conscientization process, since members of theatrical groups realise not only that, as cultural workers, they can improve their material situation, but also that they can initiate, innovate and be creatively active, thus regaining control over their own social situation.[31]

'Using' theatre

What is instructive in these varied forms of theatre is how each addresses a reality: the political theatre of Serumaga explored different modes and genres; the populist theatre of the Kampala crowds responded to the prevailing political conditions without daring to challenge them; the emergence of a critical dimension addressed both the content, the context, the style and the quality of the dramas. Just at the very moment when the dramas seem to have reached their lowest level[32] theatre practice begins to return to performance which is not simply a 'popular distraction'.[33]

Whilst there are still many many theatre companies operating in Kampala and elsewhere in Uganda, there has also been a huge upsurge in the use of Theatre for Development in Uganda where it has been promoted by government and non-government agencies in campaigns to further knowledge of sexually transmitted disease, especially AIDS. This agenda-driven theatre has tended to define much of the Theatre for Development practices in Uganda and has not allowed for the development of an open-ended theatre practice able to consider all the factors which go towards creating an environment where the transmission of AIDS can thrive.

Frank describes theatre which has been used as part of a campaign to spread information about AIDS transmission and documents the propensity of the campaign to be seen as 'successful' if the numbers seeing the performances are high enough to satisfy the international funding body. As Breitenger had earlier regretfully - if realistically - pointed out in relation to 'campaign' theatre:

> That government, non-government and international organisations are all involved in the spearheading of health-education campaigns brings its own specific pressures into the campaigns, whose officials are held responsible for producing results - 'results' which are not measured by theatrical or even medical, but by

administrative and political criteria. The investment in financial and human resources has to show results capable of being measured in terms of quantifiable data - numbers of performances, number of spectators, number of participants.[34]

More is required of the process than for it to be a series of directives from 'above', an information pack, a strategy for education or a social therapy, or what Brecht called the 'transformation of art into a pedagogical discipline' (quoted in Otty, P 92, Contemporary Theatre Review, Vol on Boal). As it is, in the short term, it has been successful in bringing about social changes[35], although so little follow-up work has been funded that it is difficult or even impossible to know. The intention of Theatre for Development was never solely as a charter for sociopolitical analysis, although it has always been a key part of its practice in its workshops and of its ideology. Theatre for Development also sought something that is altogether more powerful and more humble. It sought - and seeks - through individual experiences to bring people to a point where they gain - *and feel a sense of having gained* - some intellectual, emotional and political control over their lives.

II. Voice, transformation and encounter
Three fruitful points of contact have emerged in the relationship between practice, objectives and outcome in Theatre for Development: voice, transformation, encounter.

a) Voice: acquiring a voice; hearing a language.
The articulation of sound is a demonstration of the right to speak. Persons who feel themselves without power, do not speak, nor are they given an opportunity to speak by those who have power and who can speak - the authoritative voice, the voice of authority. Serumaga moved from experimenting with many languages onstage within a single performance to one in which it was not which *language* that was the central issue but the right to *create sound*. This approach echoes one which Dasgupta[36] notes in which Peter Brook's use of language is as a 'vehicle of action, a catalyst that renders action complete' rather than primarily as a carrier of meaning (and *a priori* as a carrier of emotion). But while Brook experimented with sound and voice as a theatrical concept devoid of direct socio-political significance, Serumaga experimented with the use of multi-lingual forms and equally with non-lingual forms of sound in order to contribute to theatricality *as political action*.

It need not primarily or solely be the *meaning* of the words which renders the spoken word effective; it is also the making of sound and *who* is making the sound. This intention - language as a vehicle of political action - finds an echo in the work of Ousmane Sembene. In his early film *'Borom Sarret'* only a voice-over - in French - is featured. In his next films, his characters spoke for themselves, but in French and after showing these early French language films to a rural audience in Senegal, Sembene wrote: 'My attitude was that there was nothing wrong with imposing the French language on the films, because French language was a fact of life. But on the other hand the peasants were quick to point out to me that I was the one who was alienated because they would have preferred the film in their own language...'[37]

Thus for Sembene, two aspects of voice - the right to speak and the right language precede a concern with *what* is said. The issue of the 'right to speak' has occupied several African filmmakers and the use of someone as a central character without the 'power of speech' was used by Sembene in *'La Noire de...'* as well as by other African filmmakers such as Souleyman Cisse in *'Den Muso/*

The Girl', and Gaston Kabori in '*Wend Kuni.*' Roy Armes has correctly observed that: 'acquiring a voice has an importance quite apart from what is actually said.'[38]

This use of their own language to speak in a context where it is not normally permitted, is sometimes the first release afforded people through the strategy of Theatre for Development as Marion Frank's description of an AIDS drama performed at a national AIDS day in 1989 in Kampala, demonstrates. In the drama, the two central characters are Oldpa, an old man, and 5-14, a young girl. 5-14 insists that children be given information about AIDS saying that children must be given the right to speak, to ask questions. 'The issue of the hierarchical nature of Ganda society, which does not encourage children to ask questions, is addressed critically here, and it is suggested that this behaviour has to change: children must be encouraged to ask questions, and have to be enlightened on sexual matters so that they have a chance to avoid infection with HIV.'[39]

With the right to speak, to ask questions and to use one's own language comes the power to hold and articulate an opinion; to cause others to listen; to choose words that carry meaning. In an essentially two-sided relationship, these rights bring with them an obligation on others to hear and to listen. It brings speakers and listeners face-to-face.

b) Transformation

Within the Theatre for Development drama, often after the impact of 'acquiring a voice', comes the physical impact of role-playing. It allows people to explore the potential of their own physical presence as they realise that *they hold within themselves* the power to present themselves in several different ways to the society. A distinctive feature of Theatre for Development is how it fictionalises the narrative which emerges from the accounts of the daily lives of the local people. In constructing the narratives, people project characters who are an amalgam of people they know - including themselves - and then go on to play the *characters* which they have created in the *story* they have created. This gives people control over content and presentation and allows individuals to 'inch forward' in the creation and presentation of a character they purport to be, and ultimately in the definition of *self*.

In a village during a Theatre for Development workshop in 1982, one of the themes in the drama concerned the right of young women to tertiary education. This was a theme which had been introduced by the wife of the headman of the village, but in later discussion several men had voiced the opinion that it was a waste of time sending girls to school because they were soon made pregnant not necessarily by fellow-students, but by their teachers. In the drama, one of the central characters is a young woman who is denied further schooling so that her father can use the money for her fees (which her mother had saved up and whose opposition to the plan is ignored) to set up her brother in business in the nearby town.

The young woman who played the character of the young girl was actually from the village, and had just begun as a first year student at the nearby college. In character (see Figure 1) she addressed her drama 'family' and the drama 'elders' within the drama, although amongst the assembled village audience was her own family and her own elders. Once on stage, the character railed against the practice of refusing to send young women for further education. She called for parity of treatment between boys and girls, for fathers to refrain from refusing their daughters the right to tertiary education. Within the drama, she was addressing her 'father' and 'mother' who, after some time sought to get her offstage so as to enable the drama to proceed, but the young

EXPRESS
STRONG &
EMOTIONALL FEALING

Figure 1.

woman, now barely distinguishing between the words of the character and her own, continued. Other actors entered trying to get her offstage: 'go now and fetch some water' one would say handing her a bucket. In character she would say, 'yes soon' and carefully put down the bucket beside her. After some time of addressing a huge assembled village audience, she picked it up and quietly said she must go and fetch water. As it was dark, this was clearly a dramatic device for leaving the stage and in doing this she reinforced the illusion that it was the character who had done all the complaining and railing against the unjust practices, but at the same time made it clear through her control, that she, as performer, meant it too.

It was a rich and rewarding experience for her to have a public forum in which to vent her frustration and express her opinion about long-established practice without having to compromise herself personally. At such transformative moments Theatre for Development achieves fulfilment in empowering people through their personal experience. This young woman would never have known that she had the ability to address the elders and the assembled village, nor would any other opportunity have presented itself whereby she *could* address them. The elders and all the men had been compelled to listen to her and recognise her ability and her analysis. Drama can offer a safe fictionalised context for real development.

c) Encounter

IT'S NOT ONLY

Nor is the transformative experience restricted to individual experiences, for it also affords an opportunity for discussion between sections of society for whom there may be no structured forum where they can meet. One example of this emerged at another of the village dramas where the issue of a water supply was paramount. A water supply is not an isolated geographical issue, but is linked to several social issues, especially gender relations. This means for example that a woman need not accept that *being a woman* intrinsically entails having to walk great distances in the search for water; it need not mean that she holds within her the duty to be 'beaten' whether this is perceived as assault or 'punishment' for failing to bring water sufficiently quickly. In other words, a distinction needs to be made between a woman's biological self and the socially ascribed behaviours to which she is subjected or selects to enjoy. If a society (and many have) finds that it has opted for women to be responsible for the duty of supplying water for the family's daily needs, then the fact that this is a *socially* determined role and not a biological one, can be focused on and the options for changing it in the face of changing resources and mores can be explored. If along with the duty of supplying water there is a concomitant *'right'* of a husband or other male member of a family unit, to 'punish' a woman for not being able to supply water irrespective of the difficulties in so doing, then that too needs to be explored.

Oga Abah has described how in one of the villages during the Benue Workshop, the initial scenes for the play showed a woman who having searched for water all day is subjected to a beating by her husband for not bringing out food to him on the farm. She tries to explain that it is because she was miles away searching for water, but he will not listen and beats her savagely. To the surprise of the performers from the Workshop, the watching audience burst out laughing at the husband's fury and the beating he dealt his wife. Abah asks: 'Did we get it all wrong? Why were they now laughing at what they described as their gravest problem? They were laughing because they saw a replica of a particular person in the village in the husband. They said that there was a man in the village who does what the husband in the skit does and for the same reason . . . we had no prior knowledge of the man...'[40]

This first performance in rehearsal generated a lot of discussion through presenting an incident with which people could identify. Initially the women were not able to take the opportunity to enter the discussion and many men said that the problem in getting water lay with the women who were 'stubborn'. Nor was it only men who failed to support the women. An elderly woman supported the right of the men to punish their wives by 'beating' them for not supplying water sufficiently quickly. However far away the water supply was, she said, the women should go for it. Abah goes on to ask why did the old woman not sympathise with the hard-worked younger women and suggests that it is because:

> She no longer goes in search of water. Her grandchildren and more significantly her children's wives do the search for her. So is she now insensitive? She must have known the agony of the problem in her youthful days... The answer . . . is... in the generation gap... She sees the traditional role of women in the society as unchanging. The search for water . . . form an integral part of the domestic chores... This is what she has known all her life and why should it change now! The woman is more of a husband than a wife now. She is the 'husband' to her son's wives. It is therefore the responsibility of these wives to find water and do most of the domestic work for this 'husband'. The woman's concept of her son's full manhood is their ability to control their wives and stay firm on what constitutes their duty.[41]

Some of the men sympathised with the women in the play, although most who did were working in the town and were no longer directly involved in the daily experience of ensuring and using a water supply, but other men, resident in the village, felt that the problem was simply that the husband had not beaten his wife 'hard enough'. In spite of there being no common response to condemn the practice of 'punishing' women for something which was not of their making, nevertheless, the very fact that the problem had been exposed in a way which made people laugh, made them angry and made them think about it anew, can only be considered as successful. An instant resolve to overturn a practice does not guarantee permanent change.

Generational difference was also portrayed in a storyline between the educated and the uneducated youth. A young man and woman decide to marry and to disregard the wishes of the leaders who have selected another young man as the woman's future husband. This was a particularly interesting example of how creatively a group can make a point within a drama without recourse to elaborate devices and just using the resources of the group. The young man who has been selected to marry the girl comes to speak to the elders. His behaviour is deferential and he bends low in his greeting to them. He is not wearing any T-shirt or other top and just a simple pair of shorts to signify how countrified he is (Figure 2). Hot on his heels comes the suave young man from the town, dressed in denim from top to toe . Instead of greeting the elders in the appropriate way, he swings in, touches a couple of the elders in a familiar manner on their arms or shoulder and saying a 'hi' to them all, grabs a chair and swinging it round from back to front, sits astride it and <u>tells</u> the elders of his intention to marry the girl (Figure 3). This was one of the most popular moments in the drama and the audience roared with laughter. The audience recognised different levels of confrontation here - the bad manners, the problem of young people wanting to marry the partner of their choice, the need for change to work in tandem with established practice rather than confront and dismiss it.

In yet another of the villages, during the performance, one of the men had not been present in the village during the preceding days and appeared not to realise that the discussion between the performers and the real elders of village was based on a fictional drama. For a time he had just watched and then gradually he came nearer and started interposing comments into the drama (Figure 4). He became angry when a 'taxi-driver' 'refused' to take a woman who had been 'bitten' by snake to the clinic unless she paid five times the usual fare. His comments were incorporated into the dialogue of the drama and after this crisis was resolved, he rushed back into his house and donned a wig and took up an elaborate fly whisk. Brandishing this, he continued to interact with the performers in the drama who neither ignored him nor let him lead them too far from the agreed storyline. He continued to 'dress up' adding an embroidered <u>riga</u> over his own clothes and was now

Figure 2.

Figure 3.

in the acting area most of the time, fully engaged with the drama. The performance came to a close with a dance which the man joined in as eagerly as anyone else (Figure 5).

Conclusion

Theatre for Development has taken many forms. It has had many results. Essentially an interactive process utilising reality and fiction to create the experience of performing, it has not always adequately recognised the transformative personal experience of its participants amongst its successes. This experience can be described as being within the frame of 'conscientizing', but something more than rationalising takes place at times during workshops as people find in themselves strengths and abilities to effect changes. Experiencing through enactment the self as powerful, is one of Theatre for Development's most important achievements to date.

Figure 4.

Figure 5.

It is only when we have tried to lift our load to our heads and found it too heavy that we turn to our neighbour and ask for help in lifting it.[42]

Notes

1. Oga S Abah, 'Perspective in Popular Theatre: Orality as a definition of New Realities', in Eckhard Breitenger (ed), *Theatre and Performance in Africa*, (Bayreuth; 1994), p. 92.
2. Oga S Abah, *From Celebration to Survival*: Report on the International Workshop on Theater of Integrated Development (TIDE), (Unpublished; 1989), p. 14.
3. Personal communication, June 1996.
4. Antonin Artaud, *The Theatre and its Double*, (London; 1959).
5. Ibid.
6. Wole Soyinka, *Myth, Literature and the African World*, (Cambridge University Press; 1976), p. 146.
7. David Kerr, 'Theatre and Social Issues in Malawi: Performers, Audiences, Aesthetics', in *New Theatre Quarterly*, (4/14, 1988), p. 174.
8. 7% of the people own 84% of the land.
9. see for example, Kerr, NTQ 4/14; 1988, 175.
10. Mbogemi Ngema, personal statement publicly to Grotowski, Copenhagen, May 1996.
11. personal communication, Karundi R. Serumaga, London, June 1996.
12. Kerr, 1988; 178

13. Kerr, 1995; 145.
14. Oga S Abah, 'Perspective in Popular Theatre: Orality as a definition of New Realities', in Eckhard Breitenger (ed), *Theatre and Performance in Africa*, (Bayreuth; 1994), pp. 89-91.
15. Ibid., p. 92.
16. *NTQ*, (46, Vol XII, May 1996).
17. Rose Mbowa, 'Artists under Siege: Theatre and the Dictatorial Regimes in Uganda', in Breitenger (ed), (Bayreuth; 1994), p. 128.
18. Ibid., p. 129.
19. Ibid.
20. Ibid.
21. Ibid., p. 132.
22. Ibid., p. 132.
23. Ibid., p. 133.
24 .   Ibid.
25. Breitenger, 1994.
26. Breitenger, 1992, p. 278.
27. Ibid., p. 289.
28. Ibid., p. 282.
29. *NTQ*, (46, Vol XII, May 1996).
30. Ibid., p. 110.
31. Breitenger, op. cit., p. 282.
32. see Mbowa, in Breitenger, op. cit., p. 133.
33. Ibid., p. 76.
34. *NTQ* (No. 31, 1992: 287)
35. Kerr, *NTQ*; Eyoh, 1993.
36. Dasgupta, 'The Man Who ...', in *Performing Arts Journal*, (Jan 1996, Vol XVIII, 1), p. 88.
37. Quoted in Roy. Armes and L. Malkmus, *Arabd and African Filmmaking*. Zed Books, London, 1991, p. 171.
38. Roy Armes, p. 169.
39. Marion Frank, 'Theatre in the service of Health Education: Case Studies from Uganda', *NTQ*, (12/46,1990), p. 112.
40. Oga S Abah, Report on Second Benue International Theatre for Development Workshop, Zaria, (unpublished, June, 1983).
41. Ibid.
42. Tiv Elder to Tar Ahura, Theatre for Development Workshop, (Benue State, Nigeria, 1983).

Product or Process: Theatre for Development in Africa

Osita Okagbu

Introduction

> 'Theatre-for-development, even that which is not popular theatre, approaches theatre from the side of the audience, and consumption is the major concern.'[1]

Michael Etherton's assertion for Theatre for Development is primarily concerned with the audience and its transformation. But I am quite concerned by the premise of the second where he concludes that 'consumption is the major concern' of Theatre for Development because in therein is contained, for me, both the paradox and consequently the failure to achieve its existential goal of affecting and, or changing the lives of the audience which Theatre for Development sets out to achieve . What I intend to do in this essay therefore is to examine the different programmes and practices of Theatre for Development across the African continent in the last twenty years or so, but with a special focus on my own experience of trying to set up a sustainable programme of Theatre for Development in Ghana in 1992. Basically, what I will be trying to do is to see to what extent the various theories, methodologies and practices have succeeded or failed in achieving the basic objective of Theatre for Development. So this essay is, as it were, a critique of my own practice in Ghana and by extension, it is a also a critique of other Theatre for Development programmes in Africa because there is an apparent similarity in its theoretical underpinning, the practical implications and tensions of its sociopolitical context with these other programmes.

Central to my thinking is a basic concern with the issue of whether an appropriate methodology and conceptualization of the form has been theorized or developed to ensure a successful realization of the objectives of the genre. Is there, for instance, a need to articulate a unique methodology and practice that takes into account the peculiarities of the African context? Which practices and methodologies work and which do not and why? Hopefully, I will be putting forward what I consider to be an ideal or more to the point, a workable theory and practice of Theatre for Development for Africa.

Ethics of Form.

I began with what I consider to be Professor Etherton's consumerist notion and aesthetic of

Theatre for Development which, as I pointed out earlier, carries with it the danger that it totally negates what should be the existential imperative of Theatre for Development which is, exist to transform the audience into makers and owners of the theatre event and experience. However, underpinning or implied in Etherton's view is both an illusionistic and an essentially capitalist conception and context in which there are producers of theatre event and consumers of its product.

My conception of Theatre for Development, inspired and informed as it is by the liberatory pedagogy of Paulo Freire, the 'theatre of the oppressed' aesthetics of Augusto Boal and a traditional African theatre aesthetic, finds a basic contradiction in a capitalist philosophy of theatre which seeks to make a distinction between the spectators and the performers, and thereby turning the former into consumers of the product of the latter. As Freire points out his 'pedagogy of the oppressed' is one, 'which must be forged with, not for , the oppressed (be they individuals or whole peoples) in the incessant struggle to regain their humanity. This pedagogy makes oppression and its causes objects of reflection by the oppressed, and from their reflection will come their necessary engagement in the struggle for their liberation.'[2]

The spate of Theatre for Development activities and programmes across the African continent seem to me to be far removed from this model since they usually operate as outside interventions that attempt to bring to target groups products and worlds that seem finished or foreclosed for them to merely consume or behold. But the central question is whether such a theatre can really liberate or empower the spectator, if it does not, in terms of Boalian aesthetics, transfer the means of production into the hands of the spectators rather than merely convert them into voyeurs of a finished spectacle, and who are thus powerless to interrupt or change the product since they neither initiate nor control the theatre process of theatrical production itself.

Boal's theatre of the oppressed is, without doubt, informed and predicated upon Freire's 'pedagogy of the oppressed' in which education and learning become a participatory collaboration between the teacher and the pupil, where the encounter between the two simply provides a context in which the two can explore with and learn from each other. Boal succeeded in transforming this liberatory pedagogy into a liberatory aesthetic that is centred around and expressed by the notion of 'theatre as a language' which the oppressed can be helped to use to articulate, not only their oppression, but their liberation from it as well.

My argument then is: that the majority of Theatre for Development programmes and practices in Africa seem not to be aiming to achieve the transformation of the theatre process into a potential context and the theatre itself into a language of exploration and expression for the deprived communities and villages in which their Theatre for Development activities are pitched; and that even when and where they are aiming to achieve this objective, they are, in the main, unable to do so. There are many reasons which can be put forward to account for this unfortunate situation. My intention will be to use my experience in Ghana to highlight these reasons and how they strongly militate against a more successful conception and practice of Theatre for Development projects within the African continent.

Theatre for Development and Government Agencies

One of the key problems confronting Theatre for Development programmes and projects seems to be the often inevitable but usually problematic alliance between Theatre for Development practitioners on the one hand and governments and non-governmental organizations on the other.

This relationship is almost always one of funding and very often it is a relationship that becomes reduced to the cynicism and impotence of the proverbial 'who pays the piper calls the tune', a situation in which the theatre project is expected to be a mouthpiece or a medium for the government or the funding agency's propaganda as was my experience with the Ghana project.

The situation in Ghana when I was invited to act as consultant for Theatre for Development was that the government through its Non-formal Education division had already completed a pilot programme of functional literacy drive in which theatre, especially role-play, had featured prominently as part of the adult literacy campaign. The seeming success of the pilot scheme convinced the government and the external funding agencies of the need in 1992 to expand the functional literacy programme into a national one with a fully developed theatre component. It was therefore apparent that there existed a fundamental difference of opinion/understanding between myself and the authorities on the nature and deployment of Theatre for Development purposes.

From the start, I was convinced that the government's approach was very limiting and restrictive as it confined the theatre input to mere role-play situations and usage within the functional literacy programme. I personally did not see any scope or prospects in this approach which I did not consider to be Theatre for Development and when I spoke to members of the Theatre Unit (a unit with the Non-formal Education Division formed to coordinate the theatre activities of the division) whose responsibility it was going to be to maintain a sustained programme of theatre activities throughout the country, I also found out that their own understanding and philosophy of Theatre for Development was firmly located within the domain of the agit-prop mode of theatre, an interventionist form of theatre which inevitably can become a pliable instrument for the government to use in pursuance its avowed development objectives. There was, therefore, basically no tension or conflict in the two views as they both are essentially concerned or view theatre as a message-bearing medium without any concern for the politics of the source. My own position does not in actual fact deny or challenge the validity of their views as I firmly believe that theatre as a form of cultural action is almost always loaded with messages and possible meanings which an audience can read into or out of it, whether these messages or meanings are intended or are unintentional is quite beside the point. Rather, what my position sought to do was take these views to a different level where the issue of the message being carried, who is responsible for it, who is carrying it, and the manner in which it is carried are paramount and definitely more important than the actual message itself. I was more concerned with ensuring that the theatre projects do not in the long run become another medium of mass indoctrination and interpellation, like television or radio have become for governments, especially in the dictatorships and one party-state politics of many African countries. The key difference between my conception and approach and that of the Theatre Unit and the government was that my emphasis was on the process of theatre itself and the possibilities contained in it as opposed to the end product which is the performance with a developmental theme or message embedded in it. In this I was guided by the basic conviction that, for all its protestations of wanting development and freedom for the masses of deprived people in Ghana, the government might in reality be scared of the possible anarchy and chaos which a critical consciousness developed through an education or theatre process that is not a one-way process of mass indoctrination can give rise to. As Freire says, people, especially those in authority, 'rarely admit their fear of freedom openly, however, tending rather to camouflage it sometimes consciously by presenting themselves as defenders of freedom. They give their doubts and misgivings an air of profound sobriety, as befitting custodians of freedom. But they confuse freedom with the maintenance of the *status quo* ; so that if conscientization threatens to place the *status quo* in question, it thereby seems to constitute a threat to freedom itself.'[3]

I find this to be the crucial dilemma for those in authority who conceive of development initiatives and practices such as Theatre for Development or functional literacy to help bring development and an improved life situation to the masses. Do they genuinely want the masses to develop a critical consciousness that would enable them understand the mechanics of their underdevelopment and deprivation? In the case of Ghana, as in many other African countries with masses of deprived, would those in power really want the masses to see clearly that there usually is a correlation between their poverty and deprivation and the relative affluence and privilege of those in positions of authority, whether political or economic? Can these really genuinely want to abolish social inequality and relations of privilege and deprivation in society? Would it not amount to committing class suicide? To giving up their privileges and power? I personally do not believe we have such altruists and revolutionaries among our politicians and all others in positions of power who would want and set in motion a process that would ultimately lead to an egalitarian social order in which there are no haves and have-nots, in which there are no subjects and objects of the historical process. These were the questions and issues that confronted me during my stay in Ghana and my final conclusion was that it was obviously just lip-service which was being paid to these and other initiatives and processes of liberation by the political and economic elite who controlled policy in Ghana.

It is inevitable that a situation such as this raises so many issues for Theatre for Development, especially the question of its ability to provide a context or become a tool that can be used by the masses of oppressed peoples in developing countries to explore and articulate or speak their concerns or issues that affect them. In this context, I believe that Boal's twin notions of 'theatre as language' and 'theatre as discourse' should become the ideal goals for Theatre for Development. It might be useful to point out here that some traditional African theatre performances already do that, and good examples of this are Okumkpa performances in Afikpo[4] and most of the masquerade performances of the Igbo of Nigeria. These theatrical performances provide a playful context within which members of the community can enter into dialogue with themselves and with their community. A context in which issues of relevance are explored, negotiated and very often resolved. But what obtains basically is that the funding situation enables the funding authorities or agencies in the end to highjack Theatre for Development projects into mediums for communicating or transmitting government propaganda programmes to target communities in a top-to-bottom/centre-to-periphery form of communication. It is they usually who set the agenda for the Theatre for Development activities which they expect the theatre workers to follow as was the case in Ghana and in many other African countries where Theatre for Development has been used as an part of development drive.

But more significantly however, the funding situation and the inevitable associations of dependence and control which it creates, as Kerr rightly concludes: 'The jargons used by popular theatre workers to describe Theatre for Development ('participatory', 'bottom-up', 'conscientization', 'liberation' and so on) derived from the combative Freirian language of popular resistance. But the actual practice had to conform to the paternalistic (or, in some cases, repressive) realities of government hegemony.'[5]

That is to say that the theatre workers constrained as they are by the one-way nature of the funding process, end up replicating a similar one-way flow of information in their encounter with their target groups. As they receive their directives from the top or centre without any input from them as to the themes of development to be covered by the theatre, so do they pass these on to the target communities without any input from the latter as to the structure and content of the theatre process.

This precisely was the situation in Ghana. Our workshop was actually officially opened by the Director of the Non-Formal Education Division who in his address painstakingly and consistently stressed the convergence between government developmental policies and strategies and those of the to be created Theatre for Development programme. Ironically, but not surprisingly, it was the same director who completely rejected the management structure which emerged from the management workshop which we felt was the best for ensuring a continued programme of Theatre for Development activities throughout the regions. The reason, I suspect, although it was never made clear to me, was that the structure threatened to take control of content and process away from government functionaries and give autonomy to individual communities and their cultural officers (the official designation for a cadre of theatre workers to be trained by us at the Theatre for Development workshop later) to develop their own programmes of theatre performances with minimal input, control or intervention from Accra. There is no denying the fact that the key thing we tried to make sure never happened was help create a situation where the theatre programmes and performances get turned into 'issue-oriented' or 'problem-solving' campaigns. And so, even though within the management structure proposed we had included mechanisms and strategies for monitoring and evaluation of regional and community programmes (a job that was to be the responsibility of members of the Theatre Unit) we collectively felt and concluded that as long as, 'the government was closely monitoring the theatre experiments, there was no likelihood of drama being used for creating genuine solidarity of peasants and workers against oppression.'[6]

The last thing we wanted was for the programme of theatre we were helping to initiate being used to legitimize the existing power structures in Ghana through giving a semblance of government interest and participation in grass-roots radical forms of cultural exploration and expression. And neither did we want the theatre to become just a medium or an instrument for putting across government messages and propaganda. We were aiming for a theatre that would cut itself loose from the purse strings of the government and thus free of its control, even if the initial impetus may have come from government functionaries.

But as I pointed out earlier with reference to our Madina plays, the demands of the government who were the sponsors of the project was for us to develop a viable and effective tool for communicating its development messages to the masses of Ghanaian people. The format of our work thus was the classic outsider-in or centre-to-periphery model of development communication. For all our stay in the community for ten days before the plays were created, we were outsiders who tried to intervene, or more accurately intrude, in the life of the people of Madina. During our research phase, we asked questions about life in the community, we probed to discover the problems plaguing the inhabitants, and we returned to our base to analyse the data we had collected. One of the things I realised personally was that even though the problems of Madina were unique to it, our group promptly analysed and neatly phrased these problems along the lines and in the terminologies of the themes already chosen by the government agencies - labels such as 'lack of health care provision', 'inadequate sanitation', 'teenage pregnancy', 'illiteracy', 'drug abuse', and 'unemployment. We then proceeded to make plays on these themes which were finally taken back to the community in the market square on the last day of our stay. Even though these were well received and probably immensely enjoyed by the spectators given the response and animated discussion that went on far into the evening after we had performed, I still do not see how our brief intrusion/intervention had significantly helped the people of Madina to understand their problems, let alone solve them better than they did before we came. And of more significance in the context of the thesis of this essay is the fact that we neither taught the people of Madina how to use theatre to explore these issues for themselves. The big irony about this failure for me was the fact that one of the major complaints which we received from various respondents was the total lack of any sense of communal identity, unity and trust among and between the different ethnic groups that make up Madina. With hindsight, I think we could have solved a major problem for Madina if we had only managed to get members of the community to come together and make a play themselves about the problems, even if these had been identified by us. The nature of theatre and the play-making process as a group sharing activity and experience carried out in an environment of fun and playfulness could have provided all the bonding and unity which members felt they needed in order to go forward, to confront and deal with issues as a community. We could have showed them that it was possible for them to work through both individual and communal problems as a group with one identity and one destiny.

The same can be said of the Samaru projects and the Marotholi Travelling Theatre work in Nigeria and Lesotho respectively. The Samaru projects, one of the earliest projects of Theatre for Development in Africa, innovative and radical in its conception and place in history, was equally a classic example of Theatre for Development very much influenced by the top-to-bottom model of development communication. The actors and the performing group in Samaru were students and lecturers from the English department of Ahmadu Bello University in Zaria. The problem in this case, as I see it, is that the group was not in any way acting as a catalyst or facilitating group. As Steve Abah, one of the leading initiators of the project, explains: 'The project intended to find a way to communicate with ordinary folk through drama made by the students. However, the students would do it in such a way that the people would recognise the voice of the plays as their own.'[7]

It is doubtful if any way can ever be found that would make it possible for the Ahmadu Bello students to speak about the problems of Samaru in such a way that the inhabitants would recognise the voices in the plays as their own. I must point out, however, that the Samaru group were aware of the class biases of the students who needed to rid themselves of these biases and perceive the problems of Samaru from the perspective of the poor deprived inhabitants before they can genuinely make contact with and impact on Samaru. But having said that , the fact remains that the project simply denied the people of Samaru the opportunity to be the actors and directors in the dramas of their lives. The same goes for Madina where the villagers neither acted nor directed, and neither did they contribute in any capacity in the making of the plays; they just watched us perform for them and only came in when we asked them to. But as Boal says of his 'poetics of the oppressed': 'The spectator delegates no power to the character (actor) either to act or to think in his place; on the contrary, he himself assumes the protagonic role, changes the dramatic action, tries out solutions, discusses plans for change - in short trains himself for real action.'[8]

The performing group in Samaru were thus simply mediums, outsiders who neither shared in the problems of Samaru in the same way that members of my workshop group did not share in the problems of our host community. Like Madina, Samaru and other such projects fell right into the trap of 'us' and 'them'. The group, like the Madina group, were the outsiders with the expert knowledge and skills to dissect the target community in order to discover the social ills that were contributing to the underdevelopment and oppression and lay these bare to the members of the community. They were the 'wonder' workers who had assumed the mantle of saviours to educate Samaru out of its poverty and slumness, that is as if the community needed to be reminded or educated about its poverty and social deprivation. Above all, it was the group of university students who were doing the plays and so in effect directing and controlling the context and content of the encounter and discourse, while the dwellers of Samaru watched them passively as they performed the dramas of their very lives! No attempts were made it seems in these earlier Samaru experiments in Theatre for Development to teach the watching community how to use the theatre as a fun way of exploring and expressing their social realities.

Again looking at Mda's accounts of the work of the Marotholi Travelling Theatre Group in Lesotho, its earlier work of agit-prop and participatory theatre were essentially limiting in their effectiveness. But as they moved toward the 'theatre of conscientization' mode, one got the impression that their work started approaching Boal's ideal of 'simultaneous dramaturgy' and the 'forum' with the attendant possibility of empowerment when the communities take over the process and the catalysts withdraw.[9] The key aim and advantage of this model is that it gradually leads to a situation where, 'participation and control increase as catalysts pull out; spectator becomes dramatic actor, then social actor.'[10]

Any method or model short of this ideal is inevitably open to the danger of being manipulated or appropriated by the funding agencies - whether governmental or non-governmental. The agit-prop and participatory models, despite their radicalism, are severely limited by the very fact that they are usually confined to specific themes - whether these be chosen from outside as in agit-prop or from inside as in participatory. The truth is that they can never lead to total freedom and ability to use and control the process and production of theatre which Boal's notion of theatre as a new language of discourse and expression aims to achieve. Moreover, the theme or issue-led approach very leads to a high degree of adhocism in the practice of Theatre for Development as we shall see later in the essay.

Communication Theory/Freirian Liberatory Pedagogy and Theatre for Development.

One of the key areas where Theatre for Development fails conceptually is in its inability and sometimes inexplicable unwillingness to work within paradigms in development communication in which real and active participation from all sides of the communication equation is the central objective and mode of practice. There are clearly significant advantages in this as Nair and White point out, 'participatory involvement of the target group in decision making, for adoption of innovation, will heighten enthusiasm and motivation. There is considerable evidence to show that grassroots participation promotes development within the acknowledged new emphasis on equality, freedom and self-reliance.'[11]

Participatory development communication which involves a sizable input from the indigenous or target community, that seeks local solutions to problems as opposed to 'expert' outside advice', and with an increased self-reliance of the people to be 'developed', is the ideal, and it is this ideal which Theatre for Development should model itself on. This ideal is 'transactional communication [which] is the opposite of a one-way persuasion process. It is a dialogue, wherein sender and receiver of messages interact over a period of time, to arrive at shared meanings.'[12]

It is an ideal which has much in common with Freire's liberatory pedagogy which eschews the 'banking system' of education in which knowledge or learning is a one-way process from teacher to pupil. In the banking system of education, as Freire (1972) argues, knowledge is perceived as a gift or a handout by those who consider themselves to be repositories and owners of knowledge upon those whom they consider to be totally lacking in or deprived of knowledge.[13] One other feature of this system also is that it is the teacher who chooses the programme content as well being the subject of the learning process while the student who has not been consulted over the choice merely has to adapt to it and invariably participates in the process as an object. But the transactional or dialogic model of communication favours a participatory or shared form of education in which the teacher is merely the catalyst of the learning context in which pupil and teacher can gain knowledge through a shared exploration and experience. For Freire, the teacher ceases to be 'the teacher' and is transformed into a 'student among students', a partner with the students in the learning process willing to learn from and with the students.

The 'diffusion of innovation' paradigm of communication which seems to be the pattern favoured by most Theatre for Development projects in Africa, including the Madina project, Samaru - in which the target communities are expected to trade comfortable old practices for new uncertainties on the basis of recommendations from external authorities or experts is simply a 'one-way persuasion process', very often a top-to-bottom or centre-to-periphery mode of communication with no contribution whatsoever from the target groups in determining what is or is not good for the groups or individuals within the groups. Freire's pedagogy, on the other hand, is one predicated upon dialogue as the best means of achieving meaningful education and communication and not a one-way indoctrination process in which the teacher constitutes in himself a bank of knowledge which is transferred into the hard-working and passively listening pupil in a one-directional flow.

Even with the much talked about follow-up action which is a key feature of Theatre for Development programmes, the fact that Theatre for Development projects in most instances use the diffusion of innovation model of communication , the follow-ups simply become nothing more than a feedback for the outside experts, a 'device to make the external manipulation more effective' and not as a mechanism for making the intervention agencies more responsive to the needs of the community.[14] The follow-ups just measure the responses of members of the target group to the new ideas or themes dealt with in the plays, assess the uptake of the development initiatives and ideas which the experts have brought in, and then fashion new plays that address areas where the first work seems not to have succeeded a or in some cases, proceed to the next phase of the development scheme or strategy as already worked out by the centre or outside agencies. The members of the community have no input whatsoever, and are not in control even of the use to which their responses are going to be put.

Looking at the plethora of Theatre for Development programmes in Africa, one really struggles to find any that in actual fact tries to get the members of the target communities to become genuine actors or participants in the theatre-making process. For some inexplicable reason, a majority of the Theatre for Development programmes in Africa fall short of Boal who rightly argues that, 'All truly revolutionary theatrical groups should transfer to the people the means of production in the theatre so that the people themselves may utilize them. The theatre is a weapon, and it is the people who should wield it.'[15]

I believe that the main goal of all Theatre for Development workers should be to find the best way of achieving this transference and not the predominantly agit-prop theatrical activities which seem to be the norm. And one of the easiest ways of transferring the theatrical process into the hands of the oppressed as we shall see later on in this chapter is by working within existing or indigenous theatre or performance forms which the target group is quite familiar with. However, for a lot of the groups, it is just enough to intervene with a performance about a community's problems after detailed research by the outside group for social awareness to be achieved as we did in Madina with our two performances. In Madina our research in the end yielded two plays - the first one had sanitation as its central theme and the second explored the theme of communal unity and identity. What we did however was to create two multi-textured plays that had a lot of themes arising from our data interwoven in them. The key thing we wanted to achieve was to point out through the plays the nature of the interconnectedness of the various problems which we found in the community - lack of adequate sanitation such as private and public toilets is the starting point of the problems for one of the characters in *Free Ranging in Angola* who while relieving himself in the bush (a practice referred to by the locals 'free ranging' and the treacherous illegal refuse site is called 'Angola') is chased by the landowner and in his haste to get away, with trousers half down falls and is cut very badly by a piece of broken glass. This situation introduces the quack doctor who charges so much only to inject all manner of concoction (ranging from expired antibiotics to water from dirty containers) into the poor man. Meanwhile, the wound begins to fester until the family rally round and on the advice of a qualified nurse he is taken to the teaching hospital where because of the advanced stage of infestation he has to have the leg amputated. The second play worked along similar lines from refuse dumping on private land to explosive fights at the only water well in the community - another key aim of *Play Two* was to highlight the fact that those in authority did not give a damn about the plight of the community, being more concerned with the political rivalry between the Assemblyman and the CDR official. Now, these two plays when we performed them at the market square were really well received, especially the undeniable comedy which we strung out of most of the characters which kept the spectators fully regaled with laughter for the duration of the performance. Also the meeting which ended the second performance in which members of the audience were invited to join the actors in having an *indaba* to debate the issue as well as adjudicate in the dispute which had been brought by the landlord to the assemblyman, proved to be quite long and very animated as people spoke with feeling about what they had seen and how close the situations in the plays came to the reality of life in Madina. The spectators even congratulated the workshop group for our ability to capture within so a short a stay the rhythm and lingo of life in Madina, but they wished we could have stayed longer so as to see more and may be make more plays with and about life in their community. Sadly, this meeting had to be stopped because we had to leave as it was our last day and it was getting rather late for some members of the workshop group who had to return to their regions that same evening.

But as I have contested elsewhere[16], this mode of intervention merely creates ripples in the pond of the oppressed which returns to its relative calm when the buzz or excitement of the ripples are gone. How, for instance, one may ask, did our performance in Madina, even with the heated and protracted 'meeting' which we had structured into the second play and which had enabled members of the community to join the group as part of the performance in order to debate the social issues and themes highlighted by the play. My argument against this type of Theatre for Development practice is that it fails to realise that in order for genuine development to occur, members of the target community need to develop a critical consciousness about themselves and their circumstances and this can only come through praxis and a conscientization process in which they, 'not as recipients, but as knowing subjects achieve a deepening awareness both of the sociocultural reality that shapes their lives and of their capacity to transform that reality.'[17] This usually is completely absent in this type of theatre. A truly 'transactional' and liberatory theatre aesthetic in which there is real participation all through the theatre process will enable both the outside theatre group and the target community to critically engage in a dialogic exploration, and not the transferral of information of the agit-prop style. And this naturally leads me to the next issue which seems to limit the possibilities or capabilities of Theatre for Development programmes and practices to genuinely make a contribution to alleviating the problems besetting the oppressed.

The Ad-hocism of the Product-Oriented Approach.

The product-oriented approach in Theatre for Development is evidently synonymous with or a direct result of the diffusion of innovation model of development communication in which the outside group act as experts who bring new ideas and development programmes to the oppressed. And in theatre terms this equates to Etherton's theory of theatre for consumption, with the outside group as makers of the theatre product and the target community as its consumers. But as Boal cautions would be practitioners of theatre for liberation purposes. 'In order to understand this *poetics of the oppressed* one must keep in mind its main objective: to change the people - 'spectators', passive beings in the theatrical phenomenon - into actors, transformers of the dramatic action.'[18]

For when the members of a community talk about their problems themselves and in their own voices, when they speak about the things that interest them it is bound to come out differently than when these same problems are spoken about by people who had never felt the pinch or burden of the problems. Not much good comes from outsiders coming to a community with a diagnostic view of and solutions to their problems - almost like coming and telling them what to do. The catalyst's job should be to help them to decide what to do, help them to find a solution and not impose one on them. And this can best be achieved through giving them the tool with which to conduct the search for answers themselves.

While working in Ghana was I felt that, on the part of the authorities who allowed my appointment, there was not really a genuine desire for a truly independent theatre movement to develop, one that would be free from any interventions from Accra. This was evident from the resistance and the ultimate rejection of the administrative structure for Theatre for Development which members of the Theatre Unit and I as consultant designed for the whole country. I had purposefully started my work in the country by spending the first ten days of my one month stay in a management workshop in which we played around with various management structures before arriving at one which contained both possibilities for freedom and a measure of accountability. These two things were necessary for Theatre for Development as I see it. The idea of freedom was essential, as I pointed out earlier, so that communities can, with time, become owners who were in complete control of the Theatre for Development process, while accountability, on the other hand, was to ensure that the cultural officers who we trained later and sent back to their respective communities to initiate theatre programmes can be monitored by the Theatre Unit and Regional Coordinators as budget holders. Again, as already argued, the monitoring was not to do with or in matters of the content of the programmes but in terms of their continuity and effectiveness in engaging and galvanizing the communities into exploring, articulating and hopefully transcending their experiences using the theatre as a language for doing so. The Organizational Chart loosely approximates to the management structure which we designed for the country.

The connecting lines, especially between the Regional Coordinators and the Regional Core Teams, do not represent a fixed and clearly defined structure of control between the boxes. The lines merely represent the possible flow of resources from the centre to the periphery until the communities take over resourcing and control of the theatre process completely. The overall plan therefore was to train a core team of trainers - five from each region - in the techniques of Theatre for Development so that they in turn will go back to their respective regions and replicate the training process for community cultural officers, with members of the Theatre Unit acting as resource persons. Again, we expected autonomy to be progressively maintained down the structure so that individual cultural officers in conjunction with members of the community are solely responsible for the nature and frequency of theatre activities in their communities. The regional core team members, together with appointed representatives of the Theatre Unit, would, from time to time, monitor the effectiveness and regularity of community theatre programmes.

One other aim of the training was to gradually move to a situation of less dependency of the

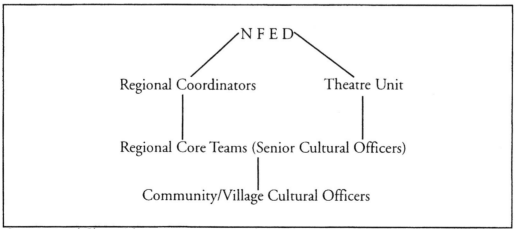

Organisational Chart. A loose approximation to the management structure designed for the country.

regions and the communities on the funding from Accra for theatre performances to happen; in fact, what I envisaged was for Accra to only be responsible for the salaries and the occasional expenses of the cultural officers. The was basically the reason why the training programme incorporated a lot of the 'poor theatre' techniques of Jerzy Grotowski (1968) - a theatre where the performer had to rely more and more on his or her body and its possibilities and less and less on the external paraphernalia of 'normal' theatre such as a 'proper' stage, costume, props, set design and lighting. Another key theme pursued during the training programme - and which it was my hope would subsequently become the guiding philosophy of the whole Theatre for Development programme in the country - was the notion of theatre as play. This to a large extent was based on my conviction that every theatre activity and process should be engaged in and realised within a play frame. Over the course of time, I have come to the conclusion that every theatre form and process represents a playful encounter between the performer and the spectator, or in the case of Theatre for Development, between a group of participants, within a unique space framed and defined by all who are involved in the process.. It is this quality which, for me, makes it theatre and differentiates it from any other form of encounter or exploration. Besides, play is disarming, but at the same time creative as it takes judgmental pressure out of whatever activity that individuals pursue within its frame. The thinking behind this was the desire to ensure that members of a community were never forced into participating, rather, their choice to be part of the theatre activity had to be volitional and primarily based on their conviction that they were going to have fun doing it, and also that they were going to be in control of some part at least, if not the entire process , and that they were to make their own rules for the game, choose whatever form they wish to use, determine what subjects they wish to explore - with minimal interference from anyone, including their local or resident cultural officer, who was only to act as the catalyst of the context, and sometimes just a participant like the rest of the community.

Unfortunately, however, the preference from the centre was for individual projects to be submitted directly to the central office for funding. What I had proposed was for the Theatre Unit to be allowed a separate annual budget which it allocated on the basis of annual proposals detailing programmes and projects from the regions or communities. This way, I had hoped that a continuous programme of performances could be organized and maintained at the village and regional levels without much interference from Accra. The performance training workshop in Madina was geared towards getting the participants to realise that theatre-making ought to be a practical and democratic process of give and take between everyone involved and also for them to realise the potential of theatre as a useful context within which a group of people can democratically explore or exchange ideas and experience. That it was a fun way of learning and that the play frame of the theatre process, because it removes pressure and imposes a 'less serious' and relaxed attitude, establishes and enhances the learning and exchange process through the creativity which it engenders. Our hope was that the workshop participants who were to become the cultural officers for the regions and communities would take this knowledge and skill of making theatre and using it creatively and pedagogically back to their respective communities where they'd begin to initiate theatre projects and performances with the villages. The object was for the communities to become solely responsible for their theatre performances with minimum or no interventions from Accra or any other outside groups who'd come as we did in Madina to essay and present it with its social ills. Most communities without doubt are already aware that they have problems and the last thing they need therefore is for outsiders to come and rub these in by pointing them out. Rather, what I hoped our programme would achieve was merely showing the communities another and potentially less stressful way of dealing with or confronting these problems. To this end, the chosen maxim of our workshop was the idea that 'outside development is no development' - meaning that salvation had to come from within both the intellectual and material/physical resources of each group of oppressed or else contexts of dependency will become established and entrenched. Our emphasis therefore was to move to a situation where individual cultural workers, while teaching their communities or villages new theatre styles and forms, were to endeavour to see to what extent they could explore or work within or with existing traditional forms as these would already be familiar to the communities - their work was merely to show the people new possibilities and strengths in what they already had. This practice is not new really; it is already being tried out by some groups on the continent as David Kerr[19] points out with reference to the conceptually better Katsina -Ala workshop in Northern Nigeria by the Ahmadu Bello Collective (the group that initiated the Samaru and Maska projects) and the use of the *Pungwe* by the Morewa Popular Theatre workshop in Zambia in 1983. I have elsewhere[20] made a case for the employment of traditional forms and styles of Theatre for Development purpose, especially as a means of avoiding the possible and unhelpful alienation which foreign theatre forms and styles tend to bring about. However, I hasten to add that foreign forms and styles should sometimes be used and taught as it can teach communities new modes of theatrical exploration and expression to add to the ones they already have.

Traditional Forms and Audience Participation in Theatre for Development

There is no doubt that the chances of audience participation can significantly be increased when the spectators are familiar with the style or form of theatre which they are watching or participating in. But having said that, I am not for one moment suggesting that employing a foreign or alien

form such as conventional western dialogic drama automatically precludes audience participation, only that when one is using such an unfamiliar form, that what is required would be a more carefully demystified practicalization since the audience would need to be educated into the codes and conventions of the form to enable any meaningful engagement to occur.

Africa is blessed with many traditional and indigenous forms and styles of performances, and some of these are already being successfully employed by Theatre for Development groups across the continent as a means of getting the communities involved in the theatre process as shown by the use of the *Pungwe* in Zimbabwe, the *Kwaghir* in the Katsina-Ala projects in Benue and the *Lifela* by the Marotholi Theatre Group in Lesotho, and the successful use of masquerade theatre style in Guinea Bissau.[21] There are also instances in other parts of the world where Theatre for Development groups have successfully employed traditional forms for their practice. Examples include the Jana Sanskriti who work with traditional Indian styles in their work with the oppressed villages around Calcutta, and the very radical and innovative theatre director, Kanhailal, also from India, who has for a long time been experimenting with the Manipuri *phunga wari*, a tradition of fireside stories[22] Theatre Dinasti which uses *wayang orang* (the traditional theatre of Indonesia) characters and structure in its Theatre for Development work. The leader of the last group, Emha Ainun Nadjib, explains the significance and effectiveness of the traditional forms when he says that, 'the power of *Wayang* cannot be underestimated. You can do modern satires for the city public, but the rural audiences cannot be moved with intellectual arguments. You have to communicate with them through their guts where *Wayang* characters like Semar, the clown live.'[23]

The *Kwaghir* is a richly stylized and complex form of 'total theatre' which emerged in the 1960s at the time of the Tiv riots in Northern Nigeria, it employs a vaudeville style and structure with a programme that combines narrative, acrobatics, dancing, puppetry etc., and these are then framed and presented as 'a mixture of traditional ritual elements and modern theatrical effects'.[24] The *Pungwe*, like the *Kwaghir*, is a popular traditional form which within its structure and aesthetics already incorporates much of the 'poetics of the oppressed' which Theatre for Development is trying to establish - evidence exists that the rural people used it effectively to mobilize against the racist and oppressive regime of Ian Smith during Zimbabwe's struggle for independence. The Marotholi, according to Mda[25] have also successfully used the traditional form of *lifela* as part of their Theatre for Development initiative. The *lifela* is a very flexible 'form of poetic self-definition created from traditional sources to express class consciousness and resistance to the controls of the migrant labour system.[26] There is also abundant evidence which suggest that traditional rituals, songs and dances were used effectively to challenge colonialism in Kenya, and recently neo-colonialism by the Kamiriithu theatre experiments of Ngugi wa Thiong'o and Ngugi wa Mere[27], an experiment which threatened the government so much that it banned both *I'll Marry When I Want* and *Mother, Sing for Me*, the two plays that came out of the Kamiriithu theatre of and by the people initiative.

One thing though is clear from the examples above - which is that some of these do not seem to be pure autochthonous forms that can be used on their own, except may be the *Pungwe* and the *lifela* and the masquerade form. However, the significant fact for my argument is that most of the traditional forms by their very nature and function seem to have the flexibility to take on board the radical and conceptual demands of Theatre for Development. Mda is still right to point out that not all the forms are usable or can adapted, but even those that can not be used in their entirety can be borrowed in part to strengthen conventional Theatre for Development structures and forms as the ABU collective did in Katsina-Ala with *Kwaghir* or the Marotholi in Lesotho with *lifela*. The masquerade form, as the *Okumkpa* of Afikpo and the Omabe of Nsukka have shown, has the both the structural and conceptual capability to embody and sustain a full theatre-for -development programme since it already serves as a context for the communities to engage in critical exploration and reflection. On the other hand, one can go the other route as I suggested we could have done with our Madina plays or as the Kamiriithu community did of structuring a play making use of a traditional performance framework of either a ritual or dance or mythology.

The Kamiriithu community experiment, although not strictly speaking, a formalised Theatre for Development initiative, managed to become for the community a tool or medium for self-reflection and self-definition. But above all, it was a good example of a context in which traditional forms rituals, dances, folklore, mythology and history were combined with conventional western theatre structures to create a unique and liberating theatre experience both for the performers and the spectators. On the other hand, the possibilities of working within the framework of structures of an existing traditional performance form such as the popular and ubiquitous *anansegoro* in Ghana was unfortunately missed by our Madina experiment. For one thing, the fact that Madina is a multi-ethnic community and a largely 'illiterate' one, working within the *anansegoro*, especially as I suggested of anchoring or building our performance on the key motifs and structural features of the genre, and possibly exploiting the well-known traits of its the central character, Ananse, who incidentally happens to be the most popular figure from folklore among the various ethnic groups in Ghana, would have been the most radical and without doubt the most effective way of reaching out to the people, some who could not understand us all the time because we performed more of the time in English. This technique of appropriating elements, characters and the ambiance from and of rituals, folklore and mythology has already been successfully done as Richard Andrews[28] work on the autodrammi (the community dramas) of Monticchiello has shown. The Teatro Povero di Monticchiello (as it is called) has enabled an impoverished community which felt politically and culturally to be deprived of a voice to create one for itself for, 'the villagers have developed a unique technique for expressing themselves on stage... or rather in their own village square... The Teatro Povero is a collective which enables the modern villagers to articulate ideas, grievances, aspirations, and anxieties into speech and action on stage.'[29]

There is clearly no doubt that there are many advantages in working within or with the traditional forms and structures. The key one I believe is the familiarity and echo of recognition which it excites in the spectators. It is a familiarity or recognition which can only be conducive to

participation. Besides, because the community already knows how to use or uses these forms or structures, are familiar with the characters as the case may be, the radicalization and perhaps intensification which a Theatre for Development deployment of the forms achieves helps to open the eyes of the community to the possibilities of using the forms in new ways to explore and express new experiences. This basically is what I believe Theatre for Development catalysts should be aiming for -

to help communities to either re-discover their forgotten traditional forms, to find new ways of employing existing forms, or when necessary teach them new forms to use to cope with contemporary realities and experience. And where they succeed in doing that, they would have achieved the greatest aspiration of Theatre for Development, which is to help oppressed or underdeveloped communities learn how to use theatre as a new language for critical self-reflection, exploration and analysis in order to articulate new directions that can lead to both individual and communal transformation. Many of the traditional forms in my opinion, have in-built mechanisms for achieving that.

Theatre for Development as Process

The main danger with the product-oriented approach to a programme of Theatre for Development is the inherent ad-hocism which it brings about; it is an adhocism born out of a consumerist and capitalist ethics _ an ethics in which there is always the necessity to differentiate between the producer and the consumer, the have and the have-not, and by extension in the context of Theatre for Development, the performer and the spectator. The implications of this essentially capitalist dualism and its compartmentalizing binary opposition are many, especially for the Theatre for Development group itself. It has often been argued that you don't have to be poor in order to work for or identify with the poor. It is true that a majority of the catalysts involved in Theatre for Development, either come from a middle class background or have become middle class by virtue of their educational attainment and so in socio-economic terms are usually better-off than the masses of oppressed peoples who are the targets of their Theatre for Development activities.

The problem and temptation then for these theatre workers in a product-driven Theatre for Development work is that very often they fall into the seductive trap of the 'saviour syndrome', in which they begin to see themselves as outside experts or redeemers who are bringing development to the oppressed through their messages of innovation and salvation. In Freirian and practical terms, this translates into the 'banking system' of education which I have already mentioned above where it is the teacher who has all the information and knowledge needed to enlighten the benighted student and in this instance, it is the outsider cultural worker who has all the ideas and means that would lead to the solutions to the problems of the poor and oppressed communities. And in development communication theory this equates to the 'dominance model of the communicator-audience relationship' in which the communicator is the source and controller of the communication context while the audience becomes simply an object of mass persuasion.[30] Its essential characteristic is that it is one-way with absolutely no input from the audience, both in terms of context and content. But as Freire rightly points out, genuine learning is never possible under this system as the mind is hardly touched, never mind being opened in any critical way. In the same way, when outside groups research into a community and go away, as we did in Madina and as many other Theatre for Development groups do, to make plays based on data from the community and then bring these back as finished products to show the community, only momentary excitement and may be recognition occurs, and even with the heated debates and discussions which this style of working may sometimes bring about, it can never achieve the same level of awareness and conscientization that can happen when the community owns and makes use of the theatre process for itself, the kind of empowerment to speak for the self which a true 'forum' can achieve. For Boal, the movement from 'simultaneous dramaturgy' (when the spectator 'writes' the dramatic action while the actor acts it as it is being written) to the forum in which 'the spectator delegates no power to the character (actor) either to act or think in his place; on the contrary, he himself assumes the protagonic role, changes the dramatic action, tries out solutions, discusses plans for change - in short trains himself for real action'[31], represents that complete ownership and control of the theatre production process by the oppressed necessary for true liberation to occur. Needless to add that it is the play environment, its tension free ambiance and its ability to release creative energy that can give a critical voice and expressive physicality to an otherwise voiceless and awkward group of oppressed and deprived people. Play is liberating as it enables participants to drop the constraints and inhibitions of daily social masks and take risks into the unknown which is the zone of knowledge. And it was for this reason that in our training workshop in Madina, we had actively sought to encourage the adoption of an attitude of play to any Theatre for Development activity. A significant part of the workshop was devoted to teaching the participants to re-learn or rediscover the spirit of play which tends to be generally lost as individuals grow move out of childhood. And in keeping with the desire to work within existing traditional forms, we wanted the cultural officers to incorporate in their subsequent theatre practice traditional games that the people play or used to play as a means of gradually introducing people into the theatre process. The games were to set the play tone which was to be maintained all through the process.

Arising from the dominance or one-way persuasion model and its attendant centre-to-periphery practicalisation in development communication, is the other danger which the product-driven approach can lead to, which is one of appropriation of the theatre by outside agencies or governments for ideological or propaganda peddling. The major difficulty for me in Ghana was the fact that the government saw Theatre for Development as just being a part of its functional literacy programme and not an activity that was meant to exist in its own right. There were key themes for development already worked out and agreed and it was these that were expected to provide the themes for the work of the theatre groups whose sole task would be to develop plays about these and feed to the communities; some of the themes include drug abuse, lack of health care provision, poor sanitation, teenage pregnancy, youth unemployment and evils of illiteracy. This policy or expectation, however, ran completely counter to my own ideas and expectations of Theatre for Development. It was obvious that what the government had in mind was more of an agit-prop style of theatre firmly developed within the mold of the diffusion of innovation paradigm of development communication. Besides, there already was in the country a theatre group, Adehyeman Theatre Group, which was employed by the government and which was using this style of theatre to work with government ministries and other non-governmental development agencies.

I recommended that this group continued with this style and but at the same time to consider expanding into 'invisible theatre' and 'guerrilla theatre' techniques. This group and others like it could be used and are being used to sell government developmental themes while the cultural officers I was training would aim to teach their respective communities how to use theatre, whether indigenous or borrowed forms, as a forum, context or language for both individual or communal exploration, analysis and expression. They were to do this by living with and being a part of their respective communities, and initiating theatre explorations and performances. Theatre was not going to be a special or rare event as it usually is with the outside intrusion or product-led method, but a living and thriving language of discourse open to everyone in the community. And because the end product was not the main thing but rather the process of it - the performance when it does happen and there are spectators who happen not to have been part of its making, should be seen as only a bonus and a means of sharing the experience of the journey and the discovery which the participants have gone through.

I find Ross Kidd's notion[32] of the 'drama-that-never-finishes' to be a very apt description of this kind of theatre, a theatre in which every interruption by a spectator reveals new dimensions to and thus new insights for the participating group into the issue being explored. The key thing here is that everyone is free to interrupt the action, in fact their interruption is actively encouraged. It is this same idea which is the philosophy underpinning Boal's forum sessions in which the 'spect-actors' continually intervene to interrogate and change the course or direction of the action of the drama once it is not to their liking until a democratically agreed solution to the problem being explored is reached, whenever that is! Nothing is ever presented as a final or finished product of the theatrical enterprise and neither is any view accepted as the final or ultimate view as there is always a general recognition and acceptance of other possibilities and directions. Boal summarizes this when he says that, 'the bourgeois theatre is a finished theatre... The bourgeoisie presents the spectacle... Popular audiences are interested in experimenting, in rehearsing, and they abhor the 'closed spectacles. In these cases they try to enter into a dialogue with the actors, to interrupt the action, to ask for explanations without waiting politely for the end of the play. Contrary to bourgeois code of manners, the people's code allows and encourages the spectator to ask questions, to dialogue, to participate.'[33]

De-emphasizing the end product therefore, because the play does not have to end, draws attention to the process which the participants are going through, especially the creative potentiality inherent in the play ambiance within which the theatre process is framed and pursued. The notion of play as an attitude to an activity or a series of activities carries with it a reduction of tension or pressure, an absence of judgment, an abandonment of holds and inhibitions, plus a clearing from the head of the cobwebs of social and cultural conditioning to enable learning and encountering new experiences to take place. All this is possible because of the volitional nature of play which predisposes every participant to push themselves and their experiences to the limits and it is only at such moments that true illumination can occur. And so a process-led Theatre for Development is fun for the people who take part in it, but it is the fun of knowing that the individual can go all the way, that there are no limits and that within the rules of the game, every individual ability as well as limitation is recognised and accommodated. In the end, there are no stars and no walk-ons, no producers and consumers, just as there are no spectators and performers. What we have is a participating group made up of members of a community, village, neighbourhood or inmates in a prison or patients in a hospital ward.

Notes

1   Michael Etherton in Mda Zakes, *When People Play People: Development Communication Through Theatre*, (Johannesburg, London and New Jersey, Witwatersrand University Press and Zed Books, 1993), p. 48.

2   Paulo Freire, *Cultural Action for Freedom*, (London, Penguin Books, 1972), also *Pedagogy of the Oppressed*, (London, Penguin Books, 1972), p. 25.

3   Idem., p. 16.

4   See Simon Ottenberg, *Masked Rituals of Afikpo: the Context of an African Art*, (Washington, Washington University Press, 1975).

5   David Kerr, *African Popular Theatre*, (London, Cape Town, Nairobi and Harare, James Currey, Heinemann, Boabab Books, David Philips and EAEP, 1995), p. 159.

6 Ibid., p. 160.

7 Abah, Oga and Etherton, Michael 'The Samaru Projects: Street Theatre in Northern Nigeria', in *Theatre Research International* (vol. VII/3, 1982), p. 226.

8 Augusto Boal, *Theatre of the Oppressed,* (London, Pluto Press. 1979), p. 122.

9 Zakes Mda, *When People Play People: Development Communication Through Theatre,* (Johannesburg, London and New Jersey, Witwatersrand University Press and Zed Books, 1993). p. 184.

10 Ibid., p. 50.

11 K. S. Nair and Shirley White, 'Participation is the Key to Development Communication', in *Media Development,* (Vol. XXXIV/ 3, 1987), p. 36.

12 Ibid., p. 37.

13 Freire op. cit., p. 46.

14 Kearl in Nair and White, op. cit., p. 36.

15 Augusto Boal, op. cit., p. 122.

16 Osita Okagbue 'A Drama of their Lives: Theatre for Development in Africa, in *Contemporary Theatre Studies,* (forthcoming, 1997).

17 Freire, op. cit., p. 93.

18 Boal, op. cit., p. 122.

19 Op. cit., p. 170.

20 Okagbue, op. cit.

21 see Kerr, 1995, op. cit., p. 157.

22 see Rustom Barucha, 'The Indigenous Theatre of Kanhailal', in *NTQ,* (vol VIII/29, 1992), p. 14.

23 Eugene van Erven, (1989) 'Beyond the Shadows of Wayang: Liberation Theatre in Indonesia', in *NTQ* (vol. V/17, 1989), p. 50.

24 Kerr, op. cit., p. 166.

25 Mda, op. cit., pp. 73-80.

26 Idem., p. 73.

27 see Cook, David and Okenimkpe, Michael, *Ngugi wa Thiong'o: An Exploration of his Writings,* (London, Heinemann, 1983); and wa Thiong'o, Ngugi *Decolonising the Mind,* (London, Heinemann. 1986).

28 Richard Andrews, 'Finding a Voice: the Community Dramas of Monticchiello', in *New Theatre Quarterly* (vol. VII/25, 1991).

29 Idem., pp. 78-83.

30 Mda, op. cit., p. 59.

31 Boal, op. cit., p. 122.

32 Ross Kidd, 'Popular Theatre, Conscientization and Popular Organization', Toronto, International Council for Adult Education (research paper, 1984), p. 13.

33 Boal, op. cit., p. 142.

Didactic Showmen: Theatre for Development in Contemporary South Africa

Page Laws

Aut prodesse volunt aut delectare poetae, aut simul et iucunda et idonea dicere vitae.

Horace, Ars Poetica[1]

If they [school children] see a clown saying 'brush your teeth daily,' they're more likely to do it.

Paul William Jacobs – Former educator and actor, Eersterrust Township

Introduction

The dictum that poetry - here, theatre - must both delight and instruct is Western, but it is equally African, Asian, universal, even commonsensical. All Theatre for Development would seem implicitly based on the premise that people learn best when the learning is somehow active and pleasurable. There are, however, different types of pleasure, ranging from the cerebral to the visceral. And there are different types of learning, ranging from the practical know-how needed to construct a good latrine to the political know-how necessary to defeat hegemonic racism.

Because apartheid so long made South Africa a sort of Evil Eden of Oppression, and because the weapons used in the struggle were so varied, there is an extraordinary range of theatrical expression which might justly qualify for the term 'Theatre for Development.' These expressions range from impromptu shows for school children on seemingly apolitical topics such as dental hygiene (mentioned in the epigraph above) to full-fledged stage musical extravaganzas such as *Sarafina 2* - a 14-million rand anti-Aids show that may have marked the apotheosis of a certain tradition, dating back to Gibson Kente's work, of musical entertainment *cum* education on South African stages.[2]

The purpose of this essay is to survey the history of didactic theatre in South Africa, using the term 'didactic' very broadly and in its positive sense. (I will use the term 'moralistic' for heavy-handed or unsuccessful didacticism.) Part Two is devoted to terms and definitions, still hotly debated by critics and theatre practitioners alike. The terms 'community theatre' and 'township theatre' are familiar to non-Africans but by no means monolithic in meaning. For many, 'township theatre' has positive connotations, but for some (such as critic Andrew Horn) the term is negative.[3] 'Town theatre' means something entirely different from 'township theatre.' ('Town theatre,' according to Michael Etherton, involves 'both blacks and whites in experimental and often highly political theatre.')[4] The term 'tribal musical,' applied to works such as *Ipi Tombi* (1975), *uMabatha* (1973), and *KwaZulu* (1973), has become a pejorative, as has 'export musical,' though with exceptions. Horn's terms 'theatre of exploitation,' 'theatre of manipulation' and 'theatre of acceptance and lament' are obviously negative. Harder to distinguish among are the many positive epithets including 'popular theatre,' 'theatre of commitment,' 'theatre of purpose,' 'theatre of criticism and confrontation,' 'theatre of defiance,' 'theater of self-realization,' 'theatre of the oppressed,' 'theatre for conscientisation,' 'comgen (for community-generated) theatre,' etc. Add to these the European terms 'epic theatre' and 'agitprop' plus the jargon associated with 'workshop' productions, and one begins to see the range of the terminology debate. [5] The term 'Theatre for Development' has itself been used in various ways by critics such as playwright/dramaturge Zakes Mda whose ideas will also be discussed.

Part Three of this essay is an extension of the definition debate in which I try to make statements that would seem to describe the highly syncretic form to be labelled 'Theatre for Development' in South Africa. Though the 'may be' format of the statements may indicate a lack of critical conviction, the variety of plays to be included under the 'big tent' of the definition requires such caution.

Part Four of the essay deals with the 'mood' of the theatre world during the winter months (June, July and August) in South Africa, 1996. I allude to the Standard Bank National Arts Festival in Grahamstown, a convenient, if arbitrary, sampling of national theatre trends. Since the *Sarafina 2* scandal was still much in the news that winter, and Zakes Mda chose to speak on it at his Grahamstown Festival lecture, I feature it in this 'freeze-frame' approach.

Part Five will be a speculation on the future of South African theatre in an era when the Truth and Reconciliation Commission Hearings still provide all-too-vivid a reminder of past horrors. Also included is a brief discussion of the far-from-resolved class and gender conflicts that promise to provide grist for didactic theatre well into the foreseeable future. It goes without saying that women are among the most important 'showmen' working in the theatre today, and the term is intended to encompass 'showpeople' of both genders.

Underlying my whole discussion is the assumption that there is something distinctive about didactic South African theatre, something I have christened in my title with the intentionally American- sounding term 'showmanship.' It, too, is intended to be a positive term, though the proximate term 'showbiz' is sometimes negative. The 'showmanship' that has characterized successful South African theatre - perhaps best exemplified in the internationally renowned two-man show *Woza Albert!* (Ngema, Mtwa and Simon, 1980) - is born of verve, audacity, and creativity under duress. It gives rise to a particular 'exaggerated' acting style found in many of the best productions. It might be seen by an outsider as a confluence of Broadway, Brecht, and *izibongo* (Zulu praise poetry, representing the oral tradition) but it exists, synergistically, beyond these component parts. It is the essence of something that elsewhere might be called 'theatricality.' 'Theatricality' in its positive sense of 'the use of the theatre medium to its utmost' is also universal, but takes a distinctively South African form south of the Limpopo.

I. A History of Didactic Theatre in South Africa

In times of upheaval, fearful and fruitful, the evenings of the doomed classes coincide with the dawns of those that are rising. It is in these twilight periods that Minerva's owl sets out on her flights.

Bertolt Brecht – Appendices to the Short Organum[6]

We don't have to make up stories.

Percy Mtwa[7]

English Language Theatre

Setting aside, for the purposes of this subheading, the rich oral performance tradition of the Khoi San and later the Bantu peoples of South Africa, the first theatre one can pin down to a conventionally understood site (i.e. *building*) was the African Theatre in Cape Town which opened in 1801.[8] The fare was presumably imported, and the tutelary relationship with Europe lasted well through that century and into the next. Missionary education promulgated the borrowed canon, although some missionaries were more forward-thinking than others. Bhekizizwe Peterson, in his 'Apartheid and the Political Imagination in Black South African Theatre,' calls the Rev. Father Bernard Huss of St. Francis College, Marianhill, 'one of the earliest and most influential pioneers of the social and pedagogical uses of theatre.'[9] Among these early 'medieval morality plays, secular European comedies, and dramatisations of Zulu oral narratives,' (p. 36) also appears a play called *Joseph in Egypt* performed by African students in the year 1904. Historians agree that H.I.E. Dhlomo's *The Girl Who Killed to Save: Nongqause the Liberator* (1935 or 1936) was the 'first published play in English by a black South African.'[10] It was to be nearly three more decades (not until 1964) before another play by a black South African appeared in print, Lewis Nkosi's *The Rhythms of Silence* (Oxford University Press), now considered a precursor of Black Consciousness Theatre.11 The end of the 1940s saw Alan Paton's novel of liberal hope, *Cry, the Beloved Country*, adapted by the American Maxwell Anderson into the Broadway musical *Lost in the Stars*, rarely mentioned any more in South African theatre histories. Its importance was clearly overshadowed by more significant types of African and American cross pollination in the arts (especially jazz) and in the nascent movements for civil rights in both countries. The 1950s saw the *Drum* generation in South Africa model itself very much on American lines. In theatre, turning points included Athol Fugard's collaboration with *Drum* writers Lewis Nkose, Nat Nakasa and Bloke Modisane to create *No-Good Friday* (1958). Aside from helping launch the career of South Africa's still preeminent playwright Athol Fugard - the 'father' against whom all subsequent playwrights have been locked in Harold Bloomsian Oedipal conflict - *No-Good Friday* features many of the characteristics that have come to be associated with at least the existential end of the didactic theatre spectrum. It is collaborative in origin, multiracial, has an urban setting, and involves victimized people further victimized by thugs (*tsotsis*). Robert Kavanagh sees the play as a conflict between *clevergeid* (use of mother wit) and *moegoegeid* (stupidity)[12] with no real resolution. He does not, however, consider it radical enough: '...It functioned principally in the interests of certain sections of the English-speaking white group, while partially reflecting the attitudes and affiliations of certain black intellectuals' (p. 83).

The years 1952-53 had seen the formation of the Union of Southern African Artists, a group of white theatre administrative professionals who recognized (some would say exploited) the talent of black performers and at least one black composer, Todd Machikiza. 1959 was a major turning point in South African theatre history with the Union Artists' production of *King Kong*, a musical composed by Machikiza with a libretto by Harry Bloom. Based on the career of a real boxer, Ezekiel Dhlamini, the protagonist at the height of his career has a fight lined up in White City (London) but falls in love with a gangster's girl played by future star Miriam Makeba. He kills a gang member, loses his big break, loses his boxing skill, kills his girl, goes to prison, and, in complete dejection, drowns himself in prison (p. 97). Kavanagh faults the piece artistically for a 'show business' (p. 106) feel at odds with its subject matter. It is politically liberal but by no means radical: 'The play was chiefly directed at white audiences.to prod gently their consciences...and touch their hearts' (p. 109). Even Kavanagh has to admire Todd Machikiza's music, however, to which he attributes the show's success among the many blacks who also saw it. *King Kong* had launched a form - the township musical - which soon had its lesser imitators and its absolute master, Gibson Kente. Having perfected his producing and directing skills working for Union Artists, in 1966 Kente broke with the union to form his own all-black production company.

Kente's career in generally split into two parts - his earlier less political works including *Manana the Jazz Prophet, Sikalo, Lifa,* and *Zwi* and his later more political works such as *How Long?* (1973) and *Too Late* (1974-75). There is a surprising difference of opinion over the political works - Robert Kavanagh, a Gramscian Marxist on most occasions, hailing *Too Late* as a break-though political masterpiece while critics such as Andrew Horn thoroughly condemn its commercialism and inauthenticity. The plot of *Too Late* involves a young country man Saduva come to Soweto to live with his shebeen-keeping aunt and his crippled girl cousin Ntanana. Saduva has trouble with his pass, falls in love with his cousin's friend, and tangles with a vengeful policeman named Pelepele. After unfair imprisonment for the aunt and Saduva, Pelepele kills the crippled Ntanana. Offside, the marginalised 'wise fool' character, prevents Saduva from killing Pelepele in revenge enabling a 'happy end' of sorts when everyone (except Ntanana) is reunited. Kavanagh admires the fact that 'No whites were involved in its staging and administration at all. Furthermore, it was not primarily created for a white audience...It is as if Todd Matshikiza were to have stepped out of *King Kong* and his subservient role in it and struggled for and won the liberty to write and direct the whole play himself.'[13] Kente's actors, who toured all over South Africa, were known for their training and discipline. Two of them touring with Kente's *Mama and the Load* (1979) caught the same itch for creative self-determination that Kente had scratched a decade before. They were Mbongeni Ngema and Percy Mtwa, the future creators with Barney Simon of *Woza Albert!* (1980), and individually of *Asinamali!* (Ngema, 1986) and *Bopha!* (Mtwa, 1985). Ngema and his Committed Artists would eventually produce the Broadway hit *Sarafina* and attempt a sequel in the already-mentioned *Sarafina 2* . Before following Ngema's career that far, it is important to backtrack a bit to the 1970s and 80s to retrieve a major thread in the non-Kente school of didactic theater, namely the Black Consciousness Movement work of Credo Mutwa (*uNosilimela*, 1973), Mthuli Ka Shezi (*Shanti*, performed in 1973 following Shezi's violent death in 1972), Maishe Maponya (*The Hungry Earth*, 1979) and Matsemela Manaka (*Egoli - The City of Gold, Survival, Imbumba, Vuka* and *Pula* - all post the Soweto uprisings of 1976.).

The Black Consciousness Movement provided South African theatre with both the rhetoric and organizing principles for protest. Although Steven Biko and fellow BCM spokesmen discouraged multi-racial collaborations, the era saw the white playwright/ actor Fugard, and his black co-creators John Kani and Winston Ntshona produce *The Island* and *Sizwe Bansi is Dead*, two of the most powerful protest dramas ever written. The white director/ critic Robert Mshengu Kavanagh formed the multiracial Workshop '71 while the Junction Avenue Theatre Company and the Company formed highly successful polemically-based mixed race groups. Says Ian Steadman, 'Characterizing all the new work were formal innovations like episodic structures, quick shifts of scene and tempo, oral narrative, music and street rhythms, jazz, and factory work-rhythms.' This era, he continues, 'signaled the maturation of the adversary tradition into popular South African performance'14.

It was an era of acronyms - BCM for Black Consciousness Movement, BPC for Black People's Conference. The UDF (United Democratic Front) founded cultural desks to inspire and track revolutionary artists. SASO (the South African Students Organization) likewise took an interest in black arts, attacking the well-intentioned but hopelessly white liberal lions Alan Paton and Nadine Gordimer. The seriousness with which the Nationalist government considered theatre is evidenced by their arrest of Strini Moodley and Saths Cooper of TECON (the Theatre Council of Natal) and Sadcque Variava and Solly Ismael of PET (People's Experimental Theatre) on charges of terrorism.[15] MDALI (the Music, Drama, Arts and Literature Institute) in Soweto was likewise forcibly disbanded.[16] Perhaps no single playwright's career summed up the BCM better than that of the ill-fated Mthuli Shezi, pushed onto railroad tracks by a white man with whom he had been arguing. Shezi's *Shanti* is the story of Thabo, a young black man illicitly in love with an Indian girl. He has to flee and serves a short time as a freedom-fighter for Frelimo, before being murdered in his Mozambique refuge. Steadman says of the play, 'It differs from earlier plays in that it was conceived in performance terms as a dynamic representation of black consciousness principles in presentational didactic form.'[17]

African Language Theatre

The study of African-language theatre in South Africa presents a complex problem of evaluation - first, because outsiders such as I must completely rely on the few talented historians and linguists - such as the standard source Albert Gerard - who have apparently mastered these languages, and secondly, because the very existence of these plays is 'tainted' by the tutelary circumstances of their composition and the exploitation of Bantu art to prop up the discredited Bantustan (homelands) policies of the Nationalist apartheid period. Having said that, the plays existed and some still exist, providing revealing links with both the unauthentic colonial past and authentic oral tradition (to be discussed in Part 4). Setting aside the pre-colonial past for a moment, Kavanagh and others mention the importance of African-language touring companies such as Esau Mthethwa's Lucky Stars from Natal. In 1929 the Lucky Stars were performing 'original didactic and satirical comedies in Zulu, based on Zulu traditional life, employing much music and dance.'[18] This 'vaudeville-like' tradition might be seen as one strand, while the written 'dramatic' tradition - highly influenced by missionary education and later the Bantustan policy - might be seen as another. Kavanagh groups the seven major African languages into conglomerates: two of the seven, Venda and Shangane (the latter also called Tsonga), he calls 'smaller and unurbanized.' Zulu and Xhosa - the largest group according to the number of speakers - comprise the Nguni conglomerate; while Sotho/Pedi and Tswana form the Sotho conglomerate (p. 41). This is, again, leaving aside the artificial but very real urban and specialized composite dialects such as '*tsotsitall*' (gangster talk), 'Soweto English' and Fanagalo (miners' dialect).

Beginning with Venda, both Albert Gerard and M.E.R Mathivha cite Titus N. Maumela's *Tshililo* (1957) about marriage customs; M.E.R. Mathivha's *Mabalanganye* (1963), about a bad prince; and Elias S. Netshilema's *Vha Musanda VhoDzegere* (*Lord Dzegere*, 1957).[19] Gerard also mentions *Vhuhosi a vhu thetshelwi* (*Chieftainship must not be challenged*, 1974) and *A hu bebwi mbilu* (*Not the heart is begotten*) about 'generations in conflict.' Finally there is E. S. Madima's *Hu na savhadina* (*Beware of Savhadina*, 1974).

In Tsonga, Gerard cites Samuel J. Baloyi's *Xaka* (*Chaka*, 1958) as does C.T.D. Marivate writing in Klein's *Guide*, though the latter gives the date of *Xaka* as 1960. Both scholars cite B.K.M. Mtombeni's *Malangavi ya mbilu* (*Flames of the heart*, 1966) about the 'painful consequences of philandering'[20] and Eric M. Nkondo's *Muhlupheki ngwanazi* which, in Marivate's words chronicles the 'attempts of Tsongas to free themselves from white oppression.'[21] Marivate also mentions *Ririmi i madlayisani* (*The tongue gets you killed*, 1964) by H. A. Mangwane about 'marital difficulties when one partner, especially the woman, is better educated than the other,' and *Gija wanuna wa matimbu* (*Gija, the strong man*, 1965) by H.S.V. Muzwayine and Bill T. Mageza about migratory labor. P. M. Makgoana's *Vugima-musi* (*The horizon*, 1975) criticizes parents interfering in marriage decisions of their children. E.G.W. Mbhombi's *Madumelani* (1976) is said to be a bit like *Macbeth*.[22]

Turning to the Sotho conglomerate languages - including Pedi (sometimes called Northern Sotho), Southern Sotho and Tswana - and beginning with Pedi, scholars concur that Elias Matlala's *Tshukudu* (*The rhinoceros*, 1941) was a landmark work. P. S. Groenewald (writing in Klein's *Guide*) calls it 'monumental'[23] and Gerard describes it as a 'verse tragedy based on the Samson and Delilah story'[24]. Matalala also wrote *Serogole I* (1948), a historical drama. Gerard notes G. H. Franz's *Maaberone* (1940), Maggie Rammala's *Rangwane ke go paletse* (*Uncle, I have beaten you*, 1971) and S.P.P. Mminele's *Ngwana wa mobu - Child of the soil*, 1967 (pp. 221-223).

Works of note in Southern Sotho include Twentyman N. Mofokeng's *Keh'ona sa joala* (*A calabash of beer*, 1939) which Gerard calls 'the first formal drama in Southern Sotho which deals with the tensions that the modern way of life generates between old and new'[25]. John Povey, writing in Klein's *Guide*, remarks on Sophonia Machabe Mofokeng's 1952 work *Senkatana*[26] and Dyke Sentso's' *Tseleng ea bophelo - The path of life*[27], 1947.

In Tswana language drama, Gerard (p. 218) and A.T. Malepe (writing in Klein) agree on the importance of *Kobo ntsho* (1968, *The black robe*) and *Pelo e ntsho* (1972, *A black heart*), both by J. M. Ntsime, and the latter about Christianity versus witchcraft. Gerard adds to Ntsime's credits *Pelo e ja serati* (*A loving heart knows no bounds*, 1965) and Malepe mentions *Lobisa radipitse* by S. A. Moroke about the dangers of alcohol.[28]

Turning finally to the two largest language groups and beginning with Xhosa, Gerard cites James J. R. Jolobe's *Amathunzi obomi* (1958, *The shadows of life*) in both his own book and his article for Klein's compendium. He also mentions Mafuya Mbidlama's *Zangen'iinkomo* (*The cattle come in*, 1954) but dismisses it as a 'rather mediocre play dramatizing a theme which is a commonplace in African-language writing, the abuses of the bride-price'[29]. Gybon B. Sinxo's *Imfene KaDebeza* (*Debeza's Baboon*) dates all the way back to the 1920s, but again, Gerard seems unimpressed with the early missionary-inspired writers: 'Their plays are inevitably moralizing and often melodramatic'[30]. *U-Manfene* (1962) is by a minister, Rev. L. M. Mbulawa, and 'depicts the intrigue that takes place when a minister of religion is unwillingly transferred from one circuit to another.' Witness K. Tamsanza's *Buzani kubawo* (*Ask my father*, 1958) again concerned traditional versus modern outlooks, and the same author wrote radio plays.[31]

The Zulu vaudeville troop Lucky Stars has already been mentioned on an early parallel course with dramatists. Kavanagh cites skits called *Umthakathi* (*Witch*) and *Ukuqomisa* (*Courting*) that were performed all over South Africa for both blacks and whites in the 1920s and 1930s.[32] Gerard notes the first written drama in Zulu as *U Gubudele namazimuzimu* (*Gubudele and the cannibals*, 1941) by Nimrod Ndebele[33]. Leonard L. J. Mncwango added *Mhla iyokwendela egodini* (*The day of going down in the grave*) in 1951 and Bethuel Blase Ndelu wrote *Mageba lazihlonza* (*I swear by Mageba*) in 1962 about a dynastic quarrel. Zulu themes, according to Gerard, often included 'permissiveness in modern education due to the breakdown of family discipline and to parental impotence and/or indifference in a city environment'[34]. Although writers glorified the past greatness of the Zulu Nation, they also pointed out the drawbacks of traditional life, including, in Gerard's words, 'its brutal authoritarianism, its inhuman customs in connection with marriage and the bride price, and its crude superstitions...'[35]

Although it is difficult for outsiders to grasp much from a series of African-language play titles, even a cursory glance at the English version of the titles or critics' brief synopses of plots indicates the strongly didactic bent of African-language drama. Many of the plays were apparently development-oriented in the authors' efforts to improve 'backward' thinking in religion, medicine, etc. Some plays, such as Eric M. Nkondo's *Muhlupeki mgwanasi* (about 'attempts of Tsongas to free themselves from white oppression') were overtly political, while the historical dramas indirectly served a political agenda which was at least negritudinist if not yet completely *au courant* BCM.

Afrikanas Language Theatre

Ezekiel Mphalele has said of the Afrikaners and their language: '...No one can reasonably be blamed for the language he speaks. On the other hand, a language commits you to a culture, real or imagined. If you use your political power to shut out your human environment and cage yourself in, your culture must shrink and with it your language.'[36] Mphalele was referring, back in 1962, to Afrikaners of the Nationalist Party ilk who now, in 1997, have been consigned by history to their proper minority status in South African political life. Their language, however, still suffers from guilt-by-association, this in spite of the fact that more non-whites speak Afrikaans than whites. A brief review of Afrikaner theatre, both conservative and liberal, might help explain to what degree this distinctive Creole of Dutch and African languages may sometimes have been the target of a 'bad rap.'

The development of early Afrikaans theatre parallels that of English theatre in its tutelage to European models - Dutch and others. In a brochure issued by the OFS Library and Museum Service Subdirectorate called 'The Earliest Afrikaans Playwrights and their Work,' Jacob Lub (1868-1926) is cited for his novel *Eenvoudige mense* (*Simple People*) which he adapted into play form in 1918. In the words of the brochure, 'It links up the theme of sociological problems, as exploited by van Bruggen and Grosskopf, although depicted in a very melodramatic way.' P.W.S. Schumann (1893-1981) wrote, among other works, *Om Lettie se ontwil* (*For Lettie's sake):* 'In these plays, Schumann focused sharply on the nature of the Poor White problem, which had already been exploited by Jochem van Bruggen in his novels and in Grosskopf's plays.'

The first flowering of Afrikaans literature occurred in the 1930s and those authors- named the *Dertigers* (the Thirtiers) after their decade - included dramatist N. P. Van Wyk Louw, author of *Germanicus* (1956) and D. J. Opperman, active in the 1940s. C. Louis Leipoldt and J.F.W. Grosskopf both lived from the 1880s into the late 1940s. Bartho Smit, born in 1924, was also important, living until 1986. The next flowering, the *Sestigers* (the Sixtiers) also included Chris Barnard, and the liberal Andre P. Brink.[37]

Temple Hauptfleisch, in his article 'Afrikaans Playwriting and the Shifting Paradigm in South African Theatre,'[38] characterizes Afrikaans writers as 'highly committed' - though usually not in the Marxist sense of the word. Their commitment has been to 'promoting and protecting the fledgling new language and culture' of the Afrikaners, and Afrikaans literature has often been an 'educational tool in the cause of nationalism'[39]. The exceptions to the conservative bent in Afrikaans-language theatre are, however, noteworthy. In her history of the Market Theatre, Pat Schwartz notes the importance of Elsa Joubert's *Die Swerfjare van Poppie Nongena*, as the 'first Afrikaans play with a majority black cast.'[40] The Market also presented the politically progressive *Diepe Grond* (*Deep Ground*, 1986). Pieter-Dirk Uys, the leading satirist of things undeservedly sacred in South Africa, found a home at the Market Theatre for Afrikaans-language works such as *Die van Aardes van Grootoor* (1979).[41]

The Market Theatre

The Market Theatre is by no means alone in its importance to the history of didactic theatre. The Junction Avenue Theatre Company, also of Johannesburg, Kavanagh's Workshop '71, the People's Space in Cape Town - all deserve their places of honour. They provided vital alternative venues when the 'official' ones - the Performing Arts Councils and other subsidized European-style theatres in several cities - had been co-opted by the Nationalist Party. What was particularly significant about the Market Theatre, however, was its consolidating, shaping influence. Schwartz cites Barrie Hough as saying, 'The Market pulled together the threads of theatre- Afrikaans, black, English.'[42] Founded in the traumatic year of 1976 by the late Barney Simon (deceased in 1995) and Mannie Manim, the Market's resident group - originally called the Company - produced valuable, cutting-edge work of its own while offering its infrastructure to outside groups, including labor and women's groups. Despite its occasional artistic failures and the 'petit-bourgeois' nature of its administrators and audience, the Market Theatre is an institution of note whose heritage is well worth exploring, even in the form of Schwartz's book, which reads like 'official' history. In the words of Mbongeni Ngema, 'Since *Woza [Albert!]*,...the Market has become a bridge for indigenous theatre from the townships to the world.'[43]

II. Defining Didactic Theatre: Terms of debate

> Majority audiences in urban environments generally expect a play to teach, reveal, comment on either moral or political issues. They require a message. They expect the driving force of the play, its cohesion and its strongest channel of communication to be music and dance. They prefer large casts, many and varied characters, a multiplicity of incidents and a clear narrative emphasis... [Such theatre is] oral not literary... public, not private. Acting is passionate and committed, energetic and heightened. Laughter is provided in the midst of tragedy - comedy depends more on movement, gesture and facial expression than on dialogue. Tears are brought by prayer and song. Anger is expressed through purple passages in English. Joy is embodied in dance.
>
> Robert Kavanagh – South African People's Plays, p. xxx.

Literature takes sides.

Ngugi wa Thiong'o [44]

Although Kavanagh's remarks are admirably succinct and go a long way towards defining didactic theatre in its South African incarnation, a review of the debate over terminology may still be helpful.

Most disagreements in terminology arise in the act of distinguishing politically valid (i.e. adversarial and liberationist, for most academic South African critics) theatre from theatre that may at first *seem* liberationist but really is not. Ian Steadman, following Ross Kidd and others, makes a useful distinction between 'popular' and 'people's' theatre. The positive term 'popular' is used to 'refer to the ways in which members of a majority oppressed group use literature and performance to conscientise audiences in relation to a broad vision of structural change in society' (p. 11).[45] On the other hand, 'people's culture' lacks this salutary effect. It is 'produced by and addressed to the oppressed people in any society, often domesticating them in a conservative way and precluding any interrogation of the structural causes of their oppression' (p. 12).

This same distinction between the genuinely radical and the merely liberal (= covertly conservative) crops up regardless of the particular term a critic or theatre practitioner might favour. The wide variety of favoured epithets ('theatre of....') has already been mentioned. Critics naturally divide on their evaluation of individual artists' works. The case of Gibson Kente (reviled by Andrew Horn as 'theatre of acceptance and lament' and revered, at least for his late work, by Robert Kavanagh) has already been mentioned. Another 'litmus' test author among critics defining what is desirable in political theatre is, not surprisingly, Athol Fugard. To some, Fugard remains forever the white liberal, hopelessly 'whiny' when it comes to social injustice - existential (even Beckettian) rather than truly radical (Brechtian). To others, Fugard is generally successful in conscientising his audience - making people think by offering no easy solutions.

Horn says of Fugard, Pieter-Dirk Uys and Robert Kirby (*It's a Boy*, 1982), that they were 'waylaid in the drawing room'[46]. He grudgingly counts their work as politically inspired but places them on a second-class 'honour roll'. First-class honours and his epithet 'theatre of criticism and confrontation' go to Zakes Mda (*Voices Ring*, 1978; *The Hill*, 1979; *The Road*, 1982) and to Matsemela Manaka's entire opus. Horn also admires Philip Mokone's *Encore Bra Joe* (1982); Maishe Maponya's *The Hungry Earth* (1980) and *Umongikazi* (*The Nurse*, 1983); Malcolm Purkey and Junction Avenue Theatre Company's *Randlords and Rotgut* (1981) and *Ilanga le so phonel abasebenzi* (*The sun will rise for the workers*, 1980); and other pieces that are generally BCM in orientation.

Keyan Tomaselli defines his 'theatre of commitment' as 'mediation rather than a reflection.'[47] It has 'no need of the conventional tools of theatre - the proscenium arch, a stage, curtains, spot lights, a separation between the audience and performers, or even intervals.. [It is] oral in tradition, construction and rendition...metonymic...not wedded to the restricting conventions of dramatic heritage or the linear demands of alphabetic logic resulting from 500 years of print literacy.' In such theatre, 'conflicts...are not always resolved in an imaginary solution. Faced with the monolithic structures of apartheid, most committed theatre ends with a song of liberation'[48]. Paraphrasing Althusser, Tomaselli speaks of an audience being empowered to perceive '*from the inside*, by an *internal distance, [his* emphasis] the very ideology in which it is held' (p. 17) There is an interchangeability among director, actors and audience (p. 18). Elsewhere [49] Tomaselli speaks of the 'dramatistic' model of the world presented in such theatre: the world is not like a stage; 'the world *is* a stage' (p. 56) It is the ultimate metonymic relationship between art and life, in Tomaselli's words 'both a methodology and an ontology' (p. 56).

When Kavanagh speaks of 'majority theatre' that would be 'dialectical' (p. 196) and 'dialogic' (p. 212), he seems very close in spirit to Tomaselli. But it remained for Zakes Mda, in his book *When People Play People*, to present the most comprehensive survey of didactic models and definitions yet attempted.

The value of Mda's book is that it is based on both theory and praxis. Thoroughly steeped in the ideas of Paolo Freire and Augusto Boal, Mda adds on a further layer of terminology (a bit less appealing to traditional literary scholars) from his graduate work in communications theory. From Freire and Boal, Mda inherits the premise that 'theatre can be utilised by all people whether they have artistic talent or not' (p. 18). Borrowing other paradigmatic terms from Ross Kidd, Michael Etherton, and Lambert (1982), Mda constructs composite charts to show the difference among Agitprop, Participatory, and Conscientisation theatre. Taking the factor of who *produces* the play or spectacle, for instance, Mda distinguishes 'Agitprop' (originally named, as most people know, for the 'Department of Agitation and Propaganda of the Central Committee of the Communist Party of the Soviet Union') as 'produced by a professional group and oriented towards the people,' while 'Participatory Theatre' is 'produced by and for the people *with* spectators' and 'Conscientisation Theatre' is 'produced by and for the people *without* spectators' (chart, p. 50). Concerning the factor of improvisation, Mda notes that in 'Agitprop' the 'actors themselves respond to the local situation;' whereas in 'Participatory Theatre' the actors improvise 'within the specific parameters of the themes,' and in 'Conscientisation Theatre' the actors improvise 'throughout, the direction never planned.' 'Agitprop,' according to Mda's chart, raises consciousness 'from *outside* on specific themes such as hygiene, human rights, nutrition, family planning, etc.' 'Participatory Theatre' raises consciousness from *inside* on specific themes such as social disputes, youth delinquency, VD, migration.' 'Theatre for Conscientisation,' on the other hand, raises consciousness 'from *inside* as *group analysis* of social reality/power relations, for example landlessness, poverty, corruption' (my emphasis). 'Agitprop' may lead to an 'informal post-performance discussion or individual action in the short term.' 'Participatory Theatre' may lead to more 'organized post-performance discussion' and perhaps some 'short of [*sic*, probably a misprint for 'short to'] medium term group action.' 'Conscientisation,' however, may lead to a 'continuing dialogue' and maybe even 'long-term organized collective action.' The implicit view of development in 'Agitprop Theatre' is that development is 'planned by individuals and families through non-formal education.' 'Participatory Theatre' implies that development is 'a planned change by transfer of knowledge and skills by non-formal education and follow up.' 'Theatre of Conscientisation,' however, assumes that development is 'structural change that can disrupt the status quo.' Mda's final comparison is made on the basis of participation and the continuity factor. In 'Agitprop,' according to the chart, there is 'no participation' and the spectacle is a 'finished product.' The actors are 'committed' but 'art comes before development.' In 'Participatory Theatre' there is 'co-operation on cue; no grassroots control; scant explanation of problems' macro-origin; pseudo-conscientisation.' 'Theatre for Conscientisation,' on the other hand, leaves its participants active: 'Participation and control increase as catalysts pull out; spectator becomes dramatic actor; then social actor' (p. 50).

In the above examples, 'Theatre for Conscientisation' is obviously the most radical, most empowering to the people and holds the greatest potential. It is also, as Mda admits, the most challenging for the 'catalysts' to pull off. The praxis part of Mda's book recounts the experiences of the Maratholi Travelling Theatre working in Lesotho. Because Lesotho is not South Africa (though located, of course, *within* South Africa's territorial bounds), it falls outside the purview of this essay. Suffice it to say that Mda's reports of the plays he and his colleagues facilitated/devised on the subjects of agricultural co-ops, rural sanitation (the Ventilated Improved Pit Latrine), trade unions and alcohol abuse, provide excellent case studies of the strengths and weaknesses of what the Maratholi Travelling Theatre people came to call 'Comgen' (Community-generated) theatre. This demanding type of work - idealistic, perilous, ideologically driven - perhaps represents the farthest, noblest end of an imaginary spectrum that might be conceived of as containing all possible mixtures and degrees of pleasure and instruction. It would seem to be close to the end representing *pure education*. And yet some modicum of pleasure (or, in Freudian terms, the promise that is *forepleasure*) must both *attract* participant audiences to the Maratholi Travelling Theatre and *hold* the participants' attention as they work towards self-actualization.

III. Synergistic Syncretism: a Non-definition of Didactic Theatre

Given the rich diversity of examples, and the disparate models presented so far, one might venture a series of descriptors that *approach,* but intentionally do not reach the status of a definition.

Theatre for Development plays may be ephemeral

Canonisation of 'theatre' into drama requires the publication of scripts, something that has been done in the case of Duma Ndlovu's *Woza Afrika!* anthology (1986), containing *Woza Albert!,* *Gangsters, Children of Asazi* (by Matsemela Manaka), *Born in the RSA* (by Barney Simon et alia), *Asinamali!* and *Bopha!*. Robert Kavanagh's *South African People's Plays* (1981) has also served to stabilise and canonise important plays of the political theatre. Yet even these published dramas are, of course, mere traces of the theatre works themselves. This is true of the written version of any play, and yet particularly true in the case of South African didactic theatre that has relied so heavily on unscriptable performance factors. Ian Steadman explains the loss in this way: 'The lived experience of literature in performance was a far richer one than that captured in textual form, because of the added dimensions of participation from audiences in the form of chanted responses to signals from the stage, emotive music, unison speaking, a metonymical rather than metaphorical construction, and language which worked as utterance rather than statement' (p. 28).

The non-identity between the performance and script in some cases spared political works from censorship, a plus at the time of the intended transgression. This very transgressive quality of the plays - if they exist in any written form, which many do not- has unfortunately been lost, however, to posterity and future scholarship. In the words of Ari Sitas, 'South African theater has left very few scripts behind. What it has left rather, is a series of powerful memories and models that have transgressed every preconceived notion of 'limit,' of 'appropriateness' and theatrical form.'[50]

To the ideologically pure, the ephemerality (and non-transferability) of this kind of theatre may be not only inevitable but almost desirable, an old play being nearly as useless as an old newspaper, and a workers' play performed for the bourgeoisie (at the Market Theatre, for instance) being utterly 'vitiated' by its separation from its natural, proletarian audience. Tomaselli explains it this way: 'Plays like *Ilanga, Egoli* and *Imbumba* arise and die in relation to the ebb and flow of worker experience in their need to expose new areas of social injustice, sensitise workers to alternative means of emancipation, and to maintain a level of consciousness which may otherwise be suppressed under state legislation and repressions' ('The Semiotics of Alternative Theatre' p. 30.

Theatre for Development may be orally based

The rich African oral tradition has already been alluded to throughout this essay, though without specific mention of forms. The Xhosa *intsomi*, and Zulu *inganekwane* and *izibongo* (praise poetry) are among the traditional oral forms most often mentioned as direct influences on modern theatre. Kofi Awoonor has analysed the patterning in Shakan praise poems for the purpose of showing a 'synthesis between traditional dramatic material and the Western stage and production technique.'[51] Anne Fuchs has also done an analysis of *Woza Albert!* (a la Vladimir Propp) showing its twenty-six scenes to be a series of four 'moves,' such as 'lack/ lack liquidated' and 'hope/disbelief.' Says Fuchs, 'The episodic structure corresponds very closely to that of the Zulu folk-tale and the Xhosa *intsomi*, which both evolve from a common Nguni heritage.'[52]

The problem with tracing the direct influence of particular oral forms that, while still practised, are rapidly becoming archaic, is rationalizing enough exposure to account for the proposed influence. Therefore the arguments of David Coplan and M. Fleischman that it is not any *particular* oral forms that prevail in influence but orality itself as a form of consciousness can seem, at times, tempting. M. Fleischman says, 'The oral system of consciousness...differs in fundamental ways from literary consciousness.'[53] Calling on the ideas of Ong, Fleischman reminds us of the utter evanescence of sound: 'Sound exists only when it is going out of existence.' Therefore, he continues, 'In an oral culture experience is intellectualised mnemonically' using rhythm, repetition formulas, etc. (p. 92). Flesichman believes that every culture lives on a continuum between primary orality (no literacy and no knowledge of literacy's existence) and high literacy. Cultures closer to primary orality have what Fleischman calls a 'verbomotor lifestyle' which produces 'personality structures that are more communal and externalized' (p. 92). While Fleischman treads dangerously close to stereotyping whole groups of people with his notion of a 'verbomotor lifestyle,' the essence of orality does seem clearer from his explanation. David Coplan wades in with what he calls the qualities of oral traditions: 'Since the times of the earliest records, and probably before, the performance traditions of Bantu-speaking people have been characterised by qualities of interconnection, visibility, imagery, and efficacy.'[54] The terms 'visibility' and 'imagery' both relate to physical and mental eye appeal. Coplan's idea of interconnection is that there is a 'synesthetic' flow of meaning among the various senses appealed to by dance, song, mime, poetry, etc. There is likewise an interconnection between and among individuals and groups involved. 'Efficacy' means even more in the way of a bond. Coplan, borrowing from Schechner (1977), explains, 'Efficacy in ritual performance represents the covenant between human and supernatural powers. Efficacy in dramatic performance means going beyond simple diversions into representation that affects audience consciousness and will to action. Performance not only reflects but also formulates and augments experience as 'part of the complicated feedback process that brings about change.' ' (p. 157).

Theatre for Development may be folk culture or myth-based

The main connection with folk culture would seem to be the complex relationship with oral tradition. But there have been notable direct uses of actual folk tales and myths in the didactic theatre tradition. Some of the African-language plays mentioned above employ folk material. Credo Mutwa's *uNosilimela* (1973) is what Coplan calls a 'somewhat specious recreation of African dramatic tradition' based on the story of a girl born of supernatural parentage who makes her way to the city, is corrupted, and must then return to purity. Fatima Dike's *The Sacrifice of Kreli* involves a

Xhosa chief who sends a diviner to the nether world for advice on recuperating from a defeat by Cape Colonial Forces (p. 171). According to Coplan, it was performed in Xhosa at Cape Town and then in Xhosa and English elsewhere. Thomas Riccio gives an interesting outsider's perspective on his collaborative creation of a folk-based play *Emandulo* at the Natal Performing Arts Council in Durban, Spring 1992. Just as interesting is his account of 'de-gentrifying' the tony institution with his young amateur actors.[55]

Theatre for Development plays may be collaborative

If the most distinctive South African plays have been more about 'the collective subject' than the 'individual subject of Western drama,'[56] then it should not prove surprising that many have been created by collective authorship. In praising the mystical union between director/facilitator, actors and even audience-members in the act of creation, the dynamics of this complex process have sometimes been overlooked. On the negative side, even some of the most ardent practitioners of the 'workshop' method soon stepped back from it to solo again. Fugard's eventual choice of individual authorship is well known, but he is not alone. Ngema left Mtwa (or vice versa). In the words of playwright/actress Gcina Mhlophe, 'Closing the door, being alone, letting your characters live on paper, hearing their voices, seeing them get dressed, that's lacking in our theatre...How many people saw Barney Simon's work-shopped play *Black Dog* (in which Gcina Mhlophe performed)? I don't know if it will ever be performed again. But if it's something that's scripted, on paper, I could be dead and the script will still be there.'[57] Collaboration does not always mean ephemerality, but the two have often coincided.

Paul Gready is one of few critics to have taken a long look at both the strengths and weaknesses of the collaborative approach. In the case of most workers' theatre (famous examples include *The sun will rises for the workers* and *The Dunlop Play*), the collaborative method turned out to be a complex 'transaction on many levels between cultural practices and forms, languages, races, classes, agendas and so on.'[58] It resulted in a 'multi-voiced, hybrid product.' What becomes important, according to Gready, is 'the tension between the desire for a single voice and the ways in which multiple voices makes themselves heard.. .raising their head as fractures, discontinuities and contradictions within a projected self-image' (p. 167).

Ian Steadman sees the same phenomenon of multi-vocality but puts a positive spin on it: 'One of the ways in which theatre can avoid the imposition of the single voice is through collaborative creative work which, while never able to guarantee objectivity, can at least ensure critical vigilance against the easy solution.'[59] Steadman identifies this 'easy solution' thinking with falling back on binary oppositions (e.g. black versus white). He hopes that collaborative work will foster, instead, 'dialectical exchange' (p. 191).

Theatre for Development may use music and a distinctive acting style

South African music is itself a richly syncretic form admired worldwide. Kofi Awoonor puts it in the following way: 'South African music is one of the most eloquent samples of the syncretic direction that African music will take, perhaps at more conscious and selective rate. South African jazz is already receiving acclaim outside the country in the work of artists such as Dollar Brand. *Kwela* music is an aspect of South African urban life...it is out of this urban and refugee reality of South African black existence that a musical such as Todd Machikiza's *King Kong* emerged'

(p. 337) The music used in the theatre under discussion has been as varied as the plays themselves, from Brecht collaborator Kurt Weill's more-Broadway-than-Brechtian score to *Lost in the Stars*, to Machikiza's work mentioned above, to folk songs, to collaboratively composed songs of liberation. Sometimes music has been used emotionally 'with the grain' of the text (perhaps in Kente) and sometimes in distancing 'epic' fashion against the grain (perhaps in certain more ideologically-driven BCM works). It is very difficult if not impossible for an outsider, especially after the fact, to judge this *most* ephemeral of theatre's ephemeral constituent parts. Is it Brecht, is it Broadway, or is it *izibongo* (i.e. the oral tradition)?

Integrally related to the use of music and the whole notion of 'showmanship' is the acting style (or styles) employed for both the spoken word and the sung. Again, one cannot assume uniformity where there is none, and the nature of the play - its literary or collaborative composition, its audience, its immediate political purpose - must be considered. There are, however, key adjectives that reoccur in the discussion of South African acting styles, including 'transgressive,' 'body-centred' and 'sensual,'[60] 'physical,' and 'acrobatic.' In the case of collaborative works created by and with the actors, there is a new ontological status created, sometimes signaled by the use of the actor's real name as his character's name. This occurs, most famously, in Fugard's *The Island*, [61] and in *Woza Albert!* Says Steadman of the ontological shift: '...Their roles as creators are interchangeable with their status as characters in the play. Signifier and signified, each of these actors plays out images of the black dispossessed - of their very own day-to-day social relations.'[62] Speaking of the collaborative element in Workshop '71's *Survival* (1976), Etherton speaks of the paradoxical result of signifier becoming signified as both 'intense engagement and emotional distancing' (p. 303)

Several explanations have been offered for the derivation of the very physical, acrobatic South African acting style in question. In his essay 'Beyond Street Theatre and Festival,' Temple Hauptfleisch mentions the 'very potent histrionic element present in... the African Christian churches' as a possible influence (p. 180) M. Fleischman believes the style may derive from some of the physical locations artists such as Gibson Kente had to use: 'The size of the performances and the vocal acrobatics can perhaps be attributed to the size of the halls in which the plays were produced and their bad acoustics' (p. 97) He also believes that improvisation itself begets a certain type of performance: 'The physical creation of the character in the process of improvisation tends to make the performance of the character more physical' (p. 102) Coplan believes there is an American strain in the style: 'The most important source of foreign influence was the performance culture of black America' (p. 159). But finally it is African: 'Acting, theme, and storyline are melodramatic, with powerful emotions expressed physically, almost acrobatically, in the rhythmical blend of farce and pathos, song, dance, and mime that is the essence of theatricality in the African tradition' (p. 168) Coplan notes that audiences, especially township audiences, demand 'complete faithfulness to social reality' (p. 168). The key to the exaggerated acting style, the showmanship of South African actors, may simply be that *reality* in South Africa has all too often been larger than life.

Theatre for Development may draw on Brechtian or Grotowskian models

But is it Brecht? Is it Grotowski's bare-chested 'theatre of the poor'?

Reacting to the similarities between Brecht's edicts on epic theatre and the style of South African committed theatre, critics have sometimes answered 'yes' to the Brecht question, but often 'no.'

Anne Fuchs describes certain epic features of *Woza Albert!* (such as direct address of the audience) but says the similarity with Brecht is 'fortuitous' (p. 36). M. Fleischman agrees, saying the episodic structure of many contemporary plays owes more to orality than to Brecht (p. 104)

If one refers to Brecht's own pronouncements on epic theatre (realizing that they change over time), one indeed finds compelling similarities, at least to Mda's categories 'Agitprop' and 'Participatory.' Mda freely admits his indebtedness to Grotowski and Brecht as do virtually all of the Western-trained-or-influenced writers (e.g. Fugard and Manaka) and directors (e.g. Barney Simon) who have shaped South African theatre. But the classic problems inherent in the epic model - problems Brecht continued to address the rest of his critical life - are especially problematic in the African context. Brecht's picture of the proper epic audience - *coolly* reasoning ways to leave the theatre and change the world - simply doesn't fit a township audience enjoying a didactic musical. (There's some question whether it ever fit a German audience, either.) There's too much emotion, too much insistence on realism, too much emphasis on entertainment in that hypothetical African crowd. Back in 1983, Arnold Blumer wrote an article entitled 'Brecht in South Africa' in which he bewailed the reluctance of South African theatres to tackle Brecht's *Lehrstuecke*, often considered his most purely political plays.[63] While the plight of the 'young comrade' (*der Junge Genosse*) in Brecht's paradigmatic *Lehrstueck, The Measures Taken (Die Massnahme)* might interestingly be compared with that of Vusi in *Survival*, the cool ratiocinations of the *Lehrstueck* form are, in the final analysis, awfully cerebral for most Westerners and most Africans alike. Brecht knew the value of entertainment and emotion. The call for pure *reason* in his early definitions of the 'epic' is dialectically balanced by later shifts towards *emotion* in his own works and his theory. He was a cagey fellow, that Brecht, and one wonders if he could not have stood up to officials of apartheid as well as he stood up to his inquisitors on the House Un-American Activities Committee.

Theatre for Development may incorporate the spectator in a distinctive fashion
Implicit in the collaborative workshop method of creation is a blurring of the traditional triadic relationship (world/author/audience) surrounding any text. But any truly polemical work - collaborative or not - targets the spectator, attempting to conscientise him or her, in a most distinctive way. Anne Fuchs, for example, speaks of the Market Theatre artists' 'obsession' with the spectator and 'his/her active response..'[64] M. Fleischman speaks of the workshop method's goal of establishing a 'homologous correspondence between consciousness of the workshop and social group' (p. 109) In the same place, Fleischman also brings in Raymond Williams' notion of a 'structure of feeling' that should unite performers and audience-members. The logical extreme of theatre that is totally at one with its audience is mentioned in Mda's definition of 'comgen' or Conscientisation Theatre. Since the community to be helped creates the play itself and receives all its benefits in the process of planning it, doing it, discussing it and taking further action (with only minimal assistance at any point in the process from the 'catalysts' or facilitators) they are, at least theoretically, their own best audience and need no other. The downside of that is, of course, the limitations placed on the even greater numbers of people who might indirectly, vicariously, benefit from mere *exposure* to the play. To use Mda's terms, Agitprop, with its imperfections, is still better than no theatre at all.

Theatre for Development may be polyglot

The Tower of Babel has become symbolic shorthand for the linguistic divisions among cultures. Most people know that the 1976 Soweto Uprising was essentially a revolt against linguistic coercion - the forced use of Afrikaans as a medium of instruction. As far back as the late 1940s, Alan Paton knew to symbolize white liberals' willingness to soften and change by the desire of one small white boy to learn an African language. (The incident of the slain Jarvis' son taking Zulu lessons is also carried over into *Lost in the Stars:* 'I know a lot of Zulu words. My father taught them to me. *Ingeli* is English,' says young Edward Jarvis to the Zulu-speaking nephew of Stephen Kumalo.)[65] Setting aside the irony of one of the white child's first words in Zulu being the word for 'English,' Paton's intent to bridge the linguistic divide is clear.

It is not surprising, then, that the didactic playwrights, both individual and collective, under discussion here have inscribed the linguistic dilemma and possible solutions in their work. The Tower of Babel is replaced by the Power of Babel. Multilingual plays show that polyglotism can unite as well as divide.

The problem, of course, is intelligibility, an especially urgent problem where the whole purpose of the play is to enlighten an audience. But which audience? Or which segment of a linguistically mixed audience? One solution is, of course, the complete translation of a play to suit each audience - the 'when-in-Rome' solution taken to its logical extreme. Some writers have allowed such translations or done them themselves, especially between English and Afrikaans. Another solution has been the attempt to render the flavour of an African language by means of using literal renderings of particular phrases into English, often with poetic effect. Gabriel Okara, in 'African Speech...[sic] English Words' advocates that technique in a Nigerian context, recommending 'May we live to see ourselves tomorrow' (a literal translation from Ijaw) instead of the more common and prosaic 'Goodnight.' Says Okara, '...A writer can use the idioms of his own language in a way that is understandable in English.'[66] A more familiar South African example would be Alan Paton's use of 'Stay well' and 'Go well' in *Cry, The Beloved Country* (and its adaptation, *Lost in the Stars*) to convey the feeling of Zulu farewells. The problem with the method is, of course, its artificiality and the exoticism factor, even when such exoticism is intended.

The third solution to the problem of polylingual audiences is the one pioneered by Fugard in his earliest works and followed by many of his more radical progeny of the BCM, namely creating plays that are a rich mixture of English, Afrikaans, various African languages and syncretic urban dialects such as *Tsotsitaal* (gangster talk) and *Fanagalo* (miners' dialect). Fugard has long insisted that he is, first and foremost, a regional writer: In an interview with Lynn Freed he says, 'Make no concessions ever to a so-called wider audience to the extent that you might water down your regionalism, try to modify your language, or avoid certain things' (p. 304). It has become standard procedure for South African published plays to include glossaries of Afrikaans and other terms bound to be unfamiliar to foreign readers. The polyglot pieces performed in South Africa frequently rely on the physical style of acting to convey the meaning of those passages unintelligible to certain members of the audience. Even this technique, however, is not without its polemical drawbacks. As Tyrone August points out, 'When some people want to swear in a play, they put in Zulu or Sotho so that only a certain section of the audience understands. And then they switch over to English when they want to speak about the serious things' (p. 273)

Theatre for Development may be covert pastoral

The term 'pastoral' is a volatile one in criticism, and to use it in the South African context demands swift and certain definition and defence. The key to using the term in a positive manner involves distinguishing between 'good' pastoral and the false, exploitative type that has come to be identified with the 'tribal musicals.'

First, one can rationalize a positive use of the term drawing on New Critic William Empson's *Some Versions of Pastoral*, still useful after three decades. Empson's key observation is that 'good proletarian art is usually Covert Pastoral.'[67]

Now the use of 'pastoral' themes in South African literature is so common that it has its own shorthand: it's the 'Jim Comes to Jo'burg' motif, named for a 1949 film by Donald Swanson of that name. [68] An innocent man (or woman, cf. *uNosilimela*) from the country goes to Johannesburg (or any other large city) and is corrupted. Sometimes he is forced into becoming what Empson, in his European context, terms a 'sympathetic criminal' and sometimes a 'sacrificial tragic hero' (p. 16) This is clearly the basis for the *Ur-text* of South African liberalism, Paton's *Cry, The Beloved Country*, but the theme also shows up in the works of black, committed writers such as Credo Mutwa *(uNosilimela)*. Even where characters are strictly urban in their roots rather than 'rural,' there is a presumed nobility and innocence about them, even (and especially) when they are forced to step outside of apartheid law in order to survive. In the inverted world of apartheid South Africa, the lovers transgressing miscegenation laws and the prisoners in their cells are far nobler than their more educated white oppressors. They become the urbanized 'swains' of pastoral and stand in a peculiarly problematic relationship with their more educated authors.

Empson describes the paradox inherent in virtually all literature celebrating (or, I might add, attempting to conscientise) the 'simpler' masses: 'Thus both versions [of pastoral], straight and comic, are based on a double attitude of the artist to the worker, of the complex man to the simple one ('I am in one way better, in another not so good'), and this may well recognise a permanent truth about the aesthetic situation. To produce pure proletarian art, the artist must be at one with the worker; this is impossible not for political reasons, but because the artist never is at one with any public' (p. 14) This might be considered sobering news for Kavanagh, Mda and other earnest theoreticians of Theatre for Development, believing, as they apparently do, in the desirability of such efficacious 'oneness'.

The abuse of the pastoral form - resulting in false, exploitative works - is also a familiar phenomenon in South Africa. Though they don't always agree on which works to place on their 'dishonour' roles, - *Ipi Tombi, uMabatha, Meropa (*a.k.a. *KwaZulu)* and *African Odyssey* make most lists - Horn, Kavanagh and other critics have condemned the insidious link between 'tribal musicals' and the former Nationalist government's 'Bantustan' or tribal homelands policy. The idea was to make the rural homelands seem 'more congenial to blacks' than the cities.[69] This was not necessarily the conscious intent of the artists involved, but all too often, in Horn's view, black artists were 'co-opted' by white management, especially when there was an opportunity to reach a lucrative export market in Europe and the United States. Bhekizizwe Peterson is unambiguous in his condemnation of tribal musicals: 'The illustration of 'traditional' cultural practices is nothing but an attempt to titillate Eurocentric minds, with various forms of 'African exoticisms' while the depiction of great chiefs differs little from standard representations of the noble savage.' [70]

Even more problematic was the practice in the latter days of apartheid of exporting higher quality, truly oppositional theatre (especially Fugard) but for the wrong reason. Ian Steadman explains it this way: 'One strategy of South African government in an era of so-called 'reform' is being seen to allow oppositional theatre to tour abroad. This creates an impression of freedom of expression which has surprised foreign audiences.' [1]

The pressure to entertain foreign audiences is still very real, post-Apartheid. What many are calling the 'seduction' of Mbogeni Ngema by the 'Great White Way' (= Broadway, but the punning epithet is intentional) brings us to the closer to the present situation.

IV. Theatre 1996: The Sarafina 2 to-Do

It is very important to keep the productive apparatus of the working-class theatre well clear of the general drug traffic conducted by bourgeois show business.

Bertolt Brecht – Schriften zum Theater [2]

It is impossible to create one play [cf. Sarafina 2] that will function throughout South Africa.

Zakes Mda – Grahamstown lecture, 1996

Siphiwe Mkhize, original chairperson for the KwaZulu Natal section of the National Association

for Community Theatre in Education and Development, reports that there are over 100 community groups, ranging in size from 10 to 40 actors each., under the NACTED umbrella.[73] Despite the number of community theatre groups working on development theatre, ephemerality and language factors make it difficult for an American outsider to give any true sense of grassroots theatre activity, other than to apologetically report the number of groups at work. Most of these grassroots groups are too limited in their resources to attend even the Fringe portion of the Standard Bank National Arts Festival in Grahamstown, the most convenient place for determined outsiders to 'take the pulse' of South African theatre. Because I have written elsewhere about the mood of the Grahamstown Festival, 1996,[74] I will restrict my remarks here to issues raised in Zakes Mda's dramatic festival lecture (attacking *Sarafina 2*).

Mda couched his Grahamstown critique of Ngema within a larger discussion of 'Theatre for Development,' which Mda prefers as a term for committed theatre *post* apartheid. (In his words, 'Development comes after Independence during Reconstruction.') His lecture remarks suggested that the whole concept behind *Sarafina 2* as a *national* anti-Aids musical, was fatally flawed. He suggested that one English-language show, extravagantly produced by professionals, could never have reached the diverse groups within South Africa nearly as well as smaller, close-to-home, grassroots efforts. Although Mda did not dwell at length on his own experience with the Maratholi

Three examples (see facing page) of Madam and Eve *by S. Francis, H. Dugmore and Rico.*

Travelling Theatre (frankly chronicled in *When People Play People*), he implied that the Maratholi model is more effective for anti-Aids work than any Broadway-type extravaganza could ever be.

Mbongeni Ngema's contribution to South African theatre (*Woza Albert!, Asinamali, Sarafina*) has been widely acknowledged. Says Ari Sitas, 'Mabongeni Ngema's craft was to take back onto the stage the performance genres that were developing in the townships around him, with their powerful orality. His distinctive contribution was to have understood and to have redrafted this orality together with the tension between the defiant body language of Black Consciousness and the strutting of urban cultures into a new style of telling stories.'[75]

As an actor himself (in *Woza Albert!*) and as the trainer of young casts for his other shows, especially *Sarafina*, Ngema became the most internationally visible proponent of the 'exaggerated' style of acting I have, throughout this essay, labelled as showmanship. This visibility, however, has made Ngema's fall from grace all the more precipitous, and the temptation to allegorize him into a tragic representative of the Black Artist Gone Awry has been considerable. Ngema's self-defence, his casting of himself as Artist Unfairly Impugned *because* of his race, has added fuel to the critical flames.

Back in 1981, Keyan Tomaselli wrote a well-known essay presenting three scenarios for the committed artist who suddenly finds himself successful.[76] In case scenario number two, he lauds the 'petty-bourgeois director-author' who faced with the popular success of his work 'decides to resist co-option.' Zakes Mda would seem to fit in this group. In case three Tomaselli lauds the 'white petty bourgeois intellectual (in Gramsci's sense) who uses the advantages of his class position, most particularly his education, ...to shape proletarian aspirations and provide them with a revolutionary thrust.' Perhaps he was thinking of Barney Simon? In his case one scenario, however, Tomaselli speaks of 'black director-authors who form part of the petty bourgeois class and whose financial success, afforded them by their plays, tends to push them towards greater aspirations for class mobility.' Tomaselli could have been thinking of Gibson Kente, but from the benefit of a 1997 perspective, Ngema would seem the classic case-one case.

Critic Bernth Lindfors has analysed the Ngema affair in a lecture he presented in summer, 1996.[77] Early on in his talk, Lindfors quotes Ngema (in a 1990 interview with Makgabutlane) speaking on the whole subject of didacticism and theatre: 'But first and foremost, theatre should entertain. When people are entertained, then they will be informed and enlightened. The vehicle we use is entertainment, first of all' (p. 7).

Sarafina 2 , starring the original actress who played Sarafina - now all grown up and Ngema's second wife - was to have been Ngema's greatest piece of entertainment. He would use the township musical form to fight the 'big A' of AIDS instead of the big A of Apartheid (the latter battle having already been won). Ngema initially estimated the cost of his proposed show at R800,000, an 'off-the-cuff estimate,' according to Lindfors' sources. But the budget grew to an astonishing 14,247,600 Rands (p. 8) drawn from funds that had been donated to fight AIDS by the European Union. Worse, standard bidding procedures had been circumvented. Ngema's fellow Zulu, Minister of Health Dr. Nkosazana Zuma, was accused of negligence for her lack of oversight in the whole affair, and the African National Congress was obliged to close ranks to defend her. Further investigation revealed R1.1 million in 'unauthorized expenditures' (p. 19). after Davis 5). Some of the big expenditures were on a luxury bus for the cast and a recording studio to be located in Ngema's home. The resulting musical production itself was faulted on the quality and even the accuracy of its anti-AIDS information. Some critics, according to Lindfors, called it 'potentially dangerous to teenagers' in that the difference between HIV, full-blown AIDS and *Ngculazi* (another disease) was blurred. Others called it 'degrading to women' (p. 16). Ngema countered the criticism with remarks to the effect that he was being racially scapegoated: 'Blacks deserve Broadway standards' (p. 21). Essays and political cartoons such as the scathingly funny 'Madam and Eve' series by S. Francis, H. Dugmore and Rico, peppered the South African press for months after the scandal broke. Outraged by what he considered to be Ngema's 'cavalier' attitude in the face of the overwhelming human tragedy that is AIDS in Africa, Lindfors said of Ngema: 'No one actually went so far as to call Ngema a murderer, but his manner of responding to the charges levelled against him, which ranged from rapacious greed and financial mismanagement to artistic incompetence and egomania, may have so alienated his national audience that he unwittingly may have put a premature end to his own spectacular career as a showman. He may have committed a form of professional suicide' (p. 1). The accuracy of Lindfors' forecast remains to be seen.[8]

V. Future South African Theatre: Exorcism and New Directions

May the truth reconcile our nation.

Truth and Reconciliation Hearing banner – Pietermaritzburg, RSA, July, 1996

It's like being in a boxing ring by myself with the gloves still on.

Athol Fugard – on being a post-Apartheid playwright[9]

News accounts of breakthrough events - such as Biko's torturers being brought to bay - cannot fully convey the intensely *dramatic* quality of even an 'ordinary' day at the Truth and Reconciliation Commission Hearings. Sitting in the audience at the Pietermaritzburg city hall for two days in July, 1996, I witnessed the half-dozen commissioners file in and take their seats behind two tables placed up on the stage. Other tables cattycorner from and on the same level as those of the commissioners would accommodate those testifying. A plastic booth stood far stage right - not to protect any Eichmann-like witness but to dampen the noise of the *Dolmetschers* doing simultaneous translation from Zulu into English and vice-versa. The huge pipes of the civic hall's organ (I also attended a concert by the King's College Singers from Cambridge, England in the very same hall) provided an ecclesiastical-looking backdrop to the proceedings. It felt like a court room.; it felt like a church. It was neither; it was both. Candles were solemnly lit as the first witness sat down at the table. Official 'comforters' - women who would pat shaking shoulders and hand over handkerchiefs to those testifying through their tears- stood at the ready. It was all-too-real oral history in the making. It was psychodrama, a Theatre of National Healing.

During the next two days I would see very ordinary-looking people, mostly black and mostly Zulu-speaking, arise from the chairs in the auditorium - sometimes from chairs on the row right in front of me, in contact with my knees - and I would hear things such as the following through my headphones:

WITNESS (describing the partial remains of a deceased loved one attacked at his house by political opponents: most accusations were against Inkatha):

Part of his liver was left at home.

COMMISSIONER (trying to comfort a witness):

We're going to take part of the pain and leave with it, so you don't have this heavy pain.

ANOTHER WITNESS (describing the death of his ANC comrade on the passenger seat of the car he was driving when they were ambushed near Ixopo – setting of *Cry, The Beloved Country*):

There was a hairpin bend and a low concrete wall. Shots fired. Reggie was lying with his head on my leg.

ANOTHER WITNESS – REGGIE'S WIDOW (describing her children's temperaments as a result of their father's murder):

They're not affectionate; they have violent tendencies; they're not caring.

ANOTHER COMMISSIONER (trying to console the woman above):

Your husband's name will go down in this country. The Commission will try to bring the death of Reggie Hebele into the public light.

ANOTHER WITNESS (the college-aged orphaned daughter, testifying with her brother, of parents who had been car bombed by South African Security agents in Mozambique):

My father's lower part was no longer there. She [my mother] was burnt and her skull had started to crack. There were two more people [in the bombed car] - my uncle and Mofit. They were not people anymore. They were ashes.

ANOTHER WITNESS (speaking of a loved one who had been murdered):

We went to hospital. I identified him. I even closed his mouth.

The point of the few snatches of testimony above is to show the depth of the horror with which some South Africans live daily. Archbishop Desmond Tutu's instinct to try to treat his nation's post-traumatic stress syndrome using a combination of religious and civic ritual - public psychodrama - seems sound, but one wonders if it can ever be enough. Exorcising public and private demons will surely keep therapists - and good playwrights - quite busy for the foreseeable future.

At the same time, there is a danger that obsession with the ills of the apartheid era can be an extension of its tyranny. As Schwartz writes in her history of the Market Theatre, 'Politics oughtn't to be THE thing. It's as though people never get born or married, as though we never have celebrations. It's as though the only thing that happens in our lives is that children get shot. Politics is a commercial quality. It guarantees success' (pp. 194-195). Ian Steadman extends a similar word of caution to critics: 'Both theatre practice and theatre scholarship undertaken in the period of colonial hegemony are guilty of inventing South Africa in terms prescribed by apartheid discourse. But even more insidiously, theatre and scholarship in the post-apartheid era are guilty of inventing South Africa in terms prescribed by the *legacy* of apartheid.'[80]

Both of these critics are part of a debate restated by Njabulo Ndebele in his 1991 book *Rediscovery of the Ordinary*. Ndebele's often quoted description of the 'spectacular' is worth repeating, particularly in light of the horrors resuscitated during the TRC Hearings: 'The spectacular documents; it indicts implicitly; it is demonstrative, preferring exteriority to interiority; it keeps the larger issues of society in our minds, obliterating the details; it provokes identification through recognition and feeling rather than through observation and analytical thought; it calls for emotion rather than conviction; it establishes a vast sense of presence without offering intimate knowledge; it confirms without necessarily offering a challenge. It is the literature of the powerless identifying the key factor responsible for their powerlessness. Nothing beyond this can be expected of it.'[81]

Having helped achieve the revolution, can South African playwrights now afford to abandon some of their rhetoric, to beat their swords into plow- (or mutual fund) shares? The answer is, of course, a dialectically tempered, temporary 'yes.' There is much to learn about and much to teach about in Ndebele's realm of the ordinary. New/old causes such as environmentalism[82] and women's rights[83] deserve the zeal once reserved for political liberation. Faculty and students at university drama departments can continue to serve as facilitators for a wide range of development/educational work.[84]

Keyan Tomaselli has made the following remark about the kind of country that breeds didactic theatre: 'This type of theatre generally thrives in countries with social problems, and where there are marked class conflicts and political despotism. In such societies content is hardly a scarce resource; it is endemic to the specific social formation. It is there waiting to be discovered, given form and to be communicated to a participant audience who are themselves part of that content.'[85]

Though the days of political despotism are over, the class conflicts in South Africa may barely have begun. There is ample need for continuing, thoughtful revolutionary rhetoric; there is ample need to promote what Brecht once called 'pleasurable learning, cheerful and militant learning' (p. 73). The walking wounded of the War against Apartheid surely need and deserve the type of therapy and clarity only great art can provide.

In his short didactic play *We Shall Sing for the Fatherland* (1993), Zakes Mda showed his usual prescience in a scene between his two hobo heroes, both of them neglected, forgotten veterans of the 'Wars of Freedom' which have liberated an unnamed African country. One hobo, Janabari, says the following to his former sergeant, now a peer in misery: 'Serge, I have been trying to tell you that our wars were not merely to replace a white face with a black one, but to change a system which exploits us, to replace it with one which will give us a share in the wealth of this country. What we need is another war of freedom, Serge - a war which will put this land back into the hands of the people.'[86] This 'second' war of freedom, if violent, could make the one against apartheid, look like a walk in the park. If a peaceful war against poverty and ignorance, however, this 'second' war for freedom - to be fought, this time, too, by playwright/soldiers - might just be a war to heal all wars.

Notes

1   This essay is dedicated to the memory of Dr. Martha H. Brown (1924-1997), friend and colleague in the National Endowment for the Humanities Summer Seminar in South Africa, 1996. The epigraph is translated by James Hynd as 'Poets wish either to benefit or to delight or to say things that are simultaneously pleasing and applicable to life.' *Ars Poetica* (*The Art of Poetry*). ll 333-334. State University of New York Press, 1974. p. 39 (Latin); p. 57 (English).

2   Mbongeni Ngema's *Sarafina 2* has met with widespread negative criticism of both its content and cost. (See Part 4.) Gibson Kente is considered the father of the 'township musical.'

3   'Community theatre' is used for black, white or nonracial theater, often performed by amateurs, in communities. 'Township theatre' is used for commercial black theater (sometimes involving white administrators) in the black communities known as 'townships.' Horn attacks certain 'township' practitioners such as Gibson Kente, in 'South African Theater: Ideology and Rebellion' (*Research in African Literatures*. vol. 17. no. 2. Summer, 1986) pp. 218-221 *passim*, and 'Ideology and the

Melodramatic Vision: Popular Theatre in Black South Africa and Nineteenth Century America,' *English in Africa* 12 no. 1 (May 1985).

4   Etherton, *The Development of African Drama*. (New York: African Publishing Co. 1982), p. 52. See also Robert Mshengu Kavanagh's work including *Theatre and Cultural Struggle In South Africa*. London: Zed Books Ltd., 1985. Kavanagh counts some early Fugard partnerships, plus the Imita Players of East London, the Ikhwezi Players of Grahamstown, and the Sechaba Players of Cape Town as 'town theatre' groups, p. 54.

5   'Popular' is used by David Kerr (1982) quoted also in Zakes Mda. See also Ian Steadman in 'Towards Popular Theatre in South Africa" in *Politics and Performance: Theatre, Poetry, and Song in Southern Africa*. ed. Liz Gunner (Johannesburg: Witwatersrand U. Press, 1994, 11-33.) 'Theater of commitment' is used by Keyan Tomaselli in 'Black South African Theatre: Text and Context' *English in Africa* 8. No. 1 (March 1980), p. 51 and in 'The Semiotics of Alternative Theatre in South Africa' *Critical Arts*. vol. 2. No. 1. July, 1981. p. 14. The Brechtian term 'Theatre of purpose' is favoured by Theatre for Africa director Nicholas Ellenbogen (phone interview, April, 1997.) 'Theatre of criticism and confrontation' is used by Andrew Horn (see above). 'Theatre of defiance' is attributed to Athol Fugard by Francis Donahue ('Apartheid's Dramatic Legacy: Athol Fugard,' *The Midwest Quarterly*. Vol. 30. No. 3. Spring 1995, p. 323.) 'Theater of self-realization' is used by David Coplan in 'Ideology and Tradition in South African Black Popular Theater' (*The Journal of American Folklore*. Vol. 99. No. 392. April-June, 1986, p. 168). 'Theatre of the oppressed' is Augusto Boal after Mda (*When People Play People: Development Communication Through Theatre*. London: Zed Books, 1993, p. 15). Mda also uses 'theater of conscientisation' and his own coinage 'comgen theatre' in that book.

6   John Willett's translation in *Brecht on Theatre: The Development of an Aesthetic*. (New York: Hill and Wang, 1964, p. 277).

7   quoted in Amiri Baraka's preface to *Woza Afrika!: An Anthology of South African Plays* ed. by Duma Ndlovu. (New York: George Braziller, 1986, p. xv.)

8   Martin Banham et al eds. *The Cambridge Guide to African and Caribbean Theatre*. (Cambridge U. Press, 1994, p. 101.)

9   Peterson's article appears in *Politics and Performance*, ed. Liz Gunner, p. 56. See also Kavanagh, p. 45, in the same volume.

10 Kavanagh, p. 47, says 1935; Steadman. p. 18., says 1936.

11 Martin Orkin. *Drama and the South African State*. (Manchester U. Press, 1991, p. 109); Steadman, p. 18.

12 Kavanagh, pp. 66-67.

13 Kavanagh, p. 113.

14 See Steadman, pp. 28-29.

15 Steadman, pp. 18 ff and Kavanagh, p. 157.

16 Peterson, p. 40.

17 Steadman, p. 25.

18 Kavanagh, p. 45.

19 M.E.R. Mathivha's article/entry appears in Leonard S. Klein ed. *African Literatures in the 20th Century: A Guide*. New York: Ungar Publishing Co., 1986, p. 181; Albert S. Gerard. *African Language Literatures*. Washington, DC, Three Continents Press, 1981, pp. 224-225.

20 Gerard's phrase, p. 220; CTD Marivate's entry in Klein, p. 178.

21 Marivate, p. 178.

22 Ibid.

23 Groenewald, p. 175.

24 Gerard, p. 221.

25 Ibid., p. 198.

26 Povey, p. 175.

27 Ibid., p. 177.

28 <alepe, p. 180.

29 Gerard, p. 212.

30 Ibid.

31 Klein, p. 183.

32 Kavanagh, p. 45.

33 Gerard, p. 214.

34 Ibid., p. 216.

35 Ibid.

36 Ezekiel Mphahlele. *The African Image*. (New York: Praeger Publishers, 1962, 1974, p. 14.)

37 A. J. Coetzee's entry in Klein, p. 167-169.

38 Hauptfleisch's article appears in *Restant* XVI (1988) 113-137.

39 Ibid., p. 119.

40 Pat Schwartz. *The Best of Company: The Story of Johannesburg's Market Theatre*. Craighall: AD. Donker (Pty) Ltd., 1988, p. 99.

41 Horn, 'South African Theatre: Ideology and Rebellion,' p. 226.

42 Schwartz, p. 196.

43 Mbongeni Ngema, p. 102.

44 Quoted in Horn, 'South African Theatre: Ideology and Rebellion,' p. 213..

45 See also Etherton, p. 321, and Ross Kidd's *The popular performing arts, non-formal education and social change in the Third World: a bibliography and review essay*. The Hague: Centre for the Study of Education in Developing Countries, 1982.o

46 Horn, p. 227.

47 Keyan G. Tomaselli, 'The Semiotics of Alternative Theatre in South Africa.' (*Critical Arts*. vol. 2 .No. 1. July, 1981, p. 18)

48 Keyan, pp. 18,19.

49 Keyan Tomaselli, 'Black South African Theatre: Text and Context.' *English in Africa* 8 No. 1 (March 1980, p. 56).

50 Ari Sitas. 'Description of a Struggle: South African Theatre Since 1970,' *World Literature Today*. Vol. 70. No. 1. 1996, p. 83.

51 Kofi Awoonor. *The Breast of the Earth: A Survey of the History, Culture, and Literature of Africa South of the Sahara*. (New York: Anchor Press/Doubleday. 1976), p. 306.

52 Anne Fuchs. 'Re-creation: One Aspect of Oral Tradition and the Theatre in South Africa,' *Commonwealth Essays and Studies*. Vol 9. No.2, Spring 1987, pp. 34-35.

53 M. Fleischman. 'Workshop Theatre as Oppositional Form,' *South African Theatre Journal*. Vol. 4. No. 1. May, 1990 , p. 91.

54 Coplan, p. 153.

55 Thomas Riccio. 'Emandulo: Process and Performance in a Changing South Africa.' (*Theatre Research International*. Vol. 19. No. 3. pp 238-261.)

56 M. Fleischman. p. 89.

57 Tyrone August. 'Interview with Gcina Mhlphe' in *Politics and Performance*, ed. Liz Gunner, p. 278.

58 Paul Gready. 'Political Autobiography in Search of Liberation. Working Class Theatre, Collaboration and the Construction of Identity' in *Politics and Performance*, p. 167.

59 Steadman, 'Performance and Politics in Process: Practices of Representation in South African Theatre.' *Theatre survey*. vol. 33. no. 2. Nov., 1992, p. 190.

60 Sitas, p. 84.

61 Etherton, pp. 128-129.

62 Steadman, 'Performance and Politics in Process,' p. 204.

63 Blumer's article appears in *Communications from the International Brecht Society*. Vol. 13. Nov. 1983.

64 Anne Fuchs, 'The Market Theatre: Drama for a new society? Targeting the Spectator,' *Matatu: Journal for African Culture and Society*. Vol. 11, 1994, p. 13.

65 Maxwell Anderson. *Lost in the Stars: The dramatization of Alan Paton's novel Cry, The Beloved Country*. London: Johnathan Cape and The Bodley Head, 1950 , p. 86. Special thanks to the Alan Paton Centre at the U. of Natal, Pietermaritzburg.

66 Gabriel Okara, 'African Speech...English Words 'in *African Writers on African Writing*. ed. G.D. Killam. (Northwestern University Press, 1973, p. 138).

67 William Empson. *Some Versions of Pastoral*. (New York: New Directions. 1960, 1968), p. 6.

68 Horn, 'South African Theatre: Ideology and Rebellion,' p. 213.

69 Horn, p. 214.

70 Peterson, 'Apartheid and the Political Imagination' in *Politics and Performance*. ed. Liz Gunner, p. 41.

71 Steadman, 'Towards popular theatre,' *Politics and Performance*, p. 30.

72 Willett's translation in *Brecht on Theatre*, pp. 88-89.

73 Phone interview , May 14, 1997. Mkhize spoke from Edendale township.

74 Page Laws. 'South Africa Through the Prism: Festival in Grahamstown, 1996,' *New Theatre Quarterly*. Vol. 12. No. 48. November, 1996, pp. 390-393. Critic Michael Arthur is currently preparing a more scholarly and in-depth study of the Grahamstown Festival over a period of several years for his University of Texas at Austin dissertation. See also Keith Bain's

'The Standard Bank National Arts Festival: Grahamstown 4-14 July 1996,' *South African Theatre Journal.* September 1996, pp. 135-147.

75 Sitas, p. 86.

76 Tomaselli, 'The Semiotics of Alternative Theatre.' The case scenarios are all found on p. 16.

77 I am basing my discussion on a July 10, 1996, lecture by Zakes Mda at the Standard Banks National Arts Festival in Grahamstown, and on a different lecture manuscript loaned to me by Bernth Lindfors entitled 'The Rise and Fall of Mbongena Ngema.' Lindfors delivered his lecture in August, 1996, at the Conference on South African Theatre at the University of London.

78 As of July, 1996, Ngema was still listed in the playbill of *uMabatha* as director for musical theatre at the Natal Playhouse in Durban where I saw the show. Although he was apparently not involved in that particular (touring) production, Ngema surely must have endorsed the show's coming to his theatre. I found this revival of Welcome Msomi's 1973 'tribal musical' disturbingly full of the negative qualities other critics have condemned in the genre. Despite a note in the same playbill by President Mandela warmly endorsing the play, it struck me as demeaningly stereotypical in its portrayal of the Zulu people. It must be said, however, that as a non-speaker of Zulu, I cannot fairly judge Welcome Msomi's script.

79 Interview on National Public Radio's 'All Things Considered,' May 14, 1997. Fugard repeated this analogy in my conversation with him on May 22, 1997, following his performance in *Valley Song* at the Kennedy Centre in Washington, D.C.

80 Steadman, 'Performance and Politics in Process,' pp. 209-210.

81 Najabulo Ndebele. *Rediscovery of the Ordinary: Essays on South African Literature and Culture.* COSAW, Africana Books, 1991, p. 46.

82 e.g. Nicholas Ellenbogen's *Guardians of Eden,* a pan-Africanist 'green' play performed at Grahamstown in 1996.

83 e.g. *You strike the woman, you strike the rock* (1986), both feminist and revolutionary in its concerns.

84 Kendall, head of the drama department at the University of Natal, Pietermaritzburg, helps with the Environmental Theatre Group in a nearby township, with her students serving a similar function at a nearby boarding school. Although it's a non-South African example, the impetus for Mda's Maratholi Travelling Theatre Company likewise came from the drama department at the National University of Lesotho.

85 Tomaselli, 'The Semiotics of Alternative Theatre in South Africa.' pp. 14-15.

86 Zakes Mda. *We Shall Sing for the Fatherland.* (Johannesburg: Ravan Press, 1993, 1995, 1996), p. 22.

Post-Colonial Theatre for Development in Algeria: Kateb Yacine's early experience

Kamal Salhi

Amateur or Professional

The subject of the 'amateur' theatre in post-colonial Algeria is of interest not only in itself but for the light it sheds on certain wider questions concerning Kateb Yacine's early work. It raises the issue of the political nature of his art and shows the extent to which it is linked with post-colonial politics. In particular, it sheds further light on how the socialist message is spread among the masses through the productions as performed by Kateb Yacine's company.

For source material I have relied chiefly on the Algerian press, and some official documents or reports which have not been published. One serious difficulty I have encountered, however, is that documents of the Algerian National Theatre (TNA), which may contain more comprehensive information than those of the Ministry of Culture and the National Secretary of the Algerian National Youth Union, have become virtually inaccessible[1]. The amateur theatre which existed in the two decades after independence (1960s, 1970s) was chiefly political for it supported the socialist reforms and the idea of the avant-garde.

The Oxford Dictionary defines an amateur as 'one who practices a thing only as a pastime'. The essence of an amateur actor is clearly to engage in theatricals 'as a pastime', but an English speaker in the twentieth century will normally expect certain other things of him as well, in particular that he should not be paid for his performances, even though he may receive handsome perquisites. In the money-centred society of the West, the word 'amateur' has even come to be somewhat derogatory and often refers to somebody whose performance is imperfect or shoddy. In its Algerian context, the concept of the amateur is rather different and should be explained further. In colonial times, the key to the future of the Algerian non-professional artist was in its insistence on superior quality. Arlette Roth asserts that young Algerian actors were eager to perfect the rudiments of their art, for they wanted to acquire further experience and training. She confirms that the pioneers of the Algerian Theatre who performed the first farces were 'all amateurs'.[2] Spare time actors or poets stress devotion to art and accept money as a reward for their effort: 'They had their jobs..and theatre was their hobby'[3]. The social system did not permit its elite to specialise too narrowly. If an amateur is defined as one who cultivates a thing 'as a pastime', then dramatists like Allalou and Ksentini were certainly amateurs. Yet the emphasis on quality and the contempt for specialisation, which were characteristic of the Algerian artist, might make 'generalist' a more appropriate word to describe the Algerian artists of the past.

The 'generalist' Mahiedine Bachetarzi was very much an elitist. It was only 'cultivated' people who attached so much importance to the universalist approach to a job and an art, and it was only people like Bachetarzi who could ever be accepted into the noblest artistic circles. Just as officialdom itself was highly elitist, apart from the professionals who carried out the basic work, so artistic groups were open only to those with a high level of education and a general as well as a particular appreciation of Art[4]. With the French influence on Algerian arts, the concept of amateurism underwent a change in emphasis. Although the idea of the generalist is not absent in the European tradition, the commercialisation of western values had, by the beginning of the century, brought to the fore the idea that an amateur is unpaid, the concern for good quality being a secondary consideration. Despite the impact of this notion in Algeria, the traditional emphasis on anti-commercialism and quality in amateur art remained strong. Moreover, spare-time artists remained an elite, at least in the city, and although they resembled Ulemas[5] followers in this respect, it was for reasons of necessity, not choice. Possibly the most important development in the first half of the century in this field was the strengthening of the idea that amateur art should be directly political. Revolutionaries after the Second World War, and those engaged in the Algerian armed struggle, saw it as a weapon which could, and should, be used on behalf of their political ideology. More than a Theatre *aux armées* the Algerian FLN party (Algerian Liberation Front) have used it as an agit-prop instrument.[6]

The socialist faction of the FLN took this notion and developed it still further, to the extent of denying that any art, whether amateur or professional, could be divorced from politics, or to have a non-political content. Roselyne Baffet[7] specifies that the actors of that theatre later became the main components of the Algerian Theatre in its present identity. She points out further features. 'It is in that theatre that the revolutionary militancy, not armed this time, but as the builder of socialism, can be found.'[8]

The socialist approach may be said to have followed on from the traditional one of the Ulemas in its treatment of amateur art as an extremely serious matter, and also, to some extent, in its attitude to the specialist. An official paper[9] of the Ulemas explains this more clearly: 'A work signed by an Algerian can interest us only from one point of view; the cause it serves and its position in the struggle against the colonialist movement.'

Boumediene (1965-1978), for instance, was perhaps not against expertise[10], but he was inclined to be wary of experts. There was a tendency among such people to begin by acquiring a highly expensive and lengthy training and then to seclude themselves in city offices where their services, no doubt extremely precious in themselves, were available only to a limited elite. In a revolutionary society this would not do, hence the constant campaigns in contemporary Algeria to send professional actors, doctors and others out into the country side, and among the people. On the other hand, Boumediene's thought was shot through with appreciation of the capabilities of non-professionals.

In its attitude to quality the socialist approach to amateur art falls somewhere between traditional attitudes and those of the modern commercial Westerner. Because amateur art is political, it must be properly performed, but a revolutionary cannot make a fetish of high standards, because he simply does not have the leisure to copy the 'cultivated' man in this respect. The point that divides the socialist ideal most sharply from earlier notions is its demand for mass participation, both in the performance and the enjoyment of art. While the Ulemas had regarded elitism as desirable, even essential, the socialist made it a central tenet that the masses must be taught artistic expression. Amateur art is no longer a prestige affair, open only to the few. On the contrary, it should be the right, and even the duty, of everybody to participate equally.

Further consideration of these concepts is necessary as it applies directly to amateur theatre, to which Kateb Yacine devoted himself from his early experience with *Le Théâtre de la mer*. He promoted the political aims of this group which, together with the high standards they achieved, led the company to its further prosperity. Such a practice could never have been perfected by the dramatist before Independence.

In the colonial period performing on the stage was considered an inferior pastime and the social status of professional players was extremely low. The amateur artists of the Ulemas placed pursuits like calligraphy and literature higher in their scale of reckoning than acting. Despite this attitude, there is quite a long tradition of amateur theatre in Algeria. Examples of people who performed on the stage can be found from early times. The best known was Bachetarzi whose love of acting resulted in his unseemly favouritism towards the performers of the *Mutribya* society and the '*Saisons Arabes de l'Opéra d'Alger*'. On special occasions, religious or National days, members of 'good families'[11] would sometimes act as non-professionals.

After Independence amateurs became fairly important in the National Theatre, and quite a few were competent enough to take up acting as a full-time occupation. Indeed, some of the best known exponents in the Algerian National Theatre of the sixties had begun their careers as amateurs. These actors were taught their art in special training schools[12] which did not last long. The instruction given there was much less demanding and rigid than that inflicted on budding professionals in the INADC (National Institute of Dramatic Arts and Choreography) , almost all of whom were young people forced into a stage career by their circumstances[13]. The main reason why this easier training did not necessarily lead to inferior standards was probably psychological: unlike very young actors, the pioneers had taken to the stage through choice and not compulsion.

The practices of this first generation survived in Algeria until after the socialists of the Boumediene Regime came to strengthen their power, and may still be found to this day in the National Theatre where old amateurs hold regular rehearsals and sometimes perform on the stage. An example of these practitioners is old Mustapha Kateb who was given the National Theatre in which to perform his plays a few months before his death. Yet the first generation was limited in two important respects. In the first place, they were never found outside a few large cities, especially Algiers, Oran and Constantine. Secondly, they were - like the amateurs of Bachetarzi's times - men of 'good family'. The poor did not enter the ranks of the first generation of theatre artists, and the system was extremely elitist. In this respect, as well as in its stress on quality and contempt for commercialisation, it followed the Ulemas' concept of the amateur, even though the idea of specialisation was not always evident.

The tension between western-European and traditional notions of amateurism is apparent in the other main kind of urban amateur acting seen in preliberation Algeria: that found among young intellectuals in schools and other organisations. This developed mainly as a result of the rise of plays spoken in Algerian Arabic from 1926 onwards. The standard of performance in many of these troupes was quite inferior, either because the members lacked interest (as in some schools run along

French lines) or because they had too little time or money to devote to acting. On the other hand, the colonial period saw the development of many amateur actors who were passionately concerned with the spoken play not only as a form of art, but as a political weapon. They used it to further the cause of anti-colonial revolution and the new culture movement and its reforms.

This type of amateur theatre was of particular importance at the beginning of the 1970s when there was a reaction against the negative style of National Theatre plays conventionally performed with the same French Stereotypes. Following the movement of that time, new groups used the government reforms as main themes. The non-professional actors, whether politically inclined or not, continued their activities in the cities throughout the 1970s, years of intensive socialist reform.

The 'Cultural Revolution', which remained chaotic in socialist Algeria, had attracted much attention since its outbreak in the late 1960s. Amateur theatre played a very significant role in this 'Revolution'. The purpose of the Cultural Revolution was to secure the future of socialism by eliminating the influence of neo-colonialism which, Boumediene believed, would eventually lead to the revival of capitalism. The function of this movement was educational, designed for the younger generation in whose hands the future of Algeria lay. The significant role of theatre, especially amateur theatre, in this Cultural Revolution was therefore acknowledged and given recognition. The National Union of Youth (UNJA) was for making a large stage out of the entire nation and setting every young Algerian actor to hunt the ghosts of neo-colonialism, imperialism and bourgeois values. A report[14] from the UNJA lists over a hundred troupes which were active in twelve counties, adding that it has been given but a small sample of the total number .

Even before the 1970s, amateur theatricals commanded a following among workers and villagers, and rural clubs were found in many parts of Algeria. With grassroots popularity, they did not fall into any of the broad categories of amateurism hitherto discussed, and were, in any case, limited to one particular branch of art. Both amateurs and professionals have since been a prime concern of the authorities in the Ministries of Culture and Labour. During this time, characterised by a policy of liberating the economic and cultural sector from foreign hands, these amateurs and professionals were also given special attention. The masses and the youth were the primary source of talent, they 'make contact with rural life, with the man in his village. It is from the ranks of these young people that the rulers of the future will arise.'[15]

There had been a strong relationship between the young creators from universities and the peasantry. Voluntary common actions among students and workers had enabled contact between these two components of the people and permitted the former to learn about rural conditions and the latter to be impart their knowledge. Therefore, 'the importance of this contact resides in the experience of the youth in the real school, which is that of life'.[16]

The practice based on collective work, which came to be widespread[17] in one way or another, transforms the relationship between professional and amateur theatre workers and the masses from which non-professionals are drawn. Specialists in theatre paid attention to the small troupes in villages and the army after Kateb Yacine's company had begun to show the effectiveness of this work. In fact, he and his company were valuable to political cause. Indeed, Kateb Yacine proved that no revolutionary writer or artist can do any meaningful work unless he is closely linked with the masses, gives form to their thoughts and feelings and serves them as a loyal spokesman. Only by speaking for the masses can he educate them, and only by being their pupil can he be their teacher. In fact, if he regards himself as their master, as an aristocrat who lords it over the lower orders, then no matter how talented he may be, he will not be needed by the masses and his work will have no future.

Post-colonial politics was associated with amateur theatre for agit-prop purposes in the unions and among Urban students and workers. A specific boost occurred when the government decided to create cultural committees within factories. A civil servant said that the commission of the Ministry of Labour and Social Affairs, of which he was a member, had the task 'of defining a cultural charter applicable to socialist enterprises'.[18] The Algerian National Theatre (TNA) had a social and cultural department in its own artistic enterprise whose aim was to bring employees in contact with artistic creation - however this aim does not appear to have been honoured by the TNA's managers. That is to say the Algerian post-colonial 'revolution' had followed trends and ambitions for which many in the Regime were half-hearted. Radical activists were allowed to take part, although marginalised, in the cultural combat.

A Theatre for Development

Kateb Yacine turned words into deeds. After joining *Le Théâtre de la mer*, a theatre group composed of students and workers, he became the leading voice of the *Action Culturelle des Travailleurs* (ACT). This was a group whose identity was more a symbol of the worker's power than of theatre itself. It played a great and vital role within factories in stimulating labour. It was also an important factor in reawakening national, political and civic consciousness among the working-class communities and rural population. The avant-garde structure of the ACT was capable of undertaking a popular theatre particularly with Algerian workers at home and abroad. ACT, whose main interest was theatre, went on a French tour and recorded a degree of success among the *émigré* audiences that no Algerian company had previously been able to realise. As the dramatist puts it: 'For eight months we worked hard to produce a play *Mohamed Prends ta Valise*, which was successful in Algeria, and was put on herein France for the immigrants in the Renault Factories and other industries in the cities. We reached 70000 people in five months. In Nanterre, for example, people danced in the hall, it is as if we really had brought Algeria to them in a suitcase.'[19]

This was undeniably due to the practice of a 'pure and hard form, with a group of amateurs'[20]. Moreover the success that the young group had enjoyed in France had further repercussions at home (with considerable results) as Kateb Yacine outlines when explaining the group's implementation: 'We had up to 10,000 people in each hall. We had our good moments: at Setif, for instance, the audience sat still in total silence. They wanted more. It was like a great party. We were guided by a kind of 'virgin' public. This is an extraordinary confirmation of what we were doing. I had no more time to write, I gave myself completely to the play with no experience of directing.'[21]

The dramatist achieved this success and 'confirmation' before gaining any experience in directing, which highlights the talent or genius he had for putting on theatre. The actors were also to share this talent because they were 'workers' of theatre, and revolutionary young people, so far as the post-Independence period was concerned. In fact artistic movements in the ill-defined socialist ideology could only be aligned in the revolutionary manner: 'there is nothing extraordinary in being revolutionary... It is simply a fact of living in reality'[22]. This conceptual ideal created a uniform amateur theatre movement from which the group ACT emerged to prominence. The interests of this group were in accordance with Kateb Yacine's desire to found a popular theatre. This agrees firstly with the dramatist's ambitions:

Given my situation in Algeria, it is obvious that political problems are behind everything since the country and society itself are in process of creation. Political problems appear at a primary level. Being concerned with politics implies a middle brow or a large public. Since there is a message to communicate, we should address a maximum number of people.[23]

and secondly with the group's performance manifesto:

The *Théâtre de la mer* aims to become a cross between a training school in theatrical research and a professional company presenting theatrical productions.[24]

This should, theoretically, have been the primary objective of the National Theatre, which had, unlike the new group, begun its life as an institution. But it remained unstable in the confusion that emerged between the problems created by Algeria in the immediate post-Independence period, and its inability to adapt to the country's needs. The outdated structure of the TNA could hardly be brought up to date despite political changes in the Algerian society. This is explained by J.M.Boeglin:

That positive asset (Nationalism), acquired on the structural level, had unfortunately brushed aside the essentials, this was to be the constant and patient transformation of structures in relation to political situation which expresses itself in the revolutionary dynamic of choice. A new ideology cannot accommodate itself within old structures. Revolution involves aesthetics.[25]

The TNA remained to all extent and purposes an 'old structure' while the amateur theatre offered the chance to experiment with better adapted forms: 'In a developing country, the theatre should help the people in a concrete manner and should have a clear and diverting form. It does not seem that, apart from a few works dictated by circumstances, the Algerian Theatre achieved these aims.'[26]

Therefore new groups took over the task of performing in accordance with the new political conditions of an emergent society. Most of these groups did not make use of writers, directors, professionals or famous actors. These amateurs organised themselves in a coherent manner in order to create plays inspired by the objective conditions of Algeria. 'The lack of production and the new social system based on land reform, and socialist management of enterprise have already given birth to a new type of creative form, 'collective creation'.'[27].

The fact is that very few professional troupes have survived throughout the history of Algerian Theatre. Amateur troupes have generally lasted longer. The first festival of Mostaghanem attracted seven amateur troupes in 1967. This festival conveyed a sense of the avant-garde in that it constituted one of the lines of post-colonial combat and was also a Manifesto for revolutionary amateur theatre policy in Algeria. The amateur theatre conference of Saïda from 31st March to 13th April 1973 defined the nature and object of collective creation. 'Amateurism (is) the democratic expression of young people who are conscious of the problems posed at all levels of revolutionary progress in its different stages.'[28]

In other words, both the conference and the festival declared that they were for a theatre whose role was, essentially, to take part in the education of the masses. Therefore, a theatre which was concerned to communicate its problems, both at home and abroad, was born. Its main concern was to inform the public and raise its consciousness. The troupes which opted for this didactic purpose demonstrated in the eleventh festival[29] of Mostaghanem that they had effectively turned

to popular tradition for methods and inspiration. Traditional modes of popular performance lay behind their scenography, characters and themes. Three distinct types of theatre developed:
- A popular theatre similar to the *Djeha*[30] theatre of the Algerian pioneers Allalou and Ksentini.
- A theatre inspired by tradition but selectively using forms which the public can relate to, such as the technique of *Al Halqa* (or closed circle).
- A realistic and revolutionary form, using documentary theatre.

These types of theatre mirror sources of inspiration. They are based on the participation of the actors as a whole and even that of the audience at a performance. These also suggests the development of the theatre towards an epic form, and reinforce its didactic character. The ACT, which later became the Regional Theatre of Sidi Bel Abbes (1976), undeniably gave these ideals their fullest expression.

Kateb Yacine's theatre presents a threefold dimension: 'It constitutes a new attitude towards culture. It begins a new period of cultural socialisation. It represents a new understanding of popular history.'[31] He showed that, with the figure of Djeha, culture ceases to be normative act and becomes performance. With a serious eloquence and ill at ease in his western and berber/bedouin dress, Djeha is a symbol for laughter. There is as much movement as speech. The people's language is revived and is vulgarised. With the establishment of Djeha as an artistic influence on the troupe's performing mode, a new cultural group consciousness has appeared. Used by Kateb Yacine in almost every performance, the figure of Djeha has remained the predominant element around which his political

satire is structured and from which the group draws its devices for subtle combination between what they are in reality and what they represent on the stage. Both states combine the true role of the group. The fact that his written scripts are available and might be performed by other actors in another style does not seem to be an important perspective for the dramatist. He was, above all, interested in the group consciousness he created and with which he remained concerned. He wanted to transform the group from one level of consciousness (amateurism) to a level of intellectually mature and artistically responsible. This was achieved through the use of Djeha whose imposing figure was adopted by every actor. The actors, acquired skills and ability to perform Djeha. This character became, unconsciously a part of them. To perform according to an authentic form and in accordance with the company's set of 'rules', an actor had to 'grow up' within the company, learn its devices and be convinced by its orientations. With Djeha, a process of intellectual evolution operates in the group's consciousness, helps the members to understand what is beyond the simple theatrical act and judge the community. This transformation implies a new rapport with the public. It is made concrete by the form of Halqa, a place around which the audience gathers in the immediacy of the performance. In fact, the judgement of the public is decisive here. It is the public who creates the value of the cultural work.

The group ACT was born as *Théâtre de la mer* on 20th August 1968 in Oran thanks to a fund of 1500 DA[32] raised by its founder members. Its young members had built up a network both to produce and perform plays, and to contribute to research on theatre. When Kateb Yacine joined the group in 1970, a few plays had already been put on (in accordance with the dramatist's view). *Mon Corps ta Voix et ta Pensée* (Your voice, its thoughts and myself) was a play whose thematic approach tackled the history of 'humanity from its origins to the advent of religion'. The play *La Valeur de l'Accord* (The Value of an Agreement) had as its main theme, 'technology as an instrument of repression'. This agreed so much with Kateb Yacine's concerns that he accepted the offer of being in charge of the group. He shared several political concerns with his friend Ali Zamoum[33], a civil servant in the Ministry of Labour who devoted himself much more to cultural activities than the service of the administration. Both men have since then shared common aims: giving the people a voice on the popular stage and building a true company of pioneering workers. These aspirations had already converged in the ideals advocated by the troupe's plays *Forma / Revolution* and *La Fourmi et l'Eléphant*. The first of these is about 'the professional training given to the Algerians since the post war period up to the beginning of Algerian independence'.[34] The second play is more international as it deals with imperialism and war, in particular Vietnam. This was the year before Kateb Yacine's play *L'Homme aux Sandales de Caoutchou*, a homage to Ho Chi Minh, was published. However, the theme that seems to have had most links with the dramatist's early commitments was emigration. A topical subject in that period, that made political relations between France and Algeria worse than ever, was the expectations of Algerian workers in France. Kateb Yacine, at that time, had almost twenty years experience with the working class abroad, and welcomed the idea of a play precisely on that social/political point. He thunders: 'How many times I had dreamt of expressing myself when I was in France!'[35] This was his reply to his friend when they first met in Algiers on his return from France, when the latter asked: 'We have a troupe, and the topical subject of emigration. Since you have lived so long (in France), why don't you write a play on that theme?'[36] (The play in question was *Mohamed Prends Ta Valise* which became a constant of the repertoire and was always being rewritten).

From that moment on Kateb Yacine embarked on a genuine experience of collective theatre. The theme was very familiar to the dramatist as well as to the troupe which, during the twenty years of the former's exile, had endured the consequences of emigration on the eye and thought of the people. In an interview Kateb explains:

> I had walked around Algerian villages, and in my native city in Guelma, I saw a young lady who was baking bread with children gathering round her like flies. I asked about her husband:
> 'He has been in France for four years.'
> 'Does he write to you?'
> 'No.'
> 'Does he come to visit you in summer?'
> 'Never, may be he is living with another woman in France.'
> My play, therefore, addresses those in Algeria who want to go to France and who, once in France, suffer there or are unable to return home.[37]

For Kateb Yacine the history of emigration matched the history of Algeria as a continuous colonial phenomenon which might prove fatal for the country; the youth of Algeria, who should build the country's future, exile themselves in order to end up with a low standard of living, being exploited or wandering about on unemployment benefit. Kateb Yacine's play questions both Algerian and French policy. He depicts the complicity of the classes, a complicity which exists between the French Bourgeoisie and those Algerians in power. Post-colonial development in his country could not be perfected if capitalist attitudes survived. For this reason, young people representing the wider sections of the population became pioneers of socialism.

Kateb Yacine established his troupe to perform in the villages through which it passed. Some members highlighted the difficulty of making a categoric distinction between amateur and professional in the revolutionary situation. Others were rather professional actors, badly paid until they received their full wages from a Ministry subsidy. For instance, in 1978 they received no pay for their work, but were compensated with some cereal and provisions given by the public before starting a performance[38]. They carried on because they wanted to tell the story of the revolution to as many peasants as possible. Kateb Yacine, clinging to the idea of a 'revolutionary' theatre, explains: 'In our country, given that the revolution is far from over, revolutionary culture is necessary... A political theatre which addresses the whole people is necessary'.[39] With this ideal in mind, his theatre began. He and his company moved to a new village every day and performed afternoon and evening. The company ate at different houses in one village and lodged with their meal time hosts. They had 'unforgettable moments with the peasants of villages'[40]. Props, travel expenses, and incidentals were all paid for on a short-lived subsidy from the Ministry. In reality one has to consider these actors as non-professionals at least until 1976 (the year of the establishment of the Regional Theatres by a Government Decree). They were either workers or students. The fact that they received no pay for their work strengthens this impression, but because they were given provision, the actors were, in fact, paid in kind.

Whether amateur, professional, or in the blurred intermediate position between the two[41], Kateb Yacine's theatre displayed certain features of particular interest because they were to be carried over very strongly into the amateur dramatic life of post-independence Algeria. Frugality was of the greatest importance. Props were simple. Theatre buildings were already in existence (inherited from the French). Stages in other places were in public areas such as village platforms, warehouses or school yards. It was usually the actors themselves who elaborated the final scripts for performances. Kateb Yacine's theatre was explicitly revolutionary and designed as an art for 'political development'. Its purpose was pioneering rather than socialist, it strengthened the belief of those already committed, and won further supporters. It appears to have been successful in these aims, and the audiences were very enthusiastic:

> We pay particular attention to the young people who represent more than half of the population and which always turns up in large numbers in our theatrical performances. Sometimes it gathered more than 10000 workers, as was the case on the Anaba industrial estate, and we remember that enthusiastic explosion.[42]

When the young actors that Kateb Yacine gathered together had acquired enough experience and gained control over the installation of the Regional Theatre of Sidi Bel Abbes, they quickly made it obvious that the great emphasis formerly placed on amateur theatricals in a few selected regions could be transferred to the whole country. These non-professional drama companies have played a significant social/political role, particularly under the influence of Kateb Yacine's theatre. This coincided with the rise of the political education of the young people, especially in regions like Algiers and Sidi Bel Abbes:

> We have noticed the rapprochement of the youth theatre with the theatre of Kateb Yacine. Thus we can see the influence of the author of *Mohamed Prends ta Valise* in every play.[43]

The most remarkable example is the amateur movement in Saïda, an important province of Sidi Bel Abbes. Within the movement, the group *Prolet-Kult* showed its strength in the performance of *Rass Es'sensla* (The Top of a Chain).[44] Although from an 'amateur conception', it probably carried out its aims to the full. The emphasis in the play was on the mechanism of history perceived through its relation to reality and the ideological discourse of the protagonists. This global conception of history, that it is composed of the people who 'make it', together with the aim to go straight to essentials, explains the choice of using a common costume, fewer props and an almost bare stage.

In the mainstream of this amateur theatre movement of the 1970s and 1980s *Debza*, a typical troupe, sprang up. It is a troupe which not only practices a very radical form of TFD but also takes its iconography from Kateb Yacine's theatre . The most important effect was exerted by Kateb's contact. 'Among the troupes which were born out of our contact, there is one *Debza*, whose leader is a young delinquent who fell in love with the theatre at first sight.'[45]

Debza is 'the Fist' in Algeria, a name which evokes much for the students of central Algeria who 'shook their fists' at the government, during several protest movements against various repressive policies of the late 1970s and 1980s. In fact bureaucracy, intolerance and mistrust have consigned the troupe to anonymity and reduced its impact. However *Debza* has always leant towards popular songs as well as theatre and so this confinement paradoxically increased the mystique of the troupe: their record or tape EL Qadia (The Matter) was so popular that stocks ran out two months after issue. *Debza* is one of the first troupes, in Algeria, to invest in two areas, theatre and song. Despite a dearth of means, they developed an artistic potential on the stage and had been trying to form a coherent cross between these two art forms. This is also one of the fundamental devices in Kateb Yacine's theatre.

In 1986, *Debza* decided to turn to political songs more than theatre and recorded their second tape, which was financed by Kateb Yacine. Prior to that, the troupe's sound repertoire[46] of 1980/

1981 reflected the political face of Algeria just after Boumediene's regime: most of the titles in their first tape picture the most critical shifting of policies of the new Algerian Government; *'Wash Rah Sayer'* (What's going on?) *'El Qadia'* (The Matter), *'Allez-y'* (Go on..), and *'Abni Qesrek'* (Raise up Your Palace). This last song refers to the most important minaret in Algiers called *Riadh el Fath*. It was built in order to impress. It therefore served to annihilate previous political influence, being a most expensive building housing the Ministry of Culture. This most luxurious and attractive new site was apparently about to be financed by what was left of the budget made by the former Government to build the remaining 'socialist villages' in accordance with socialist land reform. This turning away from the initial political objective is brought into focus in *Debza*'s tape and therefore it was banned two months after it came on the market. However this ban reinforced *Debza*'s legendary status.

After an attempt to write a play in Berber, which has never been performed because of the language in which it was spoken (the Berber language has remained a political problem for successive governments), *Debza* has invested more in song. In 1988 it produced a third more elaborate recording (this time in France). A member of the troupe explains why they went abroad: 'Debza joined the studio in July 1988 (in Algiers). The first day, three songs were recorded. On their return from a coffee break, the manager said: 'Sorry, that's it!', 'This material is too subversive'.'[47]

Almost all the troupes concerned either with theatre or in what is known as 'political song' have not escaped censorship or restrictions imposed during the twenty six years of one party state under the FLN regime. Most radical artists and authors had to rely on the first editor who made them welcome. Kateb Yacine addressed the general meeting of artists and intellectuals in response to this situation:

> Censorship creates conformity, it tames people and makes courtiers out of them, it lowers those who practice it as well as those who undergo it. Censorship leads to self censorship. It mutilates, disguises, falsifies and treats reality as a mistake to be covered according to its own view. It is the language of fear. One fears to displease. Therefore one has to do everything to please. One has to lie, or to speak to no purpose or else it is silence, the last refuge of those who refuse to be censored because their job is to shout what others do not even say. This silence, when it lasts, is a kind of continual suicide. One escapes only from exile. This is why so many artists, writers, dramatists and film makers, must make themselves heard abroad, notably in France and thus give a negative image of the independent Algeria. What is independence if not freedom?
>
> To make Algeria truly free, we should demand the abolition of censorship.[48]

With the recent democratic opening (1989) in Algeria, *Debza* hoped that restrictions would be lifted. This troupe representing the youngest generation of amateur theatre is highly talented. Its members will have much to say in the Algerian Theatre of the 1990s. Their interest clearly lies in 'political' theatre and in a genuine revival of Algerian culture. It follows the general trends of the amateur movement initiated by Kateb Yacine's group.

The diverse means used by most amateur troupes should not undermine the nature and role of the amateur theatre. These means do not simplify or reduce the amateur theatre reality to an opposition between message and technique. M.Y. Selmane explains, on the basis of Djaad's argument, that most new groups, 'fail to convey their message because they confine themselves to an easy pattern of declaiming slogans'[49]. On the contrary, a possible criticism which does not patronise[50] would contribute to the debate on amateur theatre and its future which lies in the framework of its orientations and through its different approaches and 'easy pattern'.

The social function of the amateur theatre subsumes all its other functions and can only be realised in the performance and its resulting discussion. Criticism, at an early stage, appears to have lost sight of the dimensions of the amateur theatre. The critic appears to have undermined the key to the amateur theatre. The result of the role it played in voicing the post-colonial ideology, that Selmane calls a 'disaster', explains its repetition of 'slogans', its repression and its persistence in looking for what could not be found in the National Theatre in the 1970s, and its demand for things that the National Theatre, for instance, had never considered. Amateurs have always challenged the judgement of the 'easy pattern'. Slimane Benaissa[51] even describes the pattern as: 'The principle of *flash* [slogan] and *saynette*.' Yet M.Y. Selmane says that before 1971/72, 'the amateur theatre was the pulse of Algerian society'[52]. In contrast, he asserts that after that period, 'New major political events were to affect the amateur theatre'[53]. In this way, he attributes the political change to the decline of this amateur movement towards the late 1970s. The argument can work the other way round. Kateb Yacine's group had experienced most, if not all of its successful development in that period of 'New political events'. If we recall that history is a process of life, we can show that in the case of Algeria different periods of history have shown a development from social concerns to a new political situation.

The growth in importance of the theatre is reflected in the numbers of amateur companies.[54] The nature of spare-time theatre groups makes it impossible to compile exact statistics for them, because they frequently form only for one specific production and then disband. The number of troupes in any given region might therefore fluctuate a great deal even over a short period. A few of the more approximate figures[55] make sense when placed in a historical context. The rapid rise in the number of troupes, especially in the context of the Nationalisation of Theatres since 1976, may partly reflect the emphasis placed in those years on setting up 'propaganda' networks.

The National Theatre, in this respect, did not encourage the amateur movement, for it had kept its stereotyped traditional forms, its ambition to be commercial and professional, and its conservative views. However, the spectacular growth in the number of amateur actors was fairly consistent between 1970 and 1980. Surprisingly enough, the Ministry of Culture at no time put forward a policy actively deprecating the spare-time theatre. There have been periods when it has encouraged the amateur movement with special intensity. The first of these was the year 1978. In that year the Ministry of Culture called upon party branches everywhere and at all levels to enlist the aid of suitable troupes to spread the government's message among the people, and cultural circles were among the many groups asked to take part. It was given special attention at many conferences held by the Ministry of Culture, and an authoritative report[56] on amateur troupes declared that they had already become a strong force in pioneering social policies which could not be ignored. It was therefore obvious that Kateb Yacine's company was seen in the capital and given the honour of a stage in the National Theatre to perform *Palestine Trahie* (Palestine Betrayed), a play seemingly about the betrayal of Arab Palestine while, in reality, about betrayal by Arabs themselves. The next major attempt to promote amateur theatre came during the late 1970s and 1980s. One principal characteristic was the unusual number and size of festivals held in the different regions of Algeria. The main one was that which took place in Blida in 1981. Several groups came from different regions and the festival was then the largest of its kind (after the National Festival of Mostaghanem).

During the 1970s one finds certain features in the amateur movement not present in the years between 1962 and 1970. These features, such as 'progressivist aesthetics', were clear in the turbulence of the revolutionary reform period: the emphasis on Boumediene's ideology was not seen in earlier years nor later.

One result of this attitude was a movement to combine professional and amateur. Professional troupes were encouraged to perform plays written by amateurs. One aim was to prevent professionals from looking down on people acting in their spare-time and to bring professionals closer to reality. Even though amateurs might lack a fully developed expertise in playwrighting, the fact that their main work lay in industry, professional training schools and villages enabled them to write more convincingly about real life than any person engaged in the theatre on a full-time basis. Kateb Yacine and his company fulfilled this ideal[57]: the actors, different from those in the National Theatre, had developed themselves as performers while holding other jobs. The fact that they were not 'professional' or 'professionally' trained in the usual sense of the word was not critically important. They saw their job not as to set the audience at their ease but, preferably, to alert them, to make them discover the inner and seamy side of things even if it entailed putting them over in a ludicrous way using caricature. The professionals in other theatres transferred these experiments to their distinctly conventional theatre. The well experienced 'amateur' Slimane Benaïssa summarises:

> The first years after Independence, saw an impressive theatre, of huge *décors*, distribution and imposing *mise en scene*. However, it happened that this theatre did not work and could not function. Even Brecht's theatre posed serious problems of translation and adaptation. Therefore it could not 'pass' (...). It was, finally the amateur theatre which created the pattern enabling the National Theatre to move forward.[58]

Ironically, conservative elements still considered this Theatre as a creation of the masses. A press article '*Le TNA à l'heure de la jeunesse*', describes the contradictions of the TNA. With a new administrator the Institution tried to spend money in helping and supporting several mass activities while the production of the TNA was suffering a state of marasmus. Instead of re-investing to encourage those dramatists in posts since Independence and who could produce original works, the administrator says: 'A way, for us, is to help a practical formation of amateur troupes'[59]. Some actors of the FLN troupe carried on acting in the National Theatre on the basis that they legitimately had the right and duty to continue making a contribution to the arts.

Another effect of the programme to combine professional and amateur was to set up the INADC again for both amateurs and potential professionals to attend. However, a school of this sort did not last long. Concerning professional training, we should recognise that there are as many different systems of training as there are different kinds of theatre, since theatre reflects different cultures at different stages of development. There is an important difference between needs as regards training for commercial theatre and those as regards training for rural folk theatre - for development (if training in rural theatre is even necessary). The Ministry of Culture made attempts at organising workshops in the INADC but it was at a loss to find a way of training for instance the authors and actors of oral plays. As a matter of fact oral plays are born out of community life and handed down from one generation to another. So it is not suited to the artistic training organised in that Institute by European experts. Unfortunately Europeans say that those who participate in training should follow their European experiences. There are several examples of European models being transplanted into other cultures. Molière and Shakespeare were constantly performed in classical

Arabic. The number[60] of European plays translated into Arabic and put on the National Theatre stage is greater than original plays by Algerian playwrights, and this lasted until fairly recently. We should remember that there was a time in the history of European Theatre when French Theatre was a model for all theatrical activity. On these grounds, one might now think the European Theatre a good example for other countries. This is not really true. One faces a very complex problem when it comes to the relationship between the strong structure of the established theatre and the theatre in developing Algeria. Europeans must recognise their feeling of responsibility for the African countries. Offering them European models of theatre counts for little. It is not easy to recognise the links between highly-developed urban theatre and the theatre of simple rural communities, the latter being an expression of the immediate feelings and needs of the people. Of course such links do exist, expressed by the presence of the actors and spectators, but it is very important to emphasise the necessity of different methods in the development of theatre. This recalls our initial argument concerning cultural identification. One should try to enlarge ones sense of the world. Cultural identification means not only the traditional items but the social forms within which the theatre exists. The theatre of developing Algeria does not have to pass through the same stages of development as the European Theatre. It will find its own original way into the community of the future. Perhaps, in this way, a theatre of new forms and new qualities will be born. Europeans hinder its development by forcing upon it their own examples.

Amateur theatricals were important enough to be encouraged. The Regional Theatre of Sidi Bel Abbes has been most popular among the peasants, 'uneducated' or poorer sections of the population, a fact which Kateb Yacine rightly classified as 'people's theatre'. As such it is singularly appropriate for use as agit-prop. As a matter of fact his theatre has been known as *Théâtre de combat*. The conservatives in the Algerian regime in the 1970s only considered seriously the developmental flavour of this theatre in limited 'revolutionary' fields; the promotion of land reforms and industrialisation. Comments have referred to the importance of employing amateurs: 'Theatre action will not be confined to the National Theatre. We will follow the development of the amateur theatre.'[61]

The basic principles behind Kateb Yacine's company have been spelled out in such a way that, based on voluntary and mass principles, the group has kept closely in step with Kateb Yacine's political tasks. Using forms which ordinary people love to hear and see, they carry on education, encourage and perform to the worker's enthusiasm for their work and creative skills, and greatly enliven the cultural life of the people. In this way they achieve the aim of increasing production.

In fact, Kateb Yacine's theatricals have, ideally, been much more than a form of relaxation. They have also been didactic, instilling values in the people. The same purpose also holds true for the Regional Theatres, but amateurs are even more important in this respect for three reasons. Firstly, they are, in a direct sense, part of the people and more likely to have an influence on them. Secondly, they are far more numerous and hence reach an even greater number of people. Lastly, a person who takes part in a post-colonial drama himself is more easily affected by its content than someone who merely watches.

Another objective of Kateb Yacine's theatre carried on by his company is one already made implicit in the above paragraphs - namely to increase people's consciousness. Through watching or taking part in suitable places like villages, factories and training schools, workers and others are stimulated to an understanding of their working situation and conditions. In this way members of the company are not only fighters on the literary and artistic front, but also the vanguard in increasing production and work. This theme is one aspect of the stress on ideological motivation which, to a greater or lesser degree, has characterised Algerian post-colonial orientation since its early days.

Related to this, is the aim of promoting the concept of self-help. This was put into practice during the 1970s. It had stood the pioneers in good stead ever since. In the theatrical field it implies that every theatre organisation should take as its motto something like 'take it on yourselves to instruct and perform'. They should not only perform theatricals themselves, they should write their own plays and even teach others. Recourse to such techniques is imposed upon the dramatist who is prepared to stage provocative political sketches which are efficient in the context described so far. When stimulated by the reference to their political situation and its sad history, the audience is turned into or becomes actor. The public responds to the rhythms of the performance and repeats loudly the main ideas (sounded by the chorus) and the popular songs it has heard. The debate that generally follows the performance is marked by a greater political awareness, and is also diverted from the theatrical framework.

The debate on the plays, or more precisely the particular performance, which brings together the public and actors invariably extends in unexpected ways. The play is a pretext to discuss life and its problems since these occur most frequently in the debate, something which some critics find distasteful[62]. One of Kateb Yacine's goals, this stimulating of debates with plays is certainly heretical to the conservative body of criticism. Indeed there has been a gap between that criticism and Kateb Yacine's theatre as well as all theatre of his kind. After a vigorous song[63] which ends the performance on a note of conviction that social-democracy will triumph, the public gathers together with the performers where it is practicable for them to do so. Discussions last twice as long as the performance, and before the actors actually begin their performance they have already held an inquiry about the problems of the area they are performing in. Some critics usually leave at the moment the debate starts and can hardly hide their disappointment: 'Plays should not be like seminars or lectures.. They are going down.. Kateb Yacine must re-evaluate his theatre.'[64]

While the debate is proceeding, workers, peasants, young people, unemployed and actors inform and teach each other about culture, ideology, politics, the general situation in the country and abroad, their struggles, their mobilisation, alliances, achievements, tasks, action and organisation. In the meantime, the critic in front of his paper - remote from the actual practice of the art - reaches different conclusions and finds the 'principal' reasons for this theatre's 'fiasco' is that 'the actors cannot read' or 'they (the actors) do not research on the theatre direction or on this kind of production'. Whatever the variety of reaction the popular consciousness grows up within the context mentioned above. Considering a situation experienced during the few hours of a performance, the public understands, questions, compares, elucidates, in short continues its education (if it is not already continuing while taking part in the play).

The performers in Kateb Yacine's company have educated the people not merely by turning their class consciousness into a dedication to new political concerns, but also by raising their cultural level, that is by providing them with a knowledge of Algeria and the world. Kateb Yacine's plays tackle subjects like social democracy, imperialism, colonialism, world capitalism, together with religious and social trends. In a country where so many people are illiterate, the concept of acquiring knowledge through entertainment is clearly of considerable importance. It applies in particular to the performers themselves, for whom informal education is seen as a pre-requisite to good acting.

The general intention in carrying out a popular and pioneering theatre, which can be seen to emerge from the whole discussion, is to make people more conscious citizens. One can approach this problem from different angles. On a mundane level, theatre improves people by keeping them out of mischief. This is no small point as many Algerians enjoy a considerable amount of leisure, especially in the country side. In some areas it is the norm that peasants and workers spend only about half a day on a job. In Algeria, as elsewhere, healthy educational and cultural activities are excellent ways of occupying leisure hours. Algerians think the ideological aspect is the most important. Although Kateb Yacine's theatre is professionally established with some amateur features, its themes are an important influence on people. Their healthy influence not only makes the performers more progressive in a general sense, but also leads them to more specific actions.

The Theatre Company of Sidi Bel Abbes: From Constraints to Achievements

The company functions in two main areas; urban and rural. The former is normally organised in such a way that the company acts within an individual organisation, such as a factory, an institute or training school. However, this rule is by no means invariable. The rural outreach is what makes Kateb Yacine's theatre original. Sometimes a small group is found in this company in which citizens of one particular village join together to form a nucleus of a future village troupe. Rural troupes formed in this way are virtually all non-professional. One point to make here is that the greater concentration of people in the cities would seem to make the formation of a large troupe easier in urban than in rural regions. However, I have found no definite evidence which would correlate the size of a drama troupe to its area of activity either in the city or in the country. The membership of the company in terms of occupation naturally varies according to the area where its members live. Actors come from virtually all types of factories, no matter what kind of goods they produce. Naturally most of the amateurs who join the company are simple workers.

One group of amateurs who do not join the company is that of the National People's Army. The 'agit-prop' policy propagated in some areas of government during the immediate post-independence period was continued in the period after the 1965 coup. However the role of this policy in spreading propaganda among the military - especially while the Army played a major part in land reform, urban construction and industry - and in trying to wean the people from their dependence on foreign income and the constant threat of neo-colonialism shrank in importance in the moderate conditions which followed 'socialism'. Army theatricals tended largely to be the preserve of pure amateurs.

The company of Sidi Bel Abbes encourages young people. In fact they still make up the bulk of membership. The young are more likely to have the energy for theatricals after a normal day's work. In a context where amateur dramatics are a means of educating the actor himself, young people are the most suitable participants. Finally, the enthusiasm and idealism of the young also make them suitable interpreters of the messages inherent in drama.

Naturally enough, it is politically active young men and women who are most needed. As in so many spheres of life in contemporary Algeria, activism is an important concept in the company of Sidi Bel Abbes. In this, because of the way it makes use of the theatre, students and young workers are much in demand. The students who have returned to their villages, after being involved in one way or another in Kateb Yacine's theatre experience, have joined amateur troupes. Some of these groups were often infiltrated by FLN party members. This poses the important question of how far the make up of the Algerian theatre movement was controlled by the party. The evidence strongly suggests that neither in the cities nor the rural districts did the leadership consider it desirable to allow just anyone to join, but that control was both easier and more effective in the cities than outside them. In rural areas, the controls over who was permitted to join a group were fairly relaxed; the more rigid controls of urban companies did not prevent some 'discontents' on the part of the actors themselves.

In the first place the principle of voluntary membership has always been observed. From the point of view of the party commission set up in the late 1970's to supervise and take part in the management of the Regional Theatre of Sidi Bel Abbes, an even more serious problem was posed by the fact that so called 'undesirables' found their way into the company even when this party authority supervised their membership. A report (tract) from the commission names several of those it finds as 'alcoholics', 'drug addicts' and 'homosexuals'. Although company members may carry documents proving their legal status, Algerian bureaucrats scrutinise the company because it consists mostly of the unemployed, labourers and villagers with no skills or specific training. The report even absurdly states that the 'troupe was expelled from Algiers'. It appears that conservative party members viewed Kateb Yacine's troupe as a place which encouraged avoidance of government strictures. Party members, who are students, officials, administrators or essentially 'good' elements of the corrupted party administration are urged to beware of such a company in case it adversely affects their work and morals:

> We are convinced that you share our major concern: (we wish) to preserve the party organisation from dangerous deviation, bad reputation and also from infiltration of undesirable elements, enemies of our cause, the Algerian Arabic Muslim Socialist Revolution.[66]

Clearly it appears that the party organisation[67] within the theatre of Sidi Bel Abbes, intended to prevent further movement in membership. These party members are those who have appropriated the socialist ideology or taken personal advantage of it.

Like his members, Kateb Yacine was the subject of strict opposition from those press critics who supported the traditional conservatives of the FLN. The Arabic daily newspaper *El Chaab* was the stronghold of these critics of the dramatist and his company. The reasons for their criticism are many and various, but all tend to contradict Kateb Yacine's sense of his real mission as a dramatist who sought to inform and educate his people on historical, political and social matters. In the pretence of bringing to light a movement aiming to turn the clock back, a journalist of the above daily paper accuses Kateb Yacine of 'corrupting youth, and opposing popular reform'[68]. In this way, critics have tended to disparage him, supporting their views by other pretentious assumptions, such as that, like Solzhenitsyn, he stirs up dissent, or that he is guilty of political and intellectual treason[69]. They also argue that Kateb Yacine seeks to promote divisions between people from the fact that he based his first novel and early plays upon tribalism. Here, it is necessary to re-emphasise that Kateb Yacine's first literary and dramatic work was written while Algeria was still under French colonial rule. He simply showed Algeria as it was. Therefore the expression of tribal concern in his books is a clear reflection of the Algerian nation which had remained as dissimulated tribes, an irrefutable reality that abstract ideologies have tended to deny. This is precisely where socialism and nationalism in Algeria fail to find their foundation. Therefore, different principles emerged according to different ideological conceptions. In addition to this amalgam, the language that the dramatist had used in his previous works (in French) and used in his performances (common language composed of popular Algerian Arabic and Berber) remained a matter of controversy and criticism. Beside this irrational criticism, other insults and lies came from *Al Alouan*[70], a more radical right-wing review of 'Information and Culture', which Kateb Yacine answered in his play *Mohamed Prends Ta Valise*. In fact, performances of this play often include scenes based on current topical subjects in the news but also critical scenes replying to the latest attacks on the part of the authorities or the press. This is one reason why Kateb Yacine's scripts are constantly changing.

I am looking back to the play as performed in Algiers before the move of the ACT to Sidi Bel Abbes. The play included some critical material protesting against the Algerian authorities with their policies on emigration and the consequences of the exploitation of Algerian workers in France whose misery profits only those in power in Algeria and the host country. The play was staged in Algeria after the troupe's tour of France, and performed without incident. Unusually for that period, it escaped censorship, since it had the some kind of support of the cultural commission of the Ministry of Labour.

These are the actual conditions under which both Kateb Yacine and members of the company (then known as the ACT) had to try to establish a genuine form of Popular Theatre for Development . Their artistic enterprise therefore deserves the title of '*Théâtre de Combat*' for they had a real struggle trying to survive as a drama group and establish a popular genre at the same time.

As members of a company derived from the amateur movement within a professional establishment, the actors had other feelings to express. An actor describes the situation during the decisive year of 1972, a year after the foundation of the ACT:

> A hard year's work has finally produced a great experience and a certain amount of worthwhile work, despite innumerable difficulties as well as certain weaknesses. Several qualities have been attributed to our work, but something else counts for us as well... A year has passed since the foundation of the ACT: we have put on a single production: *Mohamed Prends Ta Valise*. We have actually spared nothing of our efforts or senses. This hard work has been satisfactory to some people, taking account of our material difficulties. For others, the results could have been better with more discipline and method in their work. Taking account of the fact that our work was designed with workers in mind, our troupe has taken its present name. In taking a new name, it has taken on a new character as well.[71]

This last sentence accounts for its purpose, which the actor describes as 'bringing about the victory of the people's cause', an important function which the company has been fulfilling ever since.

A tour of the whole country was instigated, intended to reach and entertain more remote provinces and areas of the cities which were often overlooked. But the most important part of the programme was to reach villages and farms where the troupe had to use what came to hand. A few small villages could attract '15000 persons in a week'[72], despite the lack of adequate means. This lead to the decision to establish a rural theatre, a theatre for villages and other remote areas where there are no suitable buildings. Everything, even the premises that the company had at their disposal (either when they were in Algiers, or later established in Sidi Bel Abbes), was 'no longer suitable' for the new theatrical genre that Kateb Yacine and his actors had founded. As a senior actor states: 'the premises where we rehearsed proved to be inappropriate for our kind of activity'.[73] This new activity was based on the traditional and popular form of the *Halqa*.

A major attraction of this form of theatre is its simplicity. Very little is required in the way of

construction. A plane space provides the central acting area and room for the surrounding audience. This is the pattern of both the ancient village ceremonies and the everyday business of storytellers in some rural areas and in markets, and is still available for modern performers like the actors of Sidi Bel Abbes Theatre.

Al *Halqa*, 'swivel of a chain' in Arabic'[74], is a demonstration of popular culture. It tends to make use of places which are used for public gatherings for its performances, such as the town square or the *Souks* (weekly markets). The *Halqa* 'owes its form to the spontaneous initiative of men gifted in storytelling and mimicry.'[75] These men, having picked the place where they are to perform, start to attract passers-by through their words and gesture, and by the use of percussion instruments. These passers-by then become the audience and straight away form a circle around the 'comedians'. The show starts. The entertainers tell legends and other tales, accompanied by mime and percussion music. The non-existent scenery is suggested merely by word and deed. One or the other entertainer plays on the various reactions of the public, which is not slow to comment on the action. The entertainers invite the audience to join in the show; some do this readily, going barefoot onto the stage and taking up one or other of the props which are used for the performance.

The *Halqa*, because of its popular form and the kind of places where it takes place, does not alienate the audience, unlike the theatre which, as an institution and an awe-inspiring building, is alien to the ordinary public. Here it would be useful to recall past experiences which would illuminate our discussion of Kateb Yacine's experience of popular Theatre for Development. Kaki, inspired by the *Halqa* and the storyteller[76], tried to create a new genre of popular theatre. His plays are written in the form of long epic poems in spoken Arabic. The storyteller performs the poem while the other actors perform a series of tableaux illustrating the story. To Kaki, it was simply a matter of transferring the actor-audience rapport found in the *Halqa* onto the stage of the Italianate Theatre. The form and techniques of *Halqa* performances 'are recovered, classified, standardised and adapted to the modern stage'[77]. In my view, Kaki's mistake lay in wanting to make use of the traditional form of the *Halqa* for the benefit of a pictorial stage. The *Halqa*, torn from its natural environment, did not survive this re-planting on the proscenium stage. The fact that this experience thirty years ago had no influence on the development of the Algerian Theatre is also due to other directors who failed to appreciate the significance of this work. The reason I have recalled Kaki's brief experiment is to show that if Kateb Yacine and his company had confined themselves strictly to the Italianate stage, they would have received the same setback.

The form of *Halqa* as an experience represents the circumstances which permitted Kateb Yacine's troupe to perform outdoors. The confidence, which acting without unnecessary preparations reveals, shows a spirit that is very different from that which inspires the TNA's desperate imitation of the so called 'real theatre'. It was no accident that with Kateb Yacine's authentic mode of stage expression, young actors in this missionary 'adventure' sought to experiment and develop it on a larger scale. In other words one has to recognise in the devoted spirit of Kateb Yacine's enterprise the pioneer element which the actors developed and perfected to educate the public. The participation of that public in their theatre was thorough. Although rural, the areas where their experiments were conducted were of high population density.

Folk motifs serve as the 'building blocks' of the stage production, or the 'production structure' as the members of the group prefer to call it. These folk motifs comprise elements of folk rituals, such as a scene about the historical Kahena or one involving a witchcraft ritual as well as ethnographic material, and scenes from Kateb Yacine's books. The scenes from the latter are at home in the 'thousand years' of folk culture. For there to be a truly new theatre drawn from real life, the group members realised that they had to fight for a more simple and natural environment for the theatre. This has been the idea behind Kateb Yacine's theatre for years. To find a more natural setting for the theatre, the group left the city, leaving behind both theatre buildings and city streets, and sought to address themselves to people untrammelled by conventional behaviour and free from stereotyped responses indoctrinated by society. Finally, they explored avenues previously unknown to, or abandoned by, the theatre. As Mustapha Kateb recognises, Kateb Yacine's theatre 'makes [..] political and current theatre. Its form forces the abolition of conventions but also establishes others'.[78] Mustapha Kateb as a National Theatre figure recognises that these elements of practice are effectively absent in the National Theatre.

The acting 'space' to which we refer in Kateb Yacine's new form, does not mean yet another 'closed circle' bound in by rules, nor does it indicate an ordinary stage as we know it. The acting space actually means any given area, including the land and sky bound by that area. Kateb Yacine's group is not concerned with background or with idle poetic contemplation of nature. Its concern is that these elements should become living participants in the action. All things are seen just as they are depicted in folk legend - the sun, stars or earth- are given to man, not as mere objects of individual contemplation or gratuitous reflection, but as drawn into the motion of life which makes them living participants in the action. All things take part in the story, instead of being contrasted with the action as its passive background. By entering into that 'space' one can recall and perhaps even revive the essence of the word 'theatre' for 'thea' refers to 'the art of seeing'. It therefore refers to perception and must stand for knowledge, power and purity.

Their action thus resides in the importance of the public to whom they have to translate their preoccupations in comprehensible and accessible terms. The simplicity, of this form of theatre lies in its interpretation of the *Halqa* which inspires it, and which is well known to the general public. The circle is a common figure to Algerians and its centre is in their consciousness expressed naturally in every activity of their life. Architecture, for example, is traditionally designed so as to give the impression of a circle. We usually find houses built around a plane area serving as common ground to its residents, and playing an important social role in the neighbourhood. In fact, it is there in the centre that a well is built, where all the neighbourhood will draw their water, an activity which becomes a pretext for daily meetings and discussions. It is also there that family ceremonies take place, where the residents around this central area are welcomed without distinction and without invitation. It is also where reconciliations take place. Thence arises the popular consciousness. It is where the revolution and the circle of its rebellion was born.

The shape and convention of Kateb Yacine's village or 'open-air' theatre is not universal, but is inextricably bound up in more complex patterns of cultural symbolism, logic, and presentational conventions. Furthermore, theatre traditions are among the most dynamic and powerful components of any given culture. They bear a strong relationship to folk custom in that they consist of symbolic elements. These elements are made manifest through competent actors, whose purpose is to move spectators at the performance in a preconceived manner: Kateb Yacine's actors make them laugh, persuade them, create a sense of heightened reality in them and elevate their sensibilities.

Being experimental the performances of the Theatre of Sidi Bel Abbes could be faulted if rigidly conventional stage-patterns were applied. How then does the actor convey his performance all around? Everyone in the audience is close enough to detect movement and to interpret changes of expression. The actor has what seems almost a new range of subtle gestures at his command. His least expression is clear to the audience, his motives and intentions become transparent, even from the back. The 'central stage', whether in a village square or school courtyard can hardly provide an up stage or dominant position. The novelty of this situation can be illustrated by noting that young actors playing subsidiary parts in a play on a proscenium stage must frequently be told to keep still while in this central performing area they will rather be told to react with more truth or conviction, more positively. When the actors are replaced by young amateurs who join the company, the latter are provided with this new vocabulary.

The European theatre (French model) was imported and was, to a certain degree, a function of colonialism, affecting an intellectual and cultural manipulation of the colonised people. Kateb Yacine freed theatre from this cultural discrimination, and therefore 'decolonialised' the art of theatre as it existed in the 'picture-frame' stage. His style of performance did not prove to be adaptable to this proscenium arch and called for somewhere else for the theatre to take on an authentic form. An essential factor in this context is the treatment of space and audience behaviour in the traditional 'communicative art', the *Halqa*. With this form Kateb Yacine labelled his theatre. Each 'performance structure' incorporated particular spacial relationship already existent in traditional Algerian Society.

Indeed a genre of theatre was born out of the experience that Kateb Yacine had carefully developed in order to maintain the traditions of the Algerian theatre and to achieve the goals articulated in his first novel, *Nedjma*: to address his countrymen and discuss their problems. Kateb Yacine undoubtedly achieved this through putting his dramatic ideas into practice in every part of the country that could possibly be reached. However, he was not given a chance to fulfil this end easily.

Kateb Yacine explains the hardship that he and his troupe had to endure in the second stage of their transitional period:

> Our second phase started off with the change of Minister. The creation and existence of the troupe were due to the director of professional training at the Ministry of Labour. We were wholeheartedly supported. With the nomination of the new Minister, everything fell apart. Often these things are the work of just one man. The next day we were thrown out. We had actors who were married with kids. In this way I found myself once more with nine people in my two bedroom flat. We had to live as we no longer had money coming in. We lived in this uncertainty for nearly two years. On the one hand , nobody dared suppress us altogether, as we were too well-known, and on the other, the Minister did not want us.[79]

Since he was not appreciated by the new Minister of Labour in 1975/76 and was hindered by the authorities responsible for cultural affairs because of his radical ideas, Kateb Yacine was exiled to the theatre of Sidi Bel Abbes. His troupe was evicted from its premises in Bab El Oued (Algiers) and sent to join him. This 'Exile' in a remote region with a low level of political consciousness, with few artistic traditions and therefore a non-existent public, was greeted with dismay by the company in the first instance. Kateb Yacine explains their frustrating move:

> In the end they decided to send us to Sidi Bel Abbes, 500km from Algiers. Having done so, they were openly hoping for the group to break up. The place itself was interesting as it was the former stronghold of the French foreign Legion in a strategic position, as it is placed near several important towns. Now, we, who were used to creating our work around the capital had to re-create everything. What was more, the theatre in Sidi Bel Abbes was empty.
>
> Another factor was that, away from Algiers, local reaction is always very hostile. In these areas there is a bourgeoisie, behaving like feudal Lords, thinking that everything belongs to them including the theatre.[80]

The authorities's wish that the troupe would break up and their plan to send Kateb Yacine away from the centre of politics did not have the expected result. The company, in its new home, succeeded in reaching and persuading the presumed 'culturally inactive' population of Sidi Bel Abbes and the whole region. The city, being the cradle of the avant-garde, is known for its tradition of foreign communism during the French occupation. After the French left, people such as labourers and peasants developed a thirst for ideological training. The public in that region was perhaps new to the theatre but was attracted to the person of Kateb Yacine, who conveyed ideal messages to the Algerian people. The dramatist and his actors communicated with the general public, telling them of the wrongs of the independent state and the true situation of its people.

One of the important results of sending this as yet amateur *Action Culturelle des Travailleurs* (ACT) to this desert region was not foreseen by the central Authorities. This was their entertainment of the troops at military bases:

> As Sidi Bel Abbes is in a strategic area, there are several forts; so we played to the soldiers. This was good

because it allowed us not only to educate the soldiers in politics, but others as well. That has always worked well.[81]

Indeed, that helped the company to extend its influence over people, and therefore gain a larger popular following than otherwise might have been the case. The overwhelming support of the military officers of that region kept the company very active. Kateb Yacine states that they had 'often performed on a stage with army officers for an audience'.[82] His most senior actor continues emphasising:

We had to extend our tour by three days to play in front of the soldiers of the Second Military Region. We reached an audience of more than 1800 soldiers.[83]

As time went on the troupe's status evolved towards a defined regional establishment. After having made a particular impact, the troupe seemed to replace in the life of the people that 'Legion' which for Kateb Yacine seemed to make the place 'interesting'. Kateb Yacine was in charge of the management and, although he received only a small subsidy, was successful because he was aiming to establish a genuinely popular theatre. He built a theatrical practice that no Algerian theatre had succeeded in establishing before that time.

Kateb Yacine was concerned with experimental theatre. From the early days, his outlook was development and he regarded the theatre as a weapon to bring about social change. He therefore needed to reform the current state of Algerian theatre. It made no sense for Kateb Yacine that the theatre had no contact with the public at large. He wanted a theatre whose first concern was with his people. The innumerable performances that his troupe gave between 1970 and 1980, for instance, is a clear example of its impact all over the country: Other examples show interest not only from the public but also from other institutions and organisations:

We were contacted by organisations such as industrial companies, trades unions, teachers, and other authorities who wanted us to come and perform for them.[84]

Given the parameters of Kateb's theatre, it should not be difficult to see his achievement as a convention of performance which falls between traditional revivals and modern naturalistic theatre. The dramatist presents familiar material to the audience in a naturalistic fashion. The mode of linguistic expression is not esoteric. The mode of performance reproduces real life; the settings, props and costumes are designed to be comprehensible to the audience. Most importantly, however, his performance is designed to give effect to the ideological order for the audience, and to accomplish this by producing a responsive reaction. Those in the audience are placed in the position of being both symbols of the exploited workers and the repressed people unconsciously corrupted by the political system. At the conclusion of the performance, they must end up being renewed through profound sense of awakening and anger, and through their demonstration of loyalty to the ideological order which is represented by the characters in the performance. Thus the performance offers the theatrical opportunity for the audience to renew their commitment to an order of which they are already an integral part. This order does, to some extent, limit itself to political dimensions: the saga of most of the Algerian people, and the saga of independent Algeria as a whole. So the performance invites the audience to share in an act of creation. The public is no longer a mere witness of the repetition of a process. It shares in the adventure of creation and helps the actual process of creation. This is a theatrical innovation of collective action. This theatrical symbolism is closely linked to a greater symbolism: that society is still in the process of creation and it is man's duty to help in this process (and to want to change it).

The ultimate chance was given to the troupe in the mid 1970's to flood public places with people coming to hear, watch and take part in a form of theatre that was to their taste. Among the company's best achievements is the composition of its public. The debates that arise from performances make the actors realise how important is the range of their audience, which gives the actors more satisfaction. A single performance in March 8, 1973 shows how Kateb Yacine's audience varies in its make up: the troupe took part in the celebration of International Women's Day in Sidi Bel Abbes.

> 1200 women were present in our performance. Women came from the countryside for the first time in their lives. They got to know a theatre that was involved, especially with militant issues. A group of women suggested there and then that they should launch theatrical activities in their villages.[85]

These contacts that both actors and public mutually establish are those that Kateb Yacine had incessantly and eagerly looked for since his early literary combat in the novel *Nedjma*. The National Theatre could not gather the Algerian people from different classes or from both sexes, because it had advocated European, particularly French, forms bringing a bureaucratic pattern to theatre - the hallmark of the monopoly of the National Theatre. Also because the TNA's mandate was to represent and convey an official image under the wing of the authorities, Algerians had remained very wary of it as of all kinds of artistic or cultural activity which were at odds with their aspirations. This attitude on the part of the public was inherited from the French colonial administration, which used some parts of the 'Algerian' theatre as an escape from real concerns. The theatre of Bachetarzi, for instance, and his like had taught the public lessons, unwittingly, that made them so aware of cultural dangers that they deserted theatre houses whenever the production did not agree with their political views. This portrays the general situation in Algeria after independence, more particularly during the 'socialist' period. Contradictions in the political system itself allowed the TNA to remain ambiguous in the way the identity of the nation itself had remained ambiguous. In fact pretending that the Algerian people were unified into one nation state after independence is akin to pretending that Algeria was a French Nation before 1962. This amalgam of a Nation and one people has never been a reality because before independence there was no common ground for people to meet and after independence there has been no common political culture.

It was never possible for the French to unify the people, and certainly not by means of the theatre. It has also been a serious matter for successive Algerian governments to establish unity between citizens. Kateb Yacine discusses this in his novel *Nedjma*, where he predicts the destiny of his Nation. He claimed that his country was made up out of tribes and Algeria 'has not yet been born'. His search for the ideal nation in - *Nedjma* - could be achieved and fulfilled only when the people who make up this nation were freed from cultural constraints, when one addressed them in their own language and shared with them a political concern. Kateb Yacine has put his ideals into practice precisely by those means that make his theatre. Through the stage he was constantly in contact with the public in all parts of the country, and so returned to what he had always considered to be Nedjma, the symbol of the Algerian Nation, but not by encouraging tribalism. Through the shared experience of theatre Kateb Yacine intended to voice the birth pangs of his nation, either through the way he modelled his genre or through the messages that his genre conveyed. Some of his plays in fact recall a history which can only be understood by a united people aspiring to a common culture.

This very concern had become the dramatist's Nedjma, to raise political consciousness together with the people through the active use of theatre. This new form of theatre making, imbued with folk techniques, was something Kateb Yacine devotedly undertook since the popularity accorded to his first attempts with the new form in 1970 had proved the worth of this kind of cultural action. His favourite symbol, a dream during the early part of his literary quest, became a reality. Now the dramatist saw and discovered the contradictions in his nation which he perpetually sought to contest. 'Algeria' is a stage for society to act out its problems, and Kateb Yacine's theatre provides the means for people to work out the complexities of social and cultural differences whithin their homeland.

Notes

1   When I met Mustapha Kateb (Manager/Director of the TNA) in June 1989, he did not allow me to take copies of some documents. He assumed these documents were the only existing copies. Administrators responsible for insufficient documentation in the TNA leave the institution without a consistent archive behind them. This 'anarchic' situation is due to the fact that administrators are appointed to the TNA and dismissed arbitrarily. Therefore one can hardly find copies of proposals or projects which are submitted to the head office for instance. Such papers would disappear as soon as they were found to contradict a successor's ideology.

2   Arlette Roth, *Le Théâtre Algerien de Langue dialectale (1926-1954)*, (Paris: Maspero, 1967), p. 37.

3   Ibid.

4   Ibid.

5   Muslim and Arabic elite, known as the 'intelligentsia' which had been working on a reforming programme of Islam with the inclusion of literature and Music of religious praise. Its members gathered around the Cheikh Abdelhamid Ibn Badis. They promoted the *Association des Oulemas Musulmans*, from the 1920's onwards.

6   Arlette Roth, op. cit., p. 37.

7   Roselyne Baffet, *Tradition Théâtrale et Modernité en Algerie*, (Paris: L'Harmattan, 1985), p. 47.

8   Ibid.

9   Mohamed Cherif Sahli, '*Le jeune Musulman*', *Journal Officiel* of the Ulemas in French (January 2, 1953), p. 12.

10 Under Boumediene's regime (1965-1978), Algerian students were sent abroad in large numbers to further their education. Those in arts subjects were sent to socialist countries. Boumediene used to call them '*pseudo-savant*', *Discours du Président Boumediene*, (January 2, 1975 - December 23, 1975), published by the Ministry of Information and Culture, Constantine, 1976), Vol.VI, p. 115.

11 A 'good family' in Algerian society refers to any renowned family having at least one member involved in politics, religious affairs, arts or even having a position in the government so as to publicize the family name. It can also be true of singers, actors or dancers (though it sometimes takes on a pejorative sense). The expression 'good family' can also apply to notorious families which, however, fulfil their obligation to the community.

12 The INADC was closed when I went to visit it (September 1987) and remained so for an indefinite period. For unknown reasons I was told it had ceased to exist. A porter affirmed it was transferred to another place, Tipaza, a few miles away from Algiers. Officials in the Ministry of Culture were at a loss, not knowing the person in charge of the documents that I required. However, a short section of R. Baffet's *Tradition Théâtrale...*, provides some information on the INADC and its constraints, pp. 76-77.

13 The dilemma faced by Algerian youngsters who left school is due mainly to bureaucracy which made access to some careers almost impossible. Thus they either remain unemployed for many years then turn to delinquency, or find salvation in arts. However, to obtain a well paid job in arts, the administration requires specific qualifications or long experience.

14 Annual report of the Algerian National Union of Youth. 'Collection of documents concerning the Cultural Department from May 30, 1982 to December 31, 1982' (Algiers: January 1983) [mimeographed]. It includes twelve reports, a yearly synthesis and a list of active troupes which took part in the 18th National Festival of Mostaganem (July 17-26, 1984). The report of 43 pages, in Arabic, was handed to me by the Executive Secretary of the UNJA.

15 *Discours du President Boumediene* (Constantine: Ministère de l'Information et de la culture, 1975), Vol. VI, p. 115.

16 Ibid., p. 116.

17 Ali Merah, 'Experience de création collective dans le théâtre Algerien', Europe (July-August 1976), p. 176. The article suggests up until 1976, some 50 amateur troupes had experienced collective creations. These troupes, it says, were created in youth circles, universities and factories.

18 Ali Zamoum, 'Interview with the Troupe', (Tizi Ouzou; Maison de la Culture. January 18, 1990).

19 Nadia Tazi, 'Kateb Yacine', L'autre Journal (July-August 1985), p. 17.

20 Ibid.

21 Ibid.

22 J. Duflot, 'Kateb Yacine, les intellectuels, la révolution et le pouvoir', op.cit., p. 29.

23 Jacques Alessandra, 'Le théâtre révolutionnaire algerien', Travail Théâtral (December 1979), p. 100.

24 Handout of the group Théâtre de la mer handed over during the first tour of the play Mohamed Prends ta Valise. A document of 6 pages titled 'Mohamed prends ta valise' and signed, 'Avec le salut des travailleurs de l'unité d'animation culturelle' (Théâtre de la mer).

25 Jean-Marie Boeglin, 'Théâtre et politique', Partisans (February/March, 1967), p. 29.

26 Ibid., p. 97.

27 A. Merrah, 'Experience de creation collective...', op.cit., p. 176.

28 Ibid., p. 177.

29 I took part in this Festival with a local troupe of which I was in charge. Some commentaries on this festival are given in the UNJA's anual report cited above.

30 The spelling varies. Goha, Joha, Djoh'a. Djeha is a popular cunning character, known in North African legend and culture. He even expands to some Arab countries such as Egypt, Irak, Syria and others such as Turkey. Djeha is also the title of a famous play which had given a start to the Algerian popular theatre. Djeha is a humorous character, wily in the Arab-Berber manner. An Algerian audience shares with this naive and cunning buffon many popular anecdotes and exploits. In the history of many peoples we see that there are characters who are wily and cunning, who play tricks on others, laugh at their expenses, and usually come out on top. They play the fool, or naive, but know how to make use of ridiculous situation, or to make people who are high up in society, because of their jobs or apparent dignity, look ridiculous. These characters have been invented, with different features in different countries, by writers and popular oral tradition. Some have been glorified and made legendary on an historical basis. Everyone knows of Arlechino, Garagoz, Punch, and Till Eulenspiegel. Djeha represents these characters in North Africa.

31 Allalou, L'aurore du Théâtre Algerien (1926-1932), (Oran; C.D.S.H, 1982), p. III.

32 £1 is approximately 10 Algerian DA.

33 Already cited

34 Handout, Le Théâtre de la mer.

35 G. Elhadi, ` Kateb Yacine `, Interview, El Moudjahid culturel (April 4, 1975), p. 5.

36 Ibid.

37 N. Muchnik, 'Yacine et les siens', interview, Nouvel Observateur (April 10, 1972), p. 23.

38 Y. Ait Mouloud [Mouloud] said to me that in some performances the public gave any sort of food before entering. Interview with the troupe (Tizi Ouzou, August 27, 1987).

39 A.P.S., Interview with Kateb Yacine, 'De la litterature au théâtre', El Moudjahid (April 24, 1978), p. 5.

40 Ibid.

41 Slimane Benaissa considers the notions of amateur and professional, 'completely false, because there are amateurs who are profoundly creators and professionals who are only ordinary amateurs'. 'Citations. Extraits de la déclaration de Benaïssa à la presse', Algérie Actualité (June 13-19, 1985), p. 39.

42 A.P.S., Interview with Kateb Yacine, 'De la littérature au théâtre', El Moudjahid (April 14, 1978), p. 5.

43 Abdelkrim Djaâd, 'Renforcer les rangs c'est bon, structurer c'est mieux', Algerie-Actualité (August 2-9, 1978), p. 11.

44 I attended the performance of this play in Algiers in 1976 and again in the National Festival of Mostaganem in 1978. I also chaired a discussion on the play.

45 Abdelkader Djeghloul, Long interview with Kateb Yacine, 'Le livre a paraitre' Actualité de l'Emigration (January 14, 1987), p. 18.

46 Debza sings in Berber and Algerian spoken Arabic. They use very genuine rhythms. The most remarkable and popular songs are those composed for the stage.

47 Nacer Izza, 'Chanson et théâtre', Revolution Africaine (April 7, 1989), p. 49.

48 To my knowledge, the text, until 1989 had not been published. A copy was given to me by the troupe *Debza*.

49 Moussa Youcef Selmane, 'Modern Algerian theatre...', (Phd dissertation, University of Leeds, 1989), p. 31.

50 A. Djaad seems to take a paternalistic view in his argument. He says; 'One can profit from such influence only if one has adequate intellectual potentials and appropriate political training', which I believe is not true. One does not need to have that potential to appreciate works of amateurs precisely because they address the masses in their real potential of understanding. If we believed A. Djaad, then our whole argument that amateur theatre is accessible to all should be questioned from its outset. Therefore, if we consider the critic's view, we would have to deal with an 'elitist' theatre which has been the counter argument in this study. For A. Djaad's whole argument, see his article, '*Renforcer les rangs c'est bon, structurer c'est mieux*', *Algerie Actualité* (August 2-9, 1978, p. 11.

51 "*Citations. Extraits de la déclaration de Ben Aïssa à la presse*', *Algérie Actualité* (June 13-14, 1985), p. 39.

52 M.Y. Selmane, op.cit., p. 30.

53 Ibid.

54 I was in charge of a Festival of amateur theatre (1985). The event took place in the *Maison de la Culture de Tizi Ouzou*, May 5-15, 1985. I expected a limited number of troupes to participate, but in the end , we could hardly find a way to limit the number of troupes. To see such interest accorded to a local Festival is significant for the amateur theatre movement and its popularity. Nadjib Stambouli wrote an account on this event which he preferred to call '*programme théâtral*'. In his comments the journalist does not hesitate to criticise the local Theatre which normally has in its primary tasks the organisation of such events. He puts it: ' When we talk about theatre in this city, we naturally think of the *Théâtre Communal*, beautiful building at the entrance of the town, where, films are shown in one side of the building, the other side being occupied by the football league. Perhaps awaiting the fortunate day when theatre will invade stadiums...' However this situation did not prevent the public from appreciating and enjoying those 'theatrical' days which were 'expected and applauded by a public of a rare conduct '. '*Journées théâtrales de Tizi Ouzou, Les planches aux illusions*', *Algerie-Actualité* (May 16-22, 1985), p. 37.

55 An important document '*Bilan Critique*' from the *Secretariat d'Etat à la Culture et aux Arts*, gives important statistics and analysis of the different sectors of Arts in Algeria between 1965 and 1979 (Boumediene's period in office). The *Bilan* does not specify the date in which it was made, but from the various dates given in the figures, one can assume it was published one year after former President Chadli came into office (1979/1980?). The figures on theatre are provided in terms of gross subsidies, box offices and attendance. The report mentions the importance of the young theatre without listing the number of troupes. The inferences that one might draw from the figures and the overall attendance might not be very accurate. A dozen of tables are given in this Ministerial report of 74 pages (in french), pp. 23-25, 33-40.

56 An Arabic text '*Culture through the fundamantal texts of the FLN*', (January 1981), 46 pages. In one of its major articles 'Amateur theatre', Section 1 lists the objectives and importance of the role that amateur theatre should play, p. 39-40. The importance of this theatre is also stressed in the *Bulletin du colloque culturel national du 31 Mai au 5 Juin 1968*; Already mentioned. Another paper does also put stress on amateur theatre. This is a lecture (whose author is not mentioned) published by the Ministry of culture.

57 Slimane Benaissa is another dramatist to have also brought this ideal into practice. With his troupe (composed of himself, Sid Ahmed Agoumi and Omar Guendouz), they have performed everywhere where it is possible for a theatre group to gather more than a dozen people. His play *Bualem Zid el Guddam* was even performed on the sand in the Algerian desert and shown on the television after some harassments with the administration were overcome. Slimane Benaissa is one who had a long experience with amateur theatre, shared several projects with Kateb Yacine and had offered his 'master-pieces' to a large public especially in factories and remote places. The only problem with his theatre, which represents the major difference from that of Kateb Yacine, is that he performs a more dramatically consistent text than that of his colleague. There is, in his plays, too much importance given to the dynamics of dialogue, its dimension and its reception by the audience. The text is stable and the action is static. Because the audience changes, Benaissa's plays receive different responses. This divergence of interpretations causes a loss in the credibility of the message of the play and represents the author's imposition of opinion. The dramatist's communication with the public is unilateral. One spectator remarked on this during a discussion after the performance of *Babur Gh'rak* before an audience of students in 1982 (Tizi Ouzou). In fact his plays appeal to a public already aware of the traps of politics, and his forceful dramaturgy impresses the spectator in his seat, but does not raise up his participation like any of Kateb Yacine's performance would do. This is one paradox in his popular theatre, another lies in the fact that his plays are performed before audiences who have to pay for their seats some 3 or 4 times the price of those of Kateb Yacine.

58 Slimane Benaïssa, '*Citations...*', *Algérie Actualité* (June 13-19, 1985), op.cit., p. 39.

59 APS, '*Le TNA à l'heure de la jeunesse*', *El Moudjahid* (July 26-27, 1985), p.14.

60 List of plays produced by the National Theatre between 1963 and 1985, already mentioned above.

61 *Bilan critique*, document of the *Secretariat d'Etat à la Culture*, op.cit., p. 12.

62 Amar Benkima's article *'Opinions sur les opinions de Kateb Yacine'* not only finds this issue distasteful but also attempts to discredit Kateb Yacine's initiatives. *Allouan*, No. 25, 1976.

63 There is a set of songs which all Kateb Yacine's performances include in the beginning and at the end.

64 Mimeographed document of 26 pages, *'Contribution à la reflexion sur le théâtre amateur en Algérie'*, op.cit., p. 16.

65 I was given a copy of the 'Minute' that the Party commission wrote in the form of a tract.

66 Ibid.

67 Unlike some party members in the Ministry of Labour such as Ali Zamoum, who continued to support the company.

68 Abou Amine, *'Kateb Yacine'*, *El Chaab* (January 17, 1976).

69 Ibid.

70 Amar Benkima, *Alouan* (No: 25, 1976), op.cit.

71 A text written by Ait Mouloud Youcef [Mouloud], *'Reflection d'un comedien'*. Mouloud told me that this text was initially drafted to record his 'Experiences' as an actor. Mouloud is the most senior member of the company of Sidi Bel Abbes. Before that he was founding member of *Le Théâtre de la mer*. He was very close to Kateb Yacine and shared the same concerns. In fact they were such good friends that Mouloud could hardly hide his emotions when he talked about his *'Companion'*. This was evident in the emotional tone with which he read, in the conference of Tizi Ouzou January 1990, one of the poems he wrote in memory of Kateb Yacine.

72 Ibid.

73 Ibid.

74 It can also mean 'episode'.

75 Mohamed Berrad, *'Le théâtre de langue arabe et les programmes de la T.V.*, in *Le Théâtre Arabe*, (Paris: UNESCO, 1975), p. 177.

76 Algerians know the storyteller as the *Guwal* or the *Meddah*. They have basically the same functions in life. However, each one of them appear to have specific task according to the regions where they live. Under French colonialism they were confused, for they had to play a major role in the media used in rural parts of the country. The two have then formed the *Berrah* or [V]errah for the Berber. This is similar, in function, to the town-caller.

77 Sidi Lakhdar Barka, *'La chanson de geste sur la scène ou experience de Ould Abderahmane Kaki'*, in, *Etudes et Recherches sur la Littérature Maghrébine*, (Oran; University of Oran, 1981), p. 12.

78 Interview, *'13 Questions à Mustapha Kateb'*, *La Republique* (October 29, 1971), p. 16.

79 Hichem Ben Yaïche, Interview, *'Kateb Yacine: 'Notre théâtre met le doigt sur les plaies''*, *Le Matin du Sahara et du Maghreb* (December 31, 1989 - January 7, 1990). This article is among hundreds of others collected and bound by the library of the *Centre Culturel Algerien de Paris*. Exceptionally, I was given a copy of the whole file of Articles published before and after Kateb Yacine's death. This important collection of articles is filed in the CCA's library under the title, *'dossier de press: Kateb Yacine'*.

80 Ibid.

81 Ibid.

82 Hamid Barrada, Interview, *'Kateb Yacine dit tout sur son théâtre le Berbère l'Arabisation l'Islam l'Integrisme la Révolution Iranienne'*, *Jeune Afrique Magazine* (June, 1988), p. 75.

83 Y. Ait Mouloud, *'Reflection d'un comedien'*, op.cit

84 Ibid.

85 Ibid.

Uses and Abuses of Theatre for Development: political struggle and development theatre in the Ethiopia – Eritrea war

Jane Plastow

Those of us involved in Theatre for Development projects are well aware that the form has been used for many purposes. We may wish to utilise theatre as a tool of empowerment, but all too often funding and organisation of projects has been in the hands of governments or development agencies whose agendas may be overtly oppressive or at least coercive and/or propaganda oriented. TFD projects which truly achieve many practitioners' avowed aim of giving a voice to the people are probably a minority of those undertaken. In this study I shall look at experiences of people's theatre on both sides of the Ethiopia-Eritrea war of 1961-'91 in order to investigate how theatre was used as either coercive or empowering, and to analyse relationships between propaganda imperatives and popular theatre initiatives.[1]

May Day Parade – Addis Abbaba, 1986. Huge amounts of money were spent on parades involving thousands of people and massive floats

I also wish to look at some of the roots of Theatre for Development. Such a form cannot emerge spontaneously. I will be looking not only at colonial and post-colonial African cultural history in general, but also at specific examples of developments in what might be called proto-TFD (agit-prop and some political theatre), which have arisen out of situations of political reformist and liberation struggles. The work will examine what conditions provoked an interest in developing these proto-TFD forms; how successful they were in their avowed aims of mobilising people for change, and how they may have functioned in terms of providing fertile ground for later - often post-revolutionary - truly developmental theatre.

Finally, this study will seek to investigate, with primary reference to the Ethiopia-Eritrea case study, the relationship between political freedoms and the development of theatres of empowerment. This seems necessary particularly because it is a question which has been elided by many such as Penina Muhando (Tanzania), Zakes Mda (Lesotho) and Christopher Kamlongera (Malawi)[2] who have written extensively about their work with TFD-related projects. The elision is understandable given that these people wish to continue working in the countries concerned and may be fearful of reprisals if they are openly critical of political establishments. However, this only makes it the more imperative for those of us operating under fewer political constraints to take on board what seem to me fundamental questions. How useful, empowering or valid can TFD be if it is constantly fearful of engaging with some, at least, areas of debate, in case this will be seen to be meddling in politics? Is it possible, as governments such as that in Zimbabwe have required, for TFD to engage only with local community problems and to divorce these from the wider political environment? And finally, if we accept, as we must, that many African governments are repressive of attempts from the populace to engage in any form of open political debate, at what point does such repression effectively castrate TFD and make it either effectively useless, or worse, simply another vehicle for government propaganda?

Now that various forms of Theatre for Development are operating in so many countries, it seems to me that those of us working in this area must start to look beyond our own projects to investigate what pre-conditions might be necessary for the form to have a chance of being truly useful in the longer term. If TFD has often had its roots in revolutionary struggle, it is surely unacceptable to allow politicians to say such theatre must only be used for the discussion of unchallenging local issues. Likewise TFD must not become simply a means for aid and government agencies to propagate their philosophies. Theatre for Development, it seems to me, can only be empowering if it operates freely to promote debate about every aspect of peoples' lives. As soon as specific areas are declared taboo this effectively disempowers the people, and I would argue that any theatre project is then in danger of being repressive, not liberating, because people are constantly being told that in actual fact their voices, their opinions are not allowed. The roots of social and local problems so often lie in political policies that if we accept gagging in one area of debate we are surely in danger of being crippled in all others.

The joy of working in theatre in Africa is that it is important. In countries with strong oral traditions, where access to mass media is often limited and where many are illiterate, theatre has a potential power which we can only long for in the West. The flip side to this coin is that because governments recognise this power, involvement in theatre can be very dangerous when we are dealing with repressive regimes. My own interest in this study arises from having worked in both Ethiopia and Eritrea. In Ethiopia I was unable to renew my original contract at the Theatre Studies Department of Addis Ababa University in the 1980s because my attempts to produce questioning theatre were seen as too critical by the totalitarian state. When I went to work for the liberation government in Eritrea the crucial pre-condition was that the theatre produced must be free to say whatever it felt was necessary. In both countries there is now a struggle to instil democracy in the workings of the state. I think that TFD can play a major role in this endeavour, which is after all a revolutionary struggle far more significant than military victory. But, that potential can only be realised if TFD becomes part of national cultural strategy. Isolated experiments, we know, from many examples, are of only very limited use. Ethiopia and Eritrea are fortunate in that, as newly constituted nations, politically and territorially, there is a chance that they might take on such empowering initiatives. This already seems unlikely in more troubled Ethiopia, but Eritrea, which is only just forming a multi-party constitution and which is building on its tradition of theatre as a tool of liberation, is a wonderfully dynamic place in which to work. The challenge is whether, if TFD starts to raise questions perceived to be politically controversial, that theatre will be welcomed or suppressed.

Finally, this study in no way aims to trivialise the efforts made by those working in repressive regimes to utilise TFD for the benefit of the people. It simply seeks to raise unsentimental questions about how political repression works in relation to performance cultures, and whether we either can or should in various circumstances allow the two agendas to be considered separately.

The Cultural Background

It is important to state at the outset that throughout the period of Eritrea's liberation struggle, both nations involved were in many important respects isolated from significant cultural contacts with the outside world. The ruling elites of both areas have been historically Orthodox Christians surrounded by Muslim nations, and they have traditionally inhabited a region of mountain plateaux. As Semitic-Hamitic peoples they also have languages, scripts and cultures which are profoundly different from those of the Arab, Bantu or Nilotic peoples who surround them, some of whom were until very recently in a relationship of vassalage to the Amhara leadership of the Ethiopian empire. This isolation and consequent xenophobia has been a determining factor of the region's civilisation for at least thirteen hundred years.

More recently, Ethiopia's last Emperor, Haile Selassie (ruled 1930-74), took considerable pains to restrict his people's access to outside cultures for fear of political insurgency. The military government which seized power in 1974 did allow some cultural and theatrical influence from outside the country; most importantly through the employment of a number of foreigners in the Theatre Studies Department of the University of Addis Ababa. Ideas about popular theatre disseminated by staff at the University undoubtedly had an impact on subsequent arts initiatives, but projects were at all times strictly monitored and subject to political control.

Eritrea's position was rather different. The country became an Italian colony in 1890 with an apartheid style regime which precluded Eritreans from access to most educational opportunities, let alone to cultural ideologies. In 1941 the British drove out the Italians and established a care-taker regime under a U.N. mandate. The British undertook limited theatrical work with Eritreans; introducing Shakespeare and the naturalistic theatre form to schools, as in most British colonies, with the aim of inculcating British culture and promoting the English language in a small educated elite. In 1952, for political reasons, the U.N voted to federate Eritrea with Ethiopia. Within a very short space of time Haile Selassie started to undermine this federated status and in 1962 Eritrea was declared simply an Ethiopian province.

Armed struggle for liberation began in 1961 and escalated rapidly. However, whilst Ethiopia put into the field a 300,000 strong army, heavily backed throughout the late 1970s and 1980s by the USSR (and when they withdrew in 1989 following the collapse of the Eastern bloc, by Israel); the Eritreans conducted a guerilla struggle almost entirely unsupported by an outside world, whose interest in, and knowledge of, the war was minimal. Eritrean developments in theatre were therefore almost entirely devised through a process of trial-and-error, with absolutely no trained personnel or access to contemporary theatre texts or theories.

It is also necessary to understand that drama in both Ethiopia and Eritrea has until the 1990s been seen as entirely separate from traditional performance forms, which, as in all Africa, are music and dance based. Dialogue-based drama was introduced to Ethiopia in 1916 by an Ethiopian aristocrat, Tekle Hawariat, who had travelled abroad, and the form was later nurtured in high schools run by the English and French.[3] In Eritrea ideas of what constituted drama were also taken from Europe via the colonial masters. Throughout Africa, during the period of colonialism, Europeans failed to recognise African performance forms as theatre and sought to impose their drama, claiming it to be culturally superior and using the arts as one of many means of dividing the educated elite from the mass of the people who continued to practise traditional cultural forms. This drama was almost always the naturalistic form dominant in Europe in the hey-day of colonialism in Africa. It was entirely alien to most African people.

However, as Africa began to be decolonised in the 1960s, many playwrights and theatrical impresarios started to develop syncretic theatre forms which to varying degrees incorporated African theatre traditions of music, dance and story-telling with imported Western ideas of drama. For the first time this meant playwrights and theatre groups could make plays which might be accessible to the mass of their people, and which would lay the groundwork for the later evolution of the philosophies of Theatre for Development.

In Eritrea and Ethiopia this process of integration never happened. Instead theatre remained for the most part an elitist, urban form. In Ethiopia all drama was written and performed in Amharic, the language of the ruling ethnic group which constituted only 20-25% of the population. In Eritrea drama was performed predominantly in the language of the dominant Christian group which lived in the area around the capital of Asmara; Tigrinya, with occasional performances in Amharic or English. These are only a tiny minority of some seventy languages spoken in the region, and the plays performed dealt with issues generally relevant only to the urban educated classes. This is not to say that traditional performance arts were not also popular in urban areas. In both Ethiopia and Eritrea there have been strong traditions since the 1940s of various forms of variety performances which have included songs and dances from many indigenous ethnic groups, short dramatic skits and Westernised or, in the Eritrean case, often Arabised, adaptations of indigenous music using modern instruments. These were performed in the same theatres as drama and in both places had a much wider following than did the elite art form. Moreover the mass of rural peoples continued to perform their traditional arts, and imported drama forms, until the 1980s, barely penetrated outside the few major towns.

The Beginnings of Popular Theatre

I would suggest that the roots of popular theatre in Ethiopia go back to 1974 when Haile Selassie was overthrown by an army coup and Addis Ababa was in turmoil as various radical groups jockeyed, and later fought, for control over the Ethiopian Empire. One of the most important political parties was the Ethiopian People's Revolutionary Party (EPRP) which was led by intellectuals who had links with, and were influenced by, Marxist thinking from Europe. I have been unable to identify where the idea came from, but in 1974 and '75 the EPRP mounted a series of agit-prop style performances in various halls around Addis Ababa to encourage unionisation of the workers as a first step towards the political empowerment of ordinary people.

The relationship between agit-prop and popular theatre is difficult to define. Certainly this was not theatre made by communities simply in order to articulate community problems. Nor was it dispassionate and even-handed in its discussion of various issues. But, this was theatre made outside the structures of dominant power in order to participate in a national debate about how the country should develop, using 'poor theatre' techniques to try to involve the people in making choices about their future lives. Several of the most influential people behind the EPRP had spent time with European socialists in various Western nations and I have wondered whether they garnered the idea for their theatre from workers' theatre movements which might be argued to be a kind of Western Theatre for Development.

It is impossible to create a neat dividing line between Theatre for Development and agit-prop or political theatre, much though various governments may wish such a line to be drawn. If politics cannot be discussed in TFD then surely that theatre is effectively emasculated, because time after time we see that social issues have political roots. Famously Ngugi wa Thiong'o's work at Kamiriithu was suppressed because of its implied political criticisms of the Kenyan state, but *Ngaahika Ndeenda* and *Mother, Sing for Me* were empowering plays made by the people, using their languages and cultural forms. The theatre at Kamiriithu was a superb example of the best of Theatre for Development.[4] If it was also revolutionary political theatre this simply demonstrates, to me at least, that personal and community development cannot be separated from political development. Kenyan government policies of encouraging economic and social policies which impoverish the mass of the people whilst terrorising political opponents into submission clearly demonstrate this linkage.

The development of people's theatre in Zimbabwe is another example which is particularly relevant to my discussion here for two reasons.[5] Firstly during Zimbabwe's liberation struggle in the 1970s, the guerilla forces called heavily on theatre as a tool for politicisation. In order to counteract government propaganda the guerillas held *pungwes* - all night compulsory gatherings in villages - where, rather than rely on speeches and literature, fighters performed songs and plays educating people about the nature of the struggle and the evils of colonialism. Many writers on the Zimbabwean liberation struggle have commented on how powerful were these *pungwes* in mobilising people in support of the liberation struggle.[6] Within guerilla camps in Mozambique we also know that theatre was used extensively in order to debate what kind of future Zimbabwe the fighters wished to build. This was propaganda theatre, like that of the EPRP, and as we shall see later, like that of the Eritrean liberation forces, but I would like to argue that it was also a linked precursor; a kind of proto-Theatre for Development, to the vibrant community theatre movement which has blossomed throughout Zimbabwe in the post-liberation period. This propaganda/protest/discussion theatre was devised and performed by guerillas themselves using minimal amounts of the alienating paraphernalia of conventional drama. Moreover the fighters were clearly of the people, not distanced from them as had been actors on the urban proscenium stages. Most of all this theatre was talking about the people's lives in a language and form that they could understand, with the aim of assisting in freeing them from oppression. Many of the features of TFD were already present.

The second element of Zimbabwe's popular theatre development which is significant in this discussion is the element of post-colonial government distrust which has surfaced in recent years. Guerillas and children of guerillas who had become used to using theatre as a vehicle for discussing issues in their camps saw no reason to stop engaging in open discussion of contemporary issues when the war had finished. With the assistance of some experienced and very politicised TFD and protest theatre practitioners from countries such as Kenya, (Ngugi wa Mirii and Kimani Gecau) and South Africa (Robert McLaren - aka Kavanagh), Zimbabwe, in the years after liberation, drew on the performance forms developed in the war years to produce a strong community theatre movement. However, as early as 1983, the government were already wary of this new theatre. In 1983 a major theatre workshop involving numerous foreign practitioners was held at Murehwa with government support. However, when he saw the level of political criticism emerging in some of the performances generated by the people participating in that workshop, the under-secretary to the Division of Culture who came to see the work described theatre as 'a double-edged sword'.[7] Subsequently the state has tried to insist that TFD should have nothing to do with politics but should stick to 'community issues'. Another example from the many I could have described concerns Robert McLaren, who in the late 1980s made a joint production between university students and hostel dwellers in what had been a township area, Mbare, protesting about appalling living conditions in the hostels. Again government officials came to the play and offered some support, but McLaren says that:

> Strong warnings were issued by the M.P. and the City Councillor...that students should not incite the people against the government. Thus they expressed their appreciation that the students were concerning themselves with the problems of the people and participating in their development, but a fear that they might try to do this out of the context of party and government programmes and policies.'[8]

The problem lies when states try to impose boundaries between politics, society and culture. For good reasons many who have wanted to continue working have been reluctant to challenge this arbitrary boundary, for the fate of such as Ngugi is a powerful deterrent to all-out confrontation. But here the question of degree surfaces. McLaren may be able to do valuable empowering work whilst staying within government guidelines. But what happens when the government is one such as Hastings Banda's autocracy in Malawi? During Banda's regime TFD practitioners such as Chris Kamlongera were working in Malawi, but in such a totalitarian state one has to question whether any theatre work could be truly empowering or give the people any kind of meaningful voice, or whether TFD was not in fact so bland as to become in reality another means of brain-washing and oppression. The nub of the problem is that most post-colonial states in Africa have been as reluctant to engage in dialogue with the people as any colonial regime, and have tended to see criticism as attack. Yet without freedom to discuss any issue fully how can we talk about giving a voice to the people or promoting democracy and empowerment?

To return then to Ethiopia and Eritrea. The theatrical experiments of the EPRP were only short lived. In 1977-'78 the military government of the Dergue encouraged opposing groups to battle out their differences on the streets and then stepped in to mop up the EPRP as part of the campaign which was proclaimed as The Red Terror. Someone in the Dergue had, however, obviously noted the theatrical activities of the EPRP, and the propaganda tool was turned on its inventors. Suspected EPRP members who survived The Red Terror were often sent for political re-education, and one of the proofs of their satisfactory conversion was that they then made pro-government pieces of drama. This use of a similar form by oppressors and oppressed raises an important point, in that I think it is necessary to differentiate between propaganda theatre by oppressed groups which may contain many elements of, and be a precursor to, true Theatre for Development, and state sponsored propaganda theatre which is necessarily interested in the maintenance of power and the preservation of the political *status quo*.

The agit-prop tool was subsequently much more widely utilised by the Ethiopian government. Professional agit-prop productions were encouraged on the state-funded stages of Addis Ababa. Initially it appears this theatre was widely popular, for many welcomed the overthrow of the Emperor and early moves towards land and property reform. In a people crying out for information, simple agitational drama was a popular means of spreading news and new ideologies. Quickly the state encouraged the form to spread. Youth, peasants, women and workers were all compulsorily enrolled in separate mass organisations, and these organisations often had a *kinet* group which performed traditional, and later modern, dance and music. These *kinet* groups, especially the most dynamic youth groups, were encouraged to perform crude dramas in support of the state's agenda. Most importantly, in the 1970s agit-prop drama was utilised to drum up support for wars which were being fought not only against the Eritreans but also in the southern Ogaden desert against an irridentist Somalian movement.

When I first went to Ethiopia in 1984 agit-prop theatre had all but been abandoned in the capital where people were disillusioned with both the form and the government. But in the rural areas it was still spreading outwards, and many youth enjoyed for the first time being involved in making drama without apparently worrying too much about its content.

Here we see an overtly propagandist, state-supported theatre movement. But one which moved from being at least partly empowering in the mid-1970s, when it provided information in a situation which was still politically in some degree of flux, towards becoming overtly coercive, dogmatic and doctrinaire as Dergue control became increasingly absolute and social reform programmes gave way to imperialist ambition and a desire by the state to absolutely control the people.

Eritrean alternatives

The Eritrean struggle in the 1960s had been a fairly *ad hoc* affair with small groups of insurgents living in remote areas and carrying out hit-and-run attacks. By the mid 1970s the war was escalating, with two liberation fronts in the field. The first Front had been the Eritrean Liberation Front (ELF), a Muslim dominated and generally undemocratic, authoritarian movement. Disenchantment with the ELF led to the creation in 1970 of the Eritrean People's Liberation Front (EPLF). This was a much more socially far-sighted movement which combined military struggle with a plan for social revolution including prioritising education for all, women's rights and self-sufficiency. In 1980-'81 the two Fronts fought a bitter civil war which concluded with victory for the EPLF who would become the final liberators of Eritrea in 1991.

The ELF had first seen the value of the cultural tool to the struggle in the early 1970s. Several eminent local musicians and singers joined the ELF and were used as for propaganda purposes. They held concert tours for the fighters in liberated areas and in The Sudan where an increasingly huge diaspora fled from the napalm and brutalities of the Ethiopian armed forces. These early concerts were simply a matter of promoting the struggle through patriotic music and dance, and drama made scarcely any impact.

However, by 1975 the EPLF had set up a cultural department to develop the performance arts as a tool of liberation. Theatre and literary work was particularly developed by Alemseged Tesfai who was seconded to cultural work in 1981. Alemseged, once a lawyer who had trained in America, had no performance background, but he was ordered to develop the arts in the field. He read the few available texts relating to theatre, mostly naturalistic plays by such as Chekhov and Ibsen and a few general books about theatre, and tried to find ways of developing a relevant culture for the struggle.

Through the 1980s the EPLF developed a general model for its productions to both fighters and peasants in liberated areas. Shows followed the variety format I have discussed above, but with some significant modifications. An EPLF Cultural Troupe was composed of some 20-30 performers who were often multi-talented as musicians, dancers, singers, actors and writers. They were also drawn from a variety of peoples. Eritrea has nine ethnic groups within her borders, split between Muslims and Christians, highland and desert dwellers and with radically different cultural traditions. A major priority for the EPLF was to challenge divide-and-rule policies promoted under colonialism in order to weld these diverse peoples together as a nation. Each show therefore made a point of featuring song and dance from all nine nationalities with lead performers from the groups in question wherever possible, who would then teach others how to perform each traditional cultural form. As far as possible the EPLF tried to promote indigenous performance forms in order to promote pride in national culture, although Western instruments were also utilised by some musicians. This music and dance with patriotic songs written for the struggle was immensely popular with audiences watching on open hillsides, often at night and by firelight, as Cultural Troupes could frequently not appear in the daytime for fear of Ethiopian MiG aeroplane attack. Separate from the traditional forms, but in the same programme (which often lasted over four hours) would be a piece of propaganda theatre, running for anything from twenty minutes to an hour and a half.

In keeping with the joint military and social aims of the EPLF struggle, theatre dealt with two main areas of concern. On the one hand many pieces spoke directly of the military struggle; emphasising the sacrifice of fighters, the atrocities of the Ethiopian forces and the need for all to work together for eventual victory. This was straight-forward theatre of nationalist propaganda. But, on the other hand, the EPLF was committed to social revolution and a raft of plays were produced which dealt with issues such as the need for literacy, health education and the rights of women. These plays were undoubtedly a form of simple, rather didactic Theatre for Development, performed to fighters and to people in the liberated areas in order to recruit them to an appreciation of the wider, long-term aims of the EPLF.

This theatre maintained a loosely narrative, naturalistic form, and was commonly performed by fighters to the people rather than being made with them. However, within the Cultural Troupes there was considerable democracy in the process of play-making. In the early days plays were often devised around topics decided by the members of the troupe. Although more educated members might script certain parts of a play the process of working was to be open to group discussion, and each actor had considerable freedom in developing their part. This was largely because of the acute shortage of performers with any previous drama experience. Performers with Cultural Troupes have spoken repeatedly of working through a process of 'trial-and-error'.[9] However, the aspiration was always towards more polished naturalistic drama, which was seen as 'proper' theatre. In the later years of the struggle cadres such as Alemseged Tesfai and Solomon Tsehaye, who worked for the Cultural Department, increasingly wrote scripted dramas for performance by Cultural Troupes. Because their only experience was with the naturalistic form this was the style of performance they promoted, although scripts did become increasingly subtle, and Alemseged in particular has said that he was not entirely happy with the naturalism; he simply did not know how to go about producing theatre which was more closely related to the culture of the people.

The final area of interest in discussing the theatre of the EPLF is the make-up of the Cultural Troupes. Within the EPLF everyone who took to the field was described as a fighter. Everyone participated in basic military training, and all could be called upon to fight whenever necessary, but fighting was more broadly defined than engagement in the military struggle. The EPLF was fighting not only for freedom but also for a new, post-feudal Eritrea. The core of the theatre movement was the Central Cultural Troupe. This was a permanent group with members drawn from fighters observed to have particular talent. The group toured the front lines, liberated areas, and also went abroad to the diaspora in The Sudan, Europe and the U.S.A. Beyond this each brigade had a cultural troupe which operated during rest periods when troops were out of the front-line as a tool for entertaining, educating and inspiring the fighters. So far this pattern does not seem particularly far-sighted or extraordinary, but the EPLF created other groups. Orphans and children of fighters attended EPLF schools in safe areas and these schools had children's Cultural Troupes which toured in vacation periods. Many internal refugees were women, and so a women-only Cultural Troupe was formed to express women's difficulties and aspirations. In liberated areas and amongst the Eritrean diaspora in The Sudan - with whom the EPLF maintained string links - as part of an educational process encouraging social reform and national unity, the development of cultural groups amongst civilians was encouraged. Finally, the struggle resulted not only in 65,000 Eritrean dead, but also in many disabled fighters. Those who were wounded were re-deployed to jobs behind the front-line, and a group of them formed a disabled fighters Cultural Troupe. This concern to allow all groups to express themselves and the belief that everyone was of use to the struggle and had a voice worth hearing within it, seems to me a true root of TFD and a valuable springboard for post-independence development along the lines of a culture of empowerment.

Community Arts in Ethiopia

By the mid-1980s the agit-prop movement was running out of steam in Ethiopia. The country was also acquiring a growing number of trained arts personnel, who as graduates were traditionally guaranteed government employment, but who were surplus to requirement in Addis Ababa. It is unclear exactly why the Rural Arts Programme was established in 1984, but both the above factors probably had something to do with it. The Programme aimed to send trained personnel in the fine arts, literature, music and drama to each of Ethiopia's then fourteen regions, with the avowed aim of encouraging the formation of amateur arts groups and giving training in the arts in question.

In the area of theatre some work had been done to pave the way for this initiative by foreign teachers at the Theatre Arts Department of Addis Ababa University. The Department had been established in 1978, but as there was an acute shortage of suitably trained Ethiopians teachers were recruited from the West. Undoubtedly the most dynamic and influential of these was Robert McLaren, a white South African communist who had been involved in protest theatre in that country before taking his PhD in the U.K. at Leeds University, and after four years in Ethiopia moving on to Zimbabwe. Under McLaren's leadership, from 1980 to 1984, courses were introduced on theatre-in-society, and attempts were made to introduce traditional performance arts into the theatre curriculum, although these were unpopular with the academic authorities and students alike, who saw such arts

The audience, Yet Nora – *December 1987. Home-made village theatre.*

as inferior and not a suitable arena for academic study. Another foreigner, Peter Harrop from the U.K., was interested in folklore, and he promoted devised performances of traditional tales which were taken on tour to local schools.

For Ethiopia these were radical departures from a drama tradition which was confined to a few high schools and to the big state theatres of the capital. In Ethiopia the playwright and his words were all-important; actors had traditionally had minimal training and very low prestige, with actresses being seen as little better than prostitutes. For the first time high status theatre professionals were being trained in significant numbers, and their training included at least some approaches to more democratic ideas of theatre-making. It would, however, be a mistake to think that attitudes of either the public or theatre graduates had changed very radically.

When the Rural Arts Programme was established the idea was that graduates would be posted to the regions for two years before returning to work in Addis Ababa.[10] As in many African countries the capital is bigger, more sophisticated and offers far more opportunities for advancement than any other town in the country. Both graduates and the authorities at the Ministry of Culture seem to have viewed the postings as temporary periods of exile. The graduates were expected to be cultural missionaries who would be relieved from their hardship posts after a suitable time period.

In effect the Programme was little more than a sop to truly national arts development. Arts Officers were given minimal orientation and were then sent off to regional capitals to run arts development programmes with no central funding or personnel in provinces which spanned hundreds of miles and often contained people of a dozen or so ethnic groups.

When I visited Arts Officers in three provinces in 1988 I found that true development work was minimal. All drama was performed in Amharic. For want of funding, transport and support, the graduates were largely confined to the capitals of their regions. In all their activities they were subject to control by regional councils which often invented spurious figures regarding arts or *kinet* groups. For example the smallest region of Arsi claimed it had 1300 *kinet* groups, a figure which is scarcely credible and for which I saw no hard evidence. It was up to the regional councils to raise money for arts initiatives and this they did with varying enthusiasm, but again mostly with concern for the regional capital and not for development in the region as a whole. Arts officers were often expected to keep office hours carrying out administrative tasks for prestige events, and this left little time for working with amateur groups in workers' and students' leisure time. Moreover, in each of the councils a key figure was the political officer who was concerned with imposing political orthodoxy, and all arts officers I spoke with had had their work subjected to censorship. In effect, in most places, the theatre graduates ended up working with small groups of high school or higher education students, often with a group of white collar Amhara office workers who were 'exiles' like themselves, and with the regions' professional or semi-professional *kinet* groups. They frequently produced popular comedies from Addis Ababa since these were not likely to cause political questioning, although the authorities were sometimes wary of what was seen as un-Marxist levity in comic drama. Several plays were devised with youth groups about problems with schooling and teenage pregnancy, but when these plays criticised teachers they were censored. Mostly the regional councils appear to have only supported work with the main regional *kinet* groups. These were anomalous institutions. Officially amateur; effectively many of the performers were professionals, paid by the councils who would compete for the services of leading musicians and who sent out talent scouts to find the best local performers. The groups were required to perform on high-days and holidays for the regional officials, much as feudal Amhara overlords had maintained *azmaris* - a traditional entertaining caste group - as a status symbols. Plays put on by these *kinet* groups were often commissioned to reflect government campaigns, either military, or over high-priority issues such as corruption and villagisation. Given the restraints operating, especially in areas of unrest, these productions were almost entirely propaganda oriented and reflected little of the true experience of participants or audience.

I did encounter a couple of more wide-reaching attempts to create something approaching community theatre. In Kaffa province in 1986 the Ministry of Education had granted funds for a six month training programme in the arts for selected youth and workers from around the region. However, it transpired that many of the trainees were pressed men rather than volunteers. Regrettably the theatre graduate in charge of this course was one the laziest and most self-serving I ever encountered and the training programme had obviously been minimal. On paper various amateur groups had been formed as a result of the course, but there was little evidence that this bore any relation to actual activity.

The most interesting experiment I encountered was another six month programme sponsored by the Ministry, this time in 1988 in the model village of Yet Nora; Gojjam province. Here a true enthusiast, Ephraim Bekele, had been appointed to run the course in an isolated farming village. Originally the village headman had wanted the performance to be a pean of praise to his village, but with the support of his performers the trainer had resisted, and together the group had devised a play centring round the group identified issues of alcoholism and wife-beating; both widespread Ethiopian problems. The play as I saw it was a huge success with the village, and the headman was in tears by the end; saying 'This is our life.' I know of no follow-up to the project but for once at least performers and community had created a play which reflected the reality of their situation.

Ethiopian theatre intervention in Eritrea

From the 1960s there has been theatrical exchange between Eritrea and Ethiopia. Popular variety shows from Asmara toured major Ethiopian towns, although as the struggle intensified allusive comment on the Eritrean position manifested in these performances made them increasingly dangerous for the actors. The major Ethiopian theatres also took annual tours around the provinces, including Eritrea, putting on both variety performances and tours of straight narrative drama.

Throughout his reign Haile Selassie had personally supervised the censorship of the productions mounted by the state supported professional companies of Addis Ababa; censorship which grew increasingly stringent as influential productions began to criticise his rule. In Eritrea theatre was usually performed in the local language of Tigrinya which made censorship more difficult for imperial Amhara authorities, although this did not stop them imprisoning leading theatrical figures.

When the Dergue took control censorship was stepped up. The groups operating in Eritrea were almost exclusively based in the capital of Asmara and were made up of devoted amateurs, mostly with teaching backgrounds. As in Ethiopia it was the playwright's words which were seen as most important, except in the popular comedies which relied on slapstick improvisation by leading performers. Many plays were uncontroversial romances or reactionary comedy. But increasingly sympathisers with the liberation struggle produced works which through use of coded symbols and *double entendres* exhorted audiences to patriotic resistance. These plays the Dergue ruthlessly suppressed. Solomon Gebregzhier, a leading performer and devisor, was frequently imprisoned, and in 1974 matters came to a head when soldiers surrounded a theatre during one of his performances and initially threatened the entire audience of 2,000 with imprisonment as a reprisal against a guerilla attack on an Ethiopian naval base. Eventually suspected rebel sympathisers were picked out and taken off to prison. Solomon was separated from the others, taken to a field out of town and shot twenty-four times before being left for dead. Amazingly he survived, and though crippled by the incident continued to work in theatre. Such examples were crushing, and by the mid-1970s popular protest theatre was non-existent in Ethiopian controlled areas of Eritrea.[11]

In its place the Ethiopians sought to impose the most naked forms of coercive propaganda performance. During the 1980s performance companies were forcibly set up in Eritrea by the Dergue. After recovering from his injuries, Solomon Gebregzhier took a teaching post in the port town of Assab and here he was ordered to set up the Red Sea Theatre Group. The performers were told to produce songs and plays in praise of Ethiopian rule. Some traditional songs and dances in local languages were allowed to be included in order to secure an audience, and in these the performers again used symbolism and allusion to covertly express support for the liberation struggle, but this was a dangerous business which could only be carried out with extreme caution.

In Eritrea's second city of Keren, Gebrehiwot Haile spoke to interviewers of how the Dergue forced students to form pro-Ethiopian performance groups.[12] Like most Eritrean towns Keren had never had a performance troupe. Indeed if one can say anything good about Dergue policy towards promoting the arts it is that they involved many people with the idea of being performers who had never considered such a thing before. The Dergue initially tried to set up a performance group in 1978, but when students found out what it was they were required to perform some fled to join the EPLF and others were imprisoned for refusing to co-operate. In 1988 the Dergue tried again. Troops came to Gebrehiwot's school, and he, with various other students who had been identified as good musicians or potential performers, was ordered to go with the soldiers. They were given no choice in performing, and programmes were largely selected for the group. Again performances were in the variety format, including song, music and drama. Most of the work was required to be in Amharic, but because this was not popular with audiences, some traditional songs were allowed simply in order to persuade people to attend. Because the group was made up of youth and was infiltrated with Ethiopian supporters there was no opportunity for subversion of the imposed messages of the Dergue. However, support for the liberation struggle was so overwhelming that very few people came to these performances, and even fewer were seduced by the messages given out. Gebrehiwot said that everyone knew he was performing this material against his will and no one took it seriously or held it against him.

This kind of blatant propaganda in a highly politicised oppressed nation can hardly hope to be successful. Indeed it is possibly surprising that the Ethiopians enforced performances which they can have scarcely hoped would win around a population living in daily fear of torture, rape and various military atrocities and where almost everyone had relatives who were actively engaged in supporting the struggle. In such a situation theatre becomes simply another tool of oppression and has scarcely any use value to performers, audience or even colonialists.

Recent theatre initiatives

Following the collapse of the Ethiopian army in May 1991, Eritrea became a *de facto* independent state (a position legitimised after a U.N. run referendum in 1993 which showed over 99% of the

Kinèt group – Yet Nora, *1987. Performance at the end of a six-month village training scheme in the arts.*

people in favour of independence), whilst Ethiopia acquired a new government led by the Tigray people of Ethiopia's northernmost region, whose guerilla army had worked closely with the EPLF in struggling against the Dergue.

In Ethiopia the Tigray have experienced many problems in overhauling the structures of government. Ethiopia is a huge nation with no experience of democracy, and the Tigrayans had little knowledge of many of the diverse peoples with whom they now have to work. Moreover to many Ethiopians, and particularly the previously dominant Amhara, the Tigrayans are not liberators but conquerors. Cultural initiatives have taken a very low priority in the new state and theatre is still dominated by the over-staffed, conservative professional theatres of Addis Ababa. Very few new plays have emerged in recent years. Partly this is because those involved in non-traditional theatre are nearly all Amharas who have little love for the conquering Tigray, but who dare not express their resentment on stage. The other important factor is that the government itself is very wary about how much freedom of expression it wishes to allow and does not want to encourage cultural initiatives which may be outside its direct control. Professional performances remain dominated by a neo-naturalist form and seek primarily to entertain rather than to provoke or involve their audiences. I have heard of no new cultural initiatives in the regions, and the major trend of development has been a mushrooming of amateur and semi-professional groups around Addis Ababa, mostly made up of young school leavers, who are performing in local halls, trying to raise money either by putting on old favourites or scripting shows - still in naturalistic form - about their lives.

In Eritrea, however, the situation is very different. After independence Alemseged Tesfai was charged with finding the means to develop a civilian, democratic and relevant theatre for Eritrea. The trouble was that no-one in the country had any knowledge of alternative ways in which they might build such a performance culture. Consequently Alemseged invited any and everyone he met who was involved in the arts and interested in Eritrea to come to the country and discuss ways forward. I first met Alemseged in 1992 in Ethiopia when he was visiting Addis Ababa to see if it might be appropriate for Eritrea to establish a professional theatre along Ethiopian lines. After some discussion we agreed that it might be much more useful to try to initiate a bottom-up theatre model introducing Theatre for Development techniques.

This plan emerged as *The Eritrea Community-Based Theatre Project* which began work in 1995.[15] Building on the experiences of the cultural troupes and on successful models in other parts of Africa an initial three month training programme was run with 57 trainees and four British trainers. The trainees were drawn from members of the Central Cultural Troupe who are now employed in government funded Tigre and Tigrinya theatre companies and a traditional performance troupe, and from interested members of amateur groups from a number of major towns.

Our fundamental aim was to give trainees an insight into the techniques of various practitioners whose work might be useful in creating relevant popular theatre forms; to integrate traditional performance forms with drama techniques, and to give trainees the skills to devise discussion-based, participatory theatre relevant to the lives of the mass of predominately rural peoples. The work was fascinating and challenging for all concerned. Names like those of Boal, Brecht, and Ngugi wa Thiong'o were completely new to the trainees, and notion that drama could be anything other than proscenium based and dialogue dominated was initially difficult for many to grasp. However, by the end of the course highly successful plays had been devised around the group identified issues

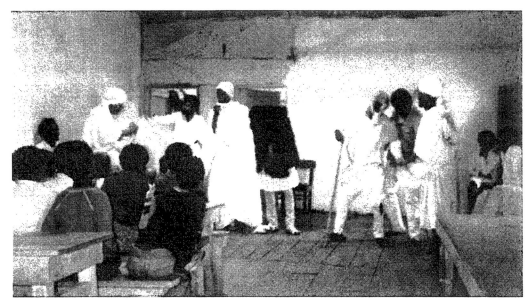

Addis Alem, Ehiopia, June 1986. Tour of folk plays to schools by university students.

of AIDS, land reform and education for women. Existing theatre groups are now experimenting with many of the new ideas, and a Community-Based Theatre group has been established which has toured extensively in Tigrinya areas and has begun teaching community and youth groups the new techniques.

As a second stage to the project a month-long Theatre-In-Education course was run in 1996 with 17 primary school teachers. Many teachers are untrained, have classes of sixty and few resources. Moreover teaching was traditionally a very authoritarian business involving much rote learning and little interactive work. Again students reacted with great enthusiasm. In future years the project has plans to extend training to other ethnic groups and to develop teaching on how to work with community and school groups, so that theatre can become a real means of discussion, problem-solving and giving a voice to people whose cultures and concerns have until very recently been rigidly suppressed. Ultimately we hope to establish a diverse nation-wide network of community-based theatre groups which can support each other and become fully independent of either state or foreign interventions.

Conclusion

The history of Eritrea and Ethiopia over the past thirty-five years demonstrates a considerable variety of attempts to utilise theatre either as a tool of rebellion and empowerment or as a means of controlling and repressing the people. As in other African countries performance cultures have been seen as important by both sides, because where the majority are illiterate and unable to gain access to the mass media, theatre can be a major means of propagating messages. Ultimately however, as has been seen in liberation struggles in Zimbabwe and South Africa as well as in this case study; theatre, music and song can only in the long term benefit the side which has mass support. In Ethiopia there was a period when workers were forced to attend agit-prop performances in the theatres, but this could only be sustained for a brief period and had no recorded impact on the audiences' views. When Ethiopians tried to use theatre as a propaganda tool in Eritrea people simply stayed away, whilst performances mounted in dangerous circumstances by EPLF liberation forces attracted audiences in their thousands.

When repressive governments realise that they cannot use theatre for their own ends they seem to react in one of two directions. Firstly, as has been in case in Ethiopia for many years, the state promotes only trivial or foreign theatre, which has no bearing on peoples' actual lives, to act as an opiate. Secondly, attempts at more empowering, controversial theatre are squashed by a variety of means ranging from denial of support through to censorship, banning and ultimately the imprisonment or murder of theatre workers.

What I continue to find most extraordinary in my practical work and reading about African theatres is the sheer resilience and conviction about the importance of their work in so many people who continue to try to use the performing arts as tools of liberation in the face of appalling difficulties. When I visited Eritrea shortly after it became independent I was almost embarrassed to be talking about theatre projects to people whose country was devastated and who were experiencing crises in dealing with fundamental problems of housing, agriculture, health and education. Yet everywhere I went culture was accorded great importance. Many people were acutely aware of the damage done to them by the Ethiopians forcing children to be educated in the foreign language of Amharic and of the dangers of losing their indigenous cultural forms of expression. Reclaiming and building relevant cultural forms which could speak to and be spoken by all was immediately recognised as an important part of building 'Free Eritrea'.[14]

The post-revolutionary, post-independence period that Eritrea and Ethiopia are now experiencing demands a reorientation from the use of theatre as a tool of propaganda. The question facing cultural authorities is how that reorientation is addressed. TFD demands that theatre is opened up to the people, using their forms, words and language in an non-elitist manner which is open to all. It also demands that in the long term at least these theatres become independent of the state and of funding agencies so that they can really produce their own voices. Such a step is difficult to take for various reasons. Political organisations which have relied on military discipline and the following of agreed policy strategies, have to be prepared to take the step of letting go and then allowing a free theatre to develop which is bound, at certain times and in certain ways, to question government lines on various issues. Secondly, funding at either amateur or professional levels has been a great problem for many TFD initiatives simply because the countries concerned are so poor that communal resources or audience receipts are bound to be minimal. Finally, such groups often require skills inputs in order to use these performance forms and build on them, which are again hard to finance.

In Ethiopia the government already appears to be closing in and restricting freedom of expression because it knows that it does not have a popular mandate outside the Tigray region. So far the Eritrean government feels broadly secure with a massive popular support base carefully nurtured throughout the years of struggle. Initial developments in training and touring discussion-based popular theatre projects have been a revelation to those used to the old forms of naturalistic drama, regularly drawing audiences of thousands to open hillside performances. Moreover structured plans are maturing to extend the programme across the major ethnic groups and to find ways of making groups independent of the state. I know of no other African nation where, to date, a cultural policy is being evolved which has such a good chance of becoming a real means of giving a voice to so many people and of allowing them to use culture to participate in nation-building.

Eritrea is therefore a very special place in which to be involved in TFD at present. What I hope this study demonstrates is that this situation did not arise in a vacuum or as the result of the efforts of a few interested individuals. The cultural possibilities in Eritrea, like the difficulties in Ethiopia, exist because of the earlier ways in which performance cultures were utilised, and because of the political choices of the governments concerned to either enforce their rule or to work with the people to build a popular base from which true democratic development might be possible.

Notes

1   One of the problems in discussing TFD concerns naming. As well as Theatre for Development writers and practitioners have referred to their work as 'popular theatre', 'theatre of the oppressed', 'community-based theatre' and 'peoples' theatre'. All these practices ideally centre around empowering people to make theatre for themselves about issues of concern to them and their communities. However, because the practice has so often fallen short of the ideal new practitioners have created new terms, often, I think, to distance themselves from forms of people-oriented theatre which have been subverted by states, churches, political parties and aid agencies to serve the funders', rather than the peoples' agendas. In this chapter I use the names as interchangeable, which I think, essentially, they are.

2   See Penina Muhando Mlama, *Culture and Development: The Popular Theatre Approach in Africa*, Nordiska Afrikainstitutet, 1991; Zakes Mda, *When People Play People: Development Communication Through Theatre*, Zed Press, 1993 and Christopher Kamlongera, *Theatre for Development in Africa with case studies from Malawi and Zambia*, German Foundation for International Development, 1989.

3   For further information on Ethiopian theatre see Jane Plastow, *Politics and African Theatre: A Comparative Study of the Evolution of Theatre in Ethiopia, Tanzania and Zimbabwe*, Rodopi Press, 1996.

4   For further information on Ngugi's work at Kamiriithu see Ingrid Bjorkman, *Mother, Sing For Me: Peoples Theatre in Kenya*, Zed Press, 1989.

5   For further information on Zimbabwean theatre see Plastow, *Politics and African Theatre*.

6   For commentary on the impact of revolutionary culture on the Zimbabwean liberation struggle see Chapter 3 of *Turmoil and Tenacity: Zimbabwe 1890-1990*, Ed, Canaan S. Banana, The College Press, Harare, 1990; *None But Ourselves: Masses vs Media in the Making of Zimbabwe*, Julie Frederike, Harare, 1982, and *Songs That Won the Liberation War*, Ed, Alec Pongweni, Harare, 1982.

7   Information given to the writer by Mrs Praxides Chikerema, then head of Community Education and Theatre of the Zimbabwe Foundation for Education with Production (ZIMFEP), in an interview in 1990.

8   Robert Kavanagh, 'Theatre for Development in Zimbabwe', in *Journal of Southern African Studies*, Vol 16, No 2, Oxford, June 1992.

9   Information about the Eritrean Cultural Troupes was gathered and interviews with members of those troupes were carried out from July to September 1995 as part an on-going research and practical project, *The Eritrea Community-Based Theatre Project*.

10 Only men were posted to work on the Rural Arts Programme, because it was thought that women would not command sufficient respect to be able to operate effectively. This judgement reflects both the traditionally low status of women in Ethiopian society and the fact that women performers have commonly been seen as little different from prostitutes.

11 Interviews with Solomon Gebregzhier, August & September 1995.

12 Interview with Gebrehiwot Haule, September 1995.

13 For further information see 'The Eritrea Community-Based Theatre Project' in *New Theatre Quarterly*, No51, Cambridge, August 1997.

14 The term 'Free Eritrea' is widely used in that country; printed on T-shirts and sprayed on shop windows. It is not just a statement of fact but a declaration that this is a new kind of country from the old feudal, colonial Eritrea.

Satires in Theatre for Development Practice in Tanzania

Juma Adamu Bakari

Introduction

In Africa today, Theatre for Development has been a major area of interest and concern not only among theatre practitioners, but also for those involved in community development. In Tanzania, since the Malya Popular Theatre for Social Development Project carried out in 1982 / 83, some organisations, both governmental and non-governmental, have used TFD in a number of projects. The argument in this essay is that 'effective communication is one of the most important factors in being successful in whatever endeavour [...] people undertake.'[1] Theatre for Development is seen not only as effective, but as an appropriate medium of communication in community development. Other communication media such as radio, television and newspapers have certain limitations. None of them offers an opportunity for direct interaction between the sender of information and the receiver. There is no interaction between individuals as everyone would be confined at home watching television, listening to the radio or reading a newspaper. 'Offended viewers of a television programme can turn-off, they can even throw a brick through the screen, but this has no effect at all on the millions of other viewers elsewhere.'[2] Theatre for Development facilitates a process whereby community members get an opportunity to identify and analyse their problems, and through discussions, lay down strategies to overcome them. Its artistic potential attracts more people than a community meeting, and thus it becomes easier to make decisions on various community issues.

However, current trends in Tanzania reveal that there is a problem of how to operate the method of Theatre for Development and sustain its process. 'The popular theatre projects seem to indicate that people are interested in community theatre but have insufficient self-confidence to carry on working in the same vein once the dominant influence of the 'experts' has gone.'[3] Community members are often at loss not knowing how to carry forward the process in the absence of the 'experts'. Therefore, I share Nyoni's opinion that there is an element of the people being robbed 'of the opportunity to voice their own concerns and do their own thinking'[4]. Although this indicates some problems in the facilitation process in that it does not permit further development by community members, the major contributing factor is the failure of practitioners to effectively use indigenous forms of theatre. Much as there has always been a will to use the popular forms of the people, current practice has shown that this has been done only to a certain extent. For example during the Malya Theatre for Social Development project the 'experts' integrated 'local Sukuma dances such as, Bugobogobo, Wigashe and Bunungule into the structure of the dramas.'[5] In another project, 'Theatre for living' by the National Arts Council in Kigoma region, in 1993, 'participants devised a piece of drama which incorporated some local songs.'[6] Such examples seem to have disregarded the dynamic forms that have evolved out of specific conditions to solve specific social problems.

There is a difference between 'experts' incorporating indigenous forms of Theatre for Development and community members themselves using their own forms to discuss their problems. With 'experts', especially if the approach is 'leadership' rather than 'partnership', community members become passive and lack confidence. In most cases, the tendency is to wait for the 'experts' to do the thinking. The local community might even fail to understand why their forms are being used. But when community members use their forms, they are confident because they know why they are using the forms and for whose interest. As this happens without being monitored by the 'experts', it is thus possible for them to carry on the process.

Various communities in Tanzania have since time immemorial used their indigenous forms of theatre as means of communicating to other community members undesirable social conditions or anti-social behaviour for possible social remedies. Mlama points out: 'dances, story-telling, mime and some rituals were effective tools through which specific values were imparted and the basis of behaviour in the society charted out.'[7] Although most of the forms were instructive and moralistic with closed ended messages and sometimes oppressive to women and children, some of them were very powerful tools in raising controversial community issues. Among these forms, satirical dramas in most communities have been powerful devices for changing people with anti-social behaviour and thus restoring the social equilibrium.

This essay examines the potential of indigenous forms of theatre, particularly satirical dramas in contemporary TFD practice. It attempts to clarify the concepts of Theatre for Development, community development and satirical drama and then looks at the history of Theatre for Development in Tanzania with particular emphasis on its major problems. It also discusses the satirical dramas, *Machonja* and *Nkhuda,* and explains what they are and how they work. Examples are given to illustrate their potential as effective communication media in Theatre for Development.

Theatre for Development

'Theatre for Development is not monolithic in its practice. On the contrary, it is so varied to make its definition difficult.'[8] This has resulted to numerous terms such as popular theatre, community theatre or peoples' theatre, which in actual fact 'describe the same thing.'[9] For the purpose of this study, Theatre for Development should be understood as a method and technique of performance creation and presentation for a specific target community. 'The people targeted for [..] are majority people in the rural areas and the urban poor, the lower classes so to speak, because of their obvious low degree of comprehension of modern social issues of governance and livelihood which are largely controlled by the upper class,'[10] The fundamental objective is, through the theatrical presentations, to stimulate and provoke members of a community to talk and discuss their problems and come up with ways and means of solving them. In this way people are enabled to free themselves from what Paulo Freire describes as the 'culture of silence'. This is a situation whereby people have internalised oppression and they do not talk about it. Subsequently they adopt a 'fear of freedom', that is, being afraid of changes as they are not sure as to whether the changes will be positive or negative. However, care must be taken so as to have a balance between artistic quality and relevance of content. There is a tendency in many Theatre for Development projects of putting more emphasis on the educative aspects than entertaining values. According to Brecht, 'the former may be useful, but only the latter is pleasant'.[11]

Theatre for Development differs in a number of ways from the mysterious conventional bourgeois theatre of audience-performer separation. Conventional theatre is mysterious in that it puts more emphasis on product than process. This product is not to be seen by the audience until it is well polished. As such, the entire process of production is hidden from the public. With the former, the attempt is to place people at the centre of their own development in terms of deciding what to do, when and how. It is a way of empowering them with the machinery of decision making and implementation. With the latter, people are told what to do, what is good and bad, and what is right and wrong.

However, for dominant authorities Theatre for Development is a threat to the status quo because the lower classes become more critical of their situation and find ways to change it. In some places where Theatre for Development has been practised effectively, addressing fundamental economic and political issues, the dominant powers have sometimes used coercive means such as putting the practitioners in detention in order to stop the practice. The demolition of the Kamiriithu community education and cultural centre, the detention of some of the leaders by the Kenyan government authorities in 1982 and the exile of Ngugi wa Thiongo and Ngugi wa Miiri demonstrates the extent to which the dominant authorities can be offended by Theatre for Development. Apart from this extreme example of the Kamiriithu in which the artists were directly confronting the ruling authorities, another typical example on a smaller scale happened in 1987 at the Bagamoyo College of Arts. Students had presented a participatory theatre performance in which they posed some of the problems at the college. One problem which sparked off hot discussion was that some tutors had a tendency of marking down students because of personal conflicts. Most tutors felt offended and they condemned the whole idea of introducing Theatre for Development in the curriculum. Their biggest argument was that Theatre for Development does nothing else but preparing students to be argumentative and disobedient to their tutors. Despite the argument, it is interesting to note that students' presentations did help to reduce problems to a certain extent.

Community Development

This is a method and a process of bringing positive changes in order to improve the living standard of the people. The community development process begins with arousing the community's consciousness of its social reality in terms of needs and resources, strengths and weaknesses. The needs of the community are fulfilled through plans and decisions designed and executed by community members. Therefore, there is a close link between Theatre for Development and community development because the major focus is participation of community members bringing about their own development.

Satirical Drama

Satirical drama is a 'type of comedy in which vice, folly, stupidity and other human weaknesses are exposed to ridicule and contempt.'[12] Satirical dramas criticise a person for transgressing socially accepted values. He or she is thus punished through people's laughter. The function of satirical dramas is twofold: to entertain and to alleviate anti-social behaviour. Performers of most traditional satirical drama are usually artists with a great sense of humour skilled enough in techniques of improvisation to enable them to act and react spontaneously during performances according to how the audience react. More often than not, they would leave spectators to make their own discoveries and judgements as to who are being ridiculed. For example, in one satirical drama of the Wazigua ethnic group in Tanzania, one elder was charged with upholding a death message that was supposed to be relayed to other relatives of the family who lived in different villages. The elder never visited the villages. The drama focused on the proceedings of the charge on how the accused failed to answer all the questions. So the performers portrayed him as a tired hen unable to catch a cockroach. In normal life, a hen would usually run after cockroaches. When it comes to the point when it fails to catch even a nearest one, it is a clear manifestation that the hen is tired. Such was a metaphorical portrayal of someone being guilty presented in a comic and funny way. Nevertheless, such a situation and such a character 'bear a readily recognisable resemblance to the same kinds of people in the world around us'[13].

I see satirical dramas having a crucial role in Theatre for Development because of their utilisation of humour in discussing community problems and their artistic licence 'to criticise and lampoon anyone in society however respectable he might be'[14] in a joyous, relaxing and entertaining way. The success of Theatre for Development relies on the participation of the people. In order for them to attend and participate in Theatre for Development projects, there is a need to use theatrical forms which have a lot of humour. When people are at ease, it becomes easier for them to discuss their problems and come up with realistic solutions.

Satirical dramas in Africa are common in many communities and they have existed for many years. David Kerr's study on pre-colonial popular theatre forms in Africa revealed the existence of the *Kote-Tlon* in Mali, a satirical drama used by the young generation to expose the antagonistic relations between the feudal old generation who owned the land and the toiling youths who owned the labour. The Bakweri people of Cameroon have the *Titi-ikoli*. This is a satirical drama performed by women against sexual humiliation from men. Across the continent from east to west and north to south, different communities have their own satirical dramas. In Tanzania, almost every ethnic group has its own satirical dramas.

Theatre for Development in Tanzania

'The use of theatre to advance popular interests has a long history in Tanzania.'[15] Prior to colonialism, dances, story-telling, rituals, heroic recitations and songs played a significant role in the life of societies and they were never separated from daily social activities. There were dances which were performed at work places, for example in the farms to encourage and mobilise people to work hard without feeling the constraints of the work. The *Bugobogobo* dance of the Wasukuma ethnic group is an example of such dances. Another theatre form is the *Kisazi*, a rites of passage dance drama of the Wazigua ethnic group performed in the bush to initiate young girls who have seen their first menstruation.

Such activities were possible because traditional societies were composed of small communities whose membership was based on family, kinship or tribal relations. As social relationships were based on brotherhood, co-operation and collective responsibility in the production process in which each able-bodied member participated, theatrical performances served the entire community and each member had an active role to play. Lihamba clarifies that 'the performances are communal because the society itself is communal.'[16] Theatre during this period was not just entertainment, but an educational institution to which each community member had access.

The colonial period witnessed a suppression of Tanzanian indigenous forms of theatre and the introduction of English drama in schools which was used 'as a tool for mastering English pronunciation, diction and language'[17]. This was an attempt to use 'the cultural bomb'. It is the most effective weapon used by imperialists to silence the majority so that they don't rise against them. 'The effect of a cultural bomb is to annihilate a peoples belief in their names, in their languages, in their environment, in their heritage of struggle, in their unity, in their capacities and ultimately in themselves'[18].

Through drama the colonialists were promoting the superiority of English culture and domesticating Africans to accept colonialism. The introduction of this kind of drama with such an imperialist philosophy was a reflection of the prevailing economic system in Europe during this particular period. When Africa became colonised, the prevailing mode of production in Europe was capitalism based on antagonistic relations between producers (the workers) and non-producers (the capitalists). As the interests of these two classes were diametrically opposed to each other, the capitalists made sure that they took into possession not only the economic base but also the superstructure with its related institutions such as the arts to be used as instruments of conserving the already established social order. Through theatre they could easily spread their propaganda, impose their ideology and safeguard their interests. As the colonial master was a representative of the metropolitan bourgeoisie, 'the introduction of the bourgeois theatre with British colonialism'[19] was geared towards serving the interests of capitalism. Most performances during the colonial period did not contribute in creating awareness for people to understand the evils of the colonial regime. In the same line of argument, Plastow puts it clearly that 'under British influence *vichekesho* was adapted to reinforce messages about the stupidity of 'backward' Africans'[20]. *Vichekesho* was a popular form of improvised drama in Tanzania during colonial era. It derives from a Swahili word 'cheka' which means laugh. Thus the meaning of *Vichekesho* is that which makes someone laugh. The result of *Vichekesho* was that the Africans failed to look at the colonialists as enemies but as the 'ideal models' because of their intelligence and cleverness. So they started to copy western ways of life in the belief that they were the 'best'. Whether this was what the colonialists wanted or not is difficult to conclude, especially taking into consideration British colonialism which operated through indirect rule. The philosophy was not to transform Africans to become English. We could have speculated such a conclusion if it were a French colony due to their policy of assimilation in which they aimed at transforming Africans to black Frenchmen and Frenchwomen. *Vichekesho* is still a popular form of drama in Tanzania but due to its colonial background, it is these days known as *Vivunja Mbavu* which means 'that which breaks your ribs' because of too much laughing.

The situation did not change immediately after independence in 1961. A year after, a ministry of National Culture and Youth was established to take care of the country's cultural affairs. This resulted into the formulation of the National Dance troupe in 1963, the National Acrobatics troupe in 1969 and the National Drama troupe in 1976. These troupes were charged with a responsibility of reviving, preserving and promoting indigenous forms of theatre which had been suppressed by the colonialists. It was believed that by creating performances and presenting them to different communities in Tanzania, people would be inspired and would have a sense of pride in their culture. This would make them confident enough to engage in such activities without any feelings of 'being inferior'. However, it is worth pointing out that much as these troupes did succeed to a certain extent in reviving some of the indigenous forms especially dance and music, 'they largely overlooked the educational and other functions of such forms.'[21] For example most performances by the National drama troupe (in which the author was an actor) never took into consideration fundamental issues like arousing consciousness among members of various communities so as to understand their reality in a more critical way. Of course this was a reflection of the bourgeois European theatre inherited from colonial theatre experts. As the actors were trained by graduates from the universities of Dar es Salaam and Makerere who studied western models of theatre, such a reflection in the performances of the National drama troupe was bound to happen.

The period after independence up to the late seventies was characterised by the travelling theatre movement pioneered by the department of Art, Music and Theatre of the University of Dar es Salaam and the National Dance, Acrobatics and Drama troupes. While the objective was taking theatre to the people, the content of most performances never addressed problems of specific communities. For example one of the productions of the National drama troupe which toured extensively was *Afande* (unpublished) by Mobali and Bakari. The play which was addressing problems of some leaders within the National Service could have been more relevant for a target audience within the army but was performed for the general public in most places it toured. The travelling theatre movement in Tanzania marked an important turning point in Theatre for Development practice. There was dissatisfaction among some theatre practitioners that the travelling theatre movement had failed to answer the needs of the people and solve their problems at the grassroots level. This was owing to its mode of operation which never took into consideration the importance of involving people in the process of identifying and discussing their problems.

During the same period, various factors within and outside Tanzania did provide the necessary conditions for theatre practitioners to shift from 'theatre for the people' to 'theatre with the people'. Outside Tanzania, this was the beginning of the popular theatre workshops in Botswana in which some practitioners from Tanzania, for example Godwin Kaduma, participated. The factors within Tanzania included a change in most of the government's policies which put more emphasis on rural development. This involved the process of villagisation in which people in most parts of the country were moved from their original places and settled in newly established Ujamaa villages. The question of empowering the people with the machinery of decision making and implementation was seen to be crucial in the success of building Ujamaa in Tanzania. This was followed by a government policy of recruiting eight thousand experts who were posted to all over the country as village managers. During the same period, a wave of critical theatre emerged in Tanzania with the production of *Harakati za Ukombozi,* a collectively devised performance by a group of dancers, musicians and actors. Under the direction of Mlama, Lihamba and the late Matteru, the play focused on Tanzanian social, economic and political problems since independence. For example one of the issues which was raised was the contradiction between politicians' behaviour on political platforms preaching the Arusha Declaration and when they were in normal life situations. The irony, which was clear to the audience, was that while politicians 'sang' socialism, they 'danced' capitalism. To most of the people who saw the play, it was a hit in the history of theatre in Tanzania as it was very critical of the ruling system.

One may associate *Harakati za Ukombozi* with the Kamiriithu's production of *Maitu Njungira* which more or less posed the same issues in the Kenyan situation and was produced collectively by peasants, workers, the unemployed and university lecturers. While there may be an influence of Kamiriithu to a certain extent, the two productions were in no way related as the conditions which gave them birth were quite different. *Maitu Njungira* was a result of a real need of the subaltern classes of Kenya to find an effective form and an appropriate language in their struggles against oppressive imperialist models of development. On the other hand, *Harakati za Ukombozi* came out of a request from Chama Cha Mapinduzi (the ruling party in Tanzania) for a play to celebrate their first anniversary. Perhaps what came out was contrary to the expectations of those who requested the performance as there were different opinions as to whether the play should be performed or not before Julius Kambarage Nyerere, the then head of state. Those who were against felt nervous thinking that the president would not enjoy the performance as it was very critical, in that case they would be answerable to whatever disappointments the president might have. However the play was eventually performed on 22nd August, 1978 in Zanzibar before the president and other top dignitaries in the government and nothing happened. Such a silence warranted subsequent productions of similar nature. These productions include *Ayubu, Lina Ubani, Mafuta* and *Mitumba ya Ndui* (by the Paukwa Theatre Association) and *Chakatu, Mwenyewe Kalala* and *Kaptula la Marx* (by the Bagamoyo College of Arts.). Still nothing happened.

Such silences may have different interpretations. The first one is that 'silence means acceptance'. That is, the ruling powers had accepted the truth and that was it. The second interpretation could be a deliberate device of cutting off the electric power supply. Instead of the ruling system feeling offended and reacting negatively by say putting a ban on the performances or arresting the artists, they opted for being positive, and as far as the magnetic theory is concerned, 'like poles always repel'. However, 'it must also be noted here that the Tanzanian government, unlike many others in the developing countries, has shown a remarkable tolerance of criticism through the arts and public discussions. This may be due to the Party's own policy of self-criticism or the realisation that such criticism has contributions to make to the general welfare of the people.'[22]

However, I am of the opinion that if the performances had gone a bit further in terms of creating a debate between performers and audience, we might have probably experienced something different. Theatre for Development is essentially participatory, enabling the audience to think and question, something which is not liked by those in power. If the performances had facilitated such a process the consequences might have been different. A good example happened in 1990 when the Bagamoyo college of Arts devised a participatory performance on the problem of corruption. The plan was to present it to members of the parliament for a discussion in order to launch a public debate on the problem but the plan never materialised. There were no reasons given, but one could assume that the experiences in one of the performances in Bagamoyo could be the major reason. In that performance, the audience reacted very bitterly and suggested radical changes of the corrupt system.

The conditions and factors so far discussed, that is, the effectiveness of theatre in traditional societies, the post-independence philosophy of promotion of indigenous forms of theatre, the limitations of the travelling theatre movements and the search for a form of theatre which could be more meaningful to people's lives gave birth to effective use of theatre in addressing community needs and problems in Tanzania. So the period beginning in the early 1980's marked the start of the effective use of theatre as a medium of education to arouse people's consciousness so as to understand their situations in a more critical way. It was thus a shift from the 'theatre for the people' model as practised by the travelling theatres to the 'theatre with the people' in which Theatre for Development practitioners together with community members engaged in a collective process of identifying and discussing community problems.

Between 1982 and 1996, a total of eleven projects have been carried out in different communities. These projects have taken place in Malya (1982-83), Bagamoyo (1983), Msoga (1985), Kerege, Kiromo, Pande and Zinga (1986), Mkambalani (1986), Nyamadoke (1988), Namionga (1991), Kisiwani (1992), Rukwa (1993), Kigoma (1993) and Kongo (1994). They have been carried out by Theatre for Development practitioners from the University of Dar es Salaam, the Bagamoyo College of Arts and the National Arts Council. All the projects used 'the community based model' in which animaters worked with people in different communities facilitating a process whereby problems were identified, discussed and strategies to overcome them laid down. This model operates through a methodology that involves research on community problems, analysis of gathered information, scenario creation and rehearsals, performances and discussions, evaluation and follow-up.

During the same period, a total of nine projects were conducted in various parts of Tanzania where TFD practitioners devised specific performances for particular target communities. Dialogue was established through performances between performers and audience in order to discuss community problems. It was a move towards creating a two-way communication among community members. Projects under this model include seven by the Bagamoyo college of Arts carried out in Kagera, Mara, Mwanza, Coast, Dar es Salaam, Tanga and Morogoro regions, one by the Lighters Arts Group carried out in Dar es Salaam, Coast, Morogoro and Tanga, and one by the Tanzania One Theatre Company Ltd carried out in Coast and Tanga regions. Issues addressed in these projects ranged from health, for example AIDS and family planning, to politics, especially civic education during Tanzania's general elections in 1995.

The projects and activities so far discussed are those undertaken by the animaters from the official established organisations based in the cities. Nevertheless, people within their own communities had continued to use their indigenous forms of theatre to address their problems. So this was yet another model of Theatre for Development, 'the theatre by the people model' in which people, on their own, created theatre to educate each other without being monitored by the 'experts'.

Looking at the Tanzania's history of Theatre for Development and the direction it has taken, a number of problems can be identified. The practice has continued to advocate the top-down approach to development as most of the projects were initiated by the 'experts' and were not 'community centred' in their objectives. For example the objectives of the Bagamoyo project 'were to train the students of the college in the popular theatre process [this was primary] as well as to involve the Bagamoyo residents in the use of theatre to discuss and analyse their problems'[23] [this was secondary]. When we look at the Msoga project we discover that the main objective was 'to serve as a continuation of the popular theatre practice building on the experiences gained in Malya and Bagamoyo'[24]. Such a situation has been contradicting the argument that 'popular theatre begins with the grassroots community with what its members think are the major concerns of their lives'.[25]

When we look at the operating models of Theatre for Development in Tanzania, that is, the Performance-based and the Community-based, it is clearly evident that for more than fifteen years the practice has not moved from the stage of 'theatre with the people', in which animaters facilitate the process, to that of 'theatre by the people' whereby community members in their own locality create theatre using their indigenous forms to discuss their problems. This is the ultimate goal of Theatre for Development. Failure to achieve this goal has given birth to difficulties in sustaining the process in many communities. Although the projects seemed to have inspired the people in looking at alternative ways of dealing with their problems 'there was no base left behind for the people to follow-up'[26]. On the same line of argument, it seems to me that Theatre for Development in Tanzania was introduced by its practitioners as a new phenomenon and its 'experts' occupied the driving seat while people in communities became the passengers. Mlama points out with regard to the Mkambalani project that 'it was organised and conducted by a team of animaters from the University of Dar es Salaam'[27]. The practitioners' failure to establish the re-claim of the function of theatre as a pedagogical institution as it used to be in traditional societies, has resulted in people perceiving Theatre for Development as a foreign concept.

Another problem with regard to the academic approach to Theatre for Development is that its operation is through a specific, and in most cases rigid, methodology in which familiarisation, data collection, data analysis and scenario creation have always been the first and foremost steps, while performance, post-performance discussion, evaluation and follow-up are considered the last steps. Most Theatre for Development projects have been carried out through such a methodology. The problem with such a systematic process is that it tends to be rigid, sounds too academic and outside the experience and comprehension of community members. Such a systematic approach may be more relevant to the academics who are only in communities for a short period. For community members this may seem irrelevant because as far as indigenous models of Theatre for Development are concerned, the whole process of identifying, analysing, presenting and discussing community problems is part and parcel of their day-to-day activities.

It is quite obvious that there exists a gap between the people with their knowledge and experience of their indigenous forms of theatre as pedagogical institutions and the academics with their 'expertise and intellectualism' of Theatre for Development. This gap has led to under-utilisation of the indigenous forms of theatre in many projects. I now turn to examine those forms in terms of their social functions and limitations.

Indigenous Models of Theatre for Development

Most Theatre for Development practitioners in Tanzania face a common problem of lack of sufficient knowledge of indigenous forms of theatre. While various factors may be attributed to this problem, the fact is that the area of indigenous African theatre forms 'has not been thoroughly researched'.[28] In Tanzania for example, apart from research projects carried out by students at the University of Dar es Salaam and Mlama's study on Tanzanian Traditional Theatre as a pedagogical Institution (1983) in which she focused on the Kaguru ethnic group, there isn't much comprehensive and well documented material available on Tanzanian indigenous forms of theatre.

However, if we want to make effective use of the indigenous forms in Theatre for Development practice, 'some mastery of the performance skills of these forms'[29] is required. In many parts of Tanzania 'people continue to use their dances, mimes, drama, recitations and story-telling to express their views about their realities, to discuss their problems, to air their fears and aspirations, to condemn and protest against injustice'[30]. Ethnic groups have always devised specific models of overcoming social problems which were categorised according to their causes such as floods, drought, and earthquake. Communities used ritual performances as an appeal to external forces which they had no control of.

By carrying out such performances everybody in the community believed that the problem would be solved. For problems which were not naturally ordained but socially determined they used ways which addressed the material world and not the spiritual one. For example among the Wasambaa, if someone was identified as a witch some chosen elders would go to the forest during the night and collect some branches from thorny trees. They would then come back singing and would dump the branches on the front door of the witch. This would not only be a notice to the witch to move to another village but a warning to stop witchcraft.

However, an analysis of most indigenous forms of theatre reveals that to a large extent they were instructive and moralistic as they never offered any opportunity for audience to be critical. Epskamp Kees says that 'the young were expected to listen and to observe and certainly not to comment on the newly acquired knowledge. This pressure to conform, in many cases, resulted in a conservative view of society with little room for active social change'[31]. Within a context of Theatre for Development whereby empowerment of people with the means of critical analysis is the main agenda, such models do not help us in promoting critical dialogue among community members. My focus is on satires in Theatre for Development, for they have the potential of raising controversial issues which need community attention. In indigenous satires, 'performances are used to expose reality, not only in its positive entirety but also in its false pretensions.'[32] I will now turn to some examples of satire from few ethnic groups.

The Wasukuma living in the northern part of Tanzania, mainly in Mwanza and Shinyanga regions, have the *Bunungule* dance. This dance originated as an association of porcupine hunters and medicine men united to 'develop ways of exterminating the porcupines which were destroying crops'[33], but later on it incorporated satirical dramas attacking people with extraordinary behaviour. For example, in one of the performances they ridicule a greedy and selfish husband who before giving some meat to his wife makes sure that he has counted all the pieces. Performance of such a drama in a community is an effective way of portraying social problems. No rural community will tolerate greedy and selfish characters especially when we consider the importance of co-operation, trust and respect for one another. The success of community development depends on the participation of every member in the process of identifying needs and priorities, deciding on what strategies to use to attain them and their full involvement in the implementation. The *Bunungule* therefore serves as a device for addressing some negative elements which may impede the community development process.

On the other hand, the Makunduchi people of Zanzibar among other art forms, have a popular satirical folk narrative called *Panjimaro*. It has been performed by famous actors such as Bwana Shaka Mussa. *Panjimaro* is a satire which ridicules power mongers in society who are prepared to do any task to further their individual ambitions. In this tale, Bwana Shaka portrays Panjimaro as a man of unbelievable energy and strength, but he is stupid because he agrees to carry out impossible duties for a king. He kills a lion, catches a dangerous poisonous snake and fights a war alone. He is eventually awarded the kingship. Bwana Shaka uses jokes and irony, and his performance is a symbolic representation of the misuse of power and authority for individual ends. In many communities there might be people with similar qualities to those of the king who would order similar Panjimaros to commit various crimes for purely personal gains. A performance of *Panjimaro* serves as a social alarm warning community members to be aware of such characters.

Looking at the Wazaramo, who are mostly found in Dar es Salaam and Coast regions, we find that they have the *Mkwaju ngoma*, a ceremonial dance for any happy occasion. During the performance, the artists present short satirical dramas ridiculing 'stupid' characters in the community. One of their famous satires is about a jealous husband who says 'goodbye' to his wife so many times that he is always late to go to work. One day, the man is asked by his friends to accompany them on a hunting expedition. Before setting off, he requests his wife to give him her vagina for him to carry. He wants to be sure that during his absence no one would fool around with his wife. As the wife knows that such a thing is impossible but finds it difficult to tell her husband so, she decides to shave her pubic hair, wraps it in a piece of cloth and gives it to her husband. In the forest, the man with his friends happen to cross a river and in the process of swimming he loses the 'vagina'. The man starts to cry and when his friends ask him as to what is the matter, he tells the story. His friends burst out laughing at his stupidity and foolishness.

Indigenous models of Theatre for Development in most parts of Africa have a lot of similarities. It is interesting that the Wazaramo tale of the lost vagina also exists within the Bamana people of Mali but with a slightly different version. Okpewho recounts: 'A woman goes to the river to wash clothes. While there, her vagina accidentally drops off and gets lost in the water. A woman goes to the river to wash clothes. While her husband cries rather disconsolately and his two sons undertake to go and find the lost organ. Having found it, they contend with their father over the right to put the vagina back to where it came from, arguing that after all the organ was their former home. The old man eventually gives in, and the play ends with the boys thrusting their hands under their mother's waist-cloth.'[34] Such examples carry invaluable philosophy and wisdom relevant to community members. The humour which is contained is an 'appetiser' for the people to grasp the educational content of the presentation. While laughing at others because of their selfishness, stupidity and other weaknesses, there is at the same time a catharsis for negative elements of our behaviour.

In 1979 when I was a village manager at Kirare village in Tanga region, I witnessed a spontaneous performance of *Ndombi* dance by a group of women addressing an immediate problem. It was a public holiday for Independence celebrations and various dance groups were entertaining the public. The village 'government' had organised some lunch for all the artists. All the groups were served with the exception of the Ndombi performers. However, this was not known to the leaders until the group performed their dance with a message contained in the following song:

Solo:	Those those those (*pointing to the leaders*)
Chorus:	Those
Solo:	Those those those
Chorus:	Those
Solo:	They are sitting in the office
Chorus:	Those
Solo:	They have locked the door
Chorus:	Those
Solo:	They are eating some food
Chorus:	Those
Solo:	While we are starving
Chorus:	Those[35]

When the women were performing we were in the village office eating because we had thought that everyone had already eaten. The moment we heard the song, we had to make arrangements for the artists to get some food.

The examples given from the different ethnic groups indicate that people have always used their indigenous forms of theatre for specific social reasons. People have always felt the need to do something whenever a problem arose and one of the most effective ways of communication have been theatrical performances. I agree with Mlama that 'there has always been close relationship between theatre and the welfare of the society. As an ideological tool it has the potential to effect change and to contribute towards bettering living conditions.'[36]

If Theatre for Development is 'meant to promote the people's own theatre practice and to use it to advance their own concerns instead of merely parroting the ideas of the ruling class'[37] it is imperative for its practitioners to enable the people to 'use the theatre which they already possess.'[38]

The very specific indigenous forms, i.e. satirical dramas, have, in my opinion, the potential for handling social, economic and political issues. Seriousness in addressing serious social issues may not necessarily yield positive results. 'Laughter can be a powerful tool of criticism'[39] and a central political weapon. The argument that Theatre for Development concentrates on the process rather than the product needs to be re-addressed. Indigenous models of Theatre for Development have both artistic qualities and relevant contents. In order for people to be attracted by theatre it must be not only relevant to their social reality, but worth watching. The urban-rural 'expertise invasion' on Theatre for Development tends to overlook some of these qualities. That is why some of the best humorous indigenous forms such as *Machonja* and *Nkhuda* have had little room in Theatre for Development practice in Tanzania.

Machonja

Machonja is a popular satirical drama form in Rufiji. Rufiji is one of the six districts of Coast region. The other districts are Bagamoyo, Kibaha, Kisarawe, Mafia and Mkuranga. There are 'six ethnic groups inhabiting Rufiji district, presently, Mndengereko, Mngido, Mmatumbi, Mpogoro, Mmwera and Mkichi. Mndengereko living in the north is far the largest,'[40] and it is within this ethnic group that *Machonja* will be examined.

Machonja among the Wandengereko means 'something that is funny' and can cause laughter. Deriving from this meaning, *Machonja* is a theatrical presentation of a social problem or a character who transgresses socially accepted values or standards. The performers use a lot of jokes with actions which are funny as a technique to relax the audience so as to put across the intended message. Whenever there is a performance, a lot of people turn up. This is not only due to the funny gestures, actions and some of the animalistic movements of the performers, but also to the relevance of the issues and problems being portrayed. It is one of the reasons why *Machonja* is a popular form of theatre among the Wandengereko.

For many years *Machonja*, among the Wandengereko, had been a powerful medium of community education. Undesirable behaviour such as excessive drinking, adultery, theft, witchcraft and laziness were condemned through *Machonja*. Such problems were considered as 'deviations from the social norms, values and standard behaviour of the society'[41]. Therefore, something had to be done as a remedy. However, during the mid-seventies, 'government leaders in the district put a ban on all *Machonja* performances because they were seen as immoral'[42]. This was due to their sharpness of language and openness in some of the actions. For example a character playing an adulterer would have a very long penis hanging down to his ankles.

The mid-seventies in Tanzania was a period in which national morals and ideals regarding culture were being questioned by the government. During this time, many Tanzanians, particularly young people, were very much affected by western influences such as wearing mini-skirts and bell-bottom trousers. The National Executive Council of the Party, then the Tanganyika African National Union (TANU) considered such 'behaviour' to be a result of indecent literature and films. Some of the books which were thought to have contributed to the problem included Charles Mangua's *Son of Woman*, David Mailu's *After 4.30* and *My Dear Bottle*, and Dr. Mamuya's *Jando na Unyago*. The language used in the books was similar to that used in pornographic literature. The approach used to convey the messages was against Tanzanians morals and beliefs on what and how should someone communicate his or her ideas to the public. Due to these factors, the books have been and are still banned in Tanzania. So the Rufiji district leaders' ban on the *Machonja* was in line with the decisions of the central government. Many performers decided to abandon the art. As a result, there is only one active group in the whole district, the Mbungi group of Bungu village from which most of my information was gathered.

Bungu is a village situated along the main road between Dar es Salaam and Lindi. It is approximately one hundred and twenty kilometres from Dar es Salaam and about thirty kilometres from Kibiti which is 'the major trading village in the district'[43]. The Mbungi group is composed of seven artists. The division of roles is made in such a way that two are singers, two are drummers and the remaining three are performers. The group's main function is to perform *ngoma za mashetani*, that is, spirit possession dances. The *Machonja* is just an accompaniment as we shall see later. In most African ethnic groups there prevails a belief that some people have got spirits which possess them at certain times. These spirits need to be appeased from time to time, a failure to carry out this ritual may cause some harm not only to the individual but to the entire community. As Kerr observes: 'Spirit possession dances were a form of physical and/or mental therapy by which a spirit medium attempted to cure his/her patient by means of extended dancing in the course of which both the patient and the doctor were possessed by powerful spirits.'[44]

According to mzee Abdallah, 'every year they have a season which usually begins four months before Ramadan.'[45] Most people in Rufiji district are Muslims and Ramadan is a time for observing the 'fast', repentance and prayers. They usually receive requests from different villages out of which they prepare a tour schedule. Their programme would normally start with the spirit possession dances at midnight. All the patients would be gathered and dances and songs would be performed until dawn. Everybody would then have a rest until 3.00 in the afternoon. At that time, the performance would resume not for the spirit possession dances any more, but for *Machonja*. In fact, the overnight performances, apart from healing the patients, serve as publicity for the *Machonja* performances.

The performers never prepare their skits before arriving in a community. After arriving in a community, they would usually conduct a brief research on current problems and main characters. For example, if they discover a problem such as laziness, they would find who are the lazy people in the community. This identification of characters involved in the problem helps them in their presentation. They would take some of their characteristics such as the way they move, talk and laugh, and portray them but in an exaggerated and distorted manner in order not to make it so obvious to the audience. Their methods of collecting data are mainly participant observation and discussions. However, according to Mzee Abdallah, 'some people sometimes volunteer to give us information about some people with disgusting behaviour such as adultery'[46]. He recalled one woman in one village who explained about her husband who was very jealous. She went on explaining that her husband had four wives and he would always trace their whereabouts from morning to evening. As a result he had no time to do productive work. For example if two of his wives went to fetch some firewood and the other two went to attend a sick person in another village, he would shuttle between the two villages. From such a situation, they presented the following *Machonja*:

A jealous man suspects his wife that she makes love with a certain man whenever she goes to the shamba. One day he decides to make an ambush. He quietly goes to the shamba before his wife and hides in a heap of grass awaiting to be burned. It was a normal habit for the wife to go to the shamba in late afternoons to burn off the grass as a process of preparing the shamba for the planting season. The husband's idea was that his wife would meet the man and during their affair he would catch them red- handed. The wife arrives at the shamba and it so happens that she begins to burn the same heap in which the husband is hiding. Suddenly, she notices someone emerging from the burning grass. She recognises him. He is her husband. Without delaying he quickly says that he was just teasing his wife trying to recall childhood memories of hide and seek games.

According to Mzee Abdallah, where ever they performed this piece, there was laughter all the way through and the most striking moment was when the husband emerges from the grass and his spontaneous reaction of pretending to tease his wife. 'The spectator laughs out of a sense of relief and superiority because he is not in the uncomfortable situation himself.'[47] By laughing at the husband, the audience view themselves as clever and intelligent. This is where the learning process occurs because what the audience is doing is attributing to themselves a high status and to the husband low status. One could anticipate that after such a performance, the audience would have obtained a message with regard to people who have similar behaviour to the jealous husband.

Another example from the group's repertoire is concerned with the problem of laziness:

Two lazy men have a habit of paying visits to their relatives in such a way that they would start with one relative at the beginning of the month and finish with another relative at the end of the month. As the relatives lived in different villages, it was not easy for them to get a clue of what was going on. However, one of the relatives sensed something. He had been keeping records of the visits for a period of time and discovered a sort of an organised schedule which alternated each month. He then concluded that, what his relatives were doing was nothing but lazing around. Their visits were an excuse for not working. So he decided to teach them a lesson. During their next visit, he asked his wife to cook the visitors' favourite meal which was a mixture of cooked bananas with meat. He told his wife that when serving them she should spare some of the food because he would like to use it for something very important. After the visitors had eaten and went to bed, at midnight, the man took the extra food and went to the visitors' bedroom. He quickly took off their trousers and underpants and put on each one's buttocks some food. Having done that, he dressed them and off he went. Before dawn, one of them woke up and noticed something unusual on his buttocks. He realised that he had shat. He woke the other in order to narrate the embarrassing story only to discover that the other one had the same problem as well. As they could not stand such an embarrassment, they decided to sneak away immediately. Since then, they never visited anyone because the story was narrated to the other relatives .

A *Machonja* presentation combines music, mime, movement, dialogue and story-telling. The music is used as a connection between scenes and also as a background when the action is mainly dominated by movement. A story-teller would introduce the performance and then from time to time would comment on what is going on. The language used is a mixture of Kindengereko and Kiswahili.

The effectiveness of *Machonja* is not only related to community education through laughter, but also to the power to attract many people in the community. The administrative structure of villages in Tanzania is such that before plans and policies are implemented, a village general assembly must be convened. The biggest problem facing most villages in Tanzania is poor attendance at such meetings. When I was a village manager, I used to organise some dance performances during meetings as a way of attracting people. All the agendas would be discussed and resolutions passed and then would follow the dance performances.

Theatre for Development is a planning and a decision making process which requires the participation of community members. 'For the people to participate meaningfully in actions of development, they must be aware of the problems, their causes and the need for possible solutions.'[48] As a popular form of theatre in Rufiji district, with its potential to ameliorate behaviour through laughter, *Machonja* has a crucial role in contemporary Theatre for Development practice.

Nkhuda

The *Nkhuda* which will be examined is of the Wazigua ethnic group. I am trying to be specific because *Nkhuda* is a popular satirical drama among the Wabondei and Wasambaa ethnic groups all of which share a common origin within the Bantu speaking group. Their customs, manners and language have more similarities than differences.

The Wazigua are found in Coast, Morogoro and Tanga regions. In Coast region, they live in Bagamoyo district . In Morogoro, they are to be found in Morogoro rural district, especially in Turiani division. In Tanga, they have occupied the districts of Handeni, Korogwe and Pangani. They are believed to have migrated from the north via Kondoa district and settled in their present areas. During this immigration, all the three ethnic groups were one but later on they split into different groups, each settling in a different environment.

The Wabondei (deriving from a Swahili word 'Bonde' which means a valley) settled in the valleys of Tanga region and the Wasambaa (from a Swahili word 'Sambaa' meaning to spread) settled in the mountains of the region. These mountains are famously known as the Usambara mountains. For the Wazigua, it is believed that the initial name was either Ziguha which means literally, 'they have taken them' (the countries) or Zigula which means 'they had not merely taken them, they had bought them by blood through fighting'[49].

Nkhuda means 'a penalty for restoration of a lost dignity caused by swear words spoken against someone. It is a method of maintaining respect and discipline among all community members regardless of age, sex or status'[50]. *Nkhuda* is a special dance drama performed after someone has insulted another person by swear words. It does not matter whether the one insulted is a child or adult. The important thing is that the one who insults and the insulted must be related to one another as father and son or mother and daughter or uncle and nephew/niece, and there has to be someone to witness from the insulted side. For example, if my uncle insults me, at least my sister or brother or cousin must be around to bear witness. She or he will then spread the news to all the brothers and sisters and *Nkhuda* will be performed.

Sometimes *Nkhuda* may be performed without necessarily arising from a spoken insult. An indecent act may provide grounds for *Nkhuda*. For example if a mother exposes the nudity of her baby in front of her father or mother, that will be taken as a physical insult. It would be interpreted that it is the grandparents' nudity which has been exposed. *Nkhuda* is performed during the night and it is supposed to be a surprise to its audience, the ones being penalised. From the moment the insult has happened, the news must spread very quietly among the performers because if the culprits discover that plans are underway for *Nkhuda*, they may quickly apologise before the performance by paying either some money or a hen, a duck, etc. In most cases, this amount will not be as much as would be collected if the performance took place. Due to this reason, its preparation process must not be done openly.

Once the insult has happened and the news has already spread, the performers will create characters, compose songs and a cast identified so that it is clear as to who is going to do what. The nature of the insult will determine the structure of the performance. If, for example, the source of the insult was a mother who exposed her baby's nudity, during the performance that will be the central point of attack. The main characters may even go as far as exposing their nudity as well. During the performance, performers move from one house to another. These are the houses of the culprits and at each house songs in vulgar language will be sung accompanied by improvisations based on the insult. As the songs, movements and gestures are rough and to the point, the culprits would usually hurry up to pay the 'apology fines'. In fact this is the main reason why the performance must be done during the night because children would have already gone to bed. The humour in the performance creates an atmosphere in which the culprits, much as they are being attacked and paying the apology fines, enjoy the jokes and join in the laughter. The audience are happy and relaxed but at the same time absorb the educational content of the performance.

In 1981, I participated in *Nkhuda* which was performed at my home village, Maurui. The village is about eight miles from Korogwe (the district headquarters), along the Tanga-Moshi railway. What follows is a description of the situation which resulted into *Nkhuda* and the way it was performed:

My elder brother was getting married. Two days before, our aunt insulted our young brother. Idirisa is his name. Idirisa was playing with his toys and was very much involved in the game. This made him smile from time to time. Our aunt happened to be passing nearby Idirisa. When she saw him smiling, she commented, 'Idirisa, are you smiling because you are so excited of the wife you will be having in two days?' When aunt was saying these words, our sister who was coming from the market was a witness. The words were taken as an insult to us because considering the age of Idirisa, who by then was thirteen, they did not mean anything to him. So the message of the insult was conveyed to all the sisters and brothers and during the evening, Nkhuda was performed. Our elder brother was the main character dressed like a bridegroom with a fake erect penis big enough to be seen by everybody. We sang, danced and improvised moving from house to house. The songs were full of swear words. The dancing and the improvisations were very embarrassing as they symbolised consummation of marriage. This is illustrated in the following song:

SOLO: Idirisa what are you laughing at!

Boys what are you laughing at!

Girls what are you laughing at!

CHORUS: We are waiting for a new vagina![51]

The effectiveness of *Nkhuda* can be seen from the fact that after one performance, a long time will pass before the next one. Through jokes and laughter, community members are not only ridiculed but warned so as to be careful not to commit such offences in future. There are some similarities between the *Nkhuda* and the *Titi-ikoli* of the Bakweri people of Cameroon. *Titi-ikoli* is a satirical drama of women against men. It is performed in order to restore women's dignity after they have been insulted by men. 'These insults may take various forms but the most typical envisaged is the accusation that the sexual parts of women smell. A Bakweri woman so insulted before a witness must call out the other women of the village. Converging on the offender dressed in vines, they demand immediate recantation and a recompense of a pig, plus something extra for the woman who has been directly insulted. The women surround him and sing songs which are often obscene by the allusion, and accompany them by vulgar gestures.'[52]

Quite obviously the men would not stand such a shameful performance, watching a group of women in which their wives, sisters, sisters-in-law and old women are dancing. So they would run away leaving behind the one who uttered the insult. This act of running away indicates a learning process taking place manifested by the action of moving away from the event.

There may be a problem of using *Nkhuda* in contemporary Theatre for Development practice. As pointed earlier, the interval between two *Nkhuda* is normally very long because its performance must arise out of a specific reason and also due to its effectiveness. It is quite obvious that within a contemporary situation, there have to be some slight changes in its use. One possibility is that it can be used as a form but with a different content discussing contemporary community problems. For example, a Theatre for Development project that is being carried out among the Wazigua dealing with problems such as forced marriages, early pregnancies and rape could utilise *Nkhuda* both as a form and method of posing the problems for discussion. This will not only make community members participate confidently and comfortably in the problem solving process, but also demonstrate to them how their form could be used to address contemporary issues.

Machonja and *Nkhuda* are examples of the many indigenous satirical dramas to be found in many ethnic groups in Tanzania. There may be some limitations in using satires as they, in most cases, tend to be negative, ridiculing and making fun of people. However, Lihamba sums up: 'The comical, ironical elements are used not only to elicit laughter but to give man a different perspective of his activities. The sense of play which is inherent in all performances is heightened. Incongruities of behaviour, thought and ideas are shown through the words and actions of the performances. The desired result is a realisation of pretensions and satirised vices in order to attain corrective measures.'[53] If people can be offended because their negative behaviour have been laughed at in public and out of that laughter they make attempts to change those behaviour, then satire would have worked effectively.

Conclusion

Various communities where Theatre for Development projects have been carried out do fail to sustain the Theatre for Development process especially when 'experts' are absent from the field. The major factor contributing to this problem is that there is a gap between the people with their knowledge and experiences of their indigenous forms as pedagogical institutions and the academic expertise and 'intellectualism' on Theatre for Development. This gap has resulted into under-utilisation of indigenous forms of theatre in many projects. Indigenous models of Theatre for Development must be seen in terms of their social functions and limitations. Most indigenous theatre forms are moralistic and instructive as they do not promote debate. However, indigenous satires are seen to be not only powerful in raising controversial issues but also attractive to community members due to their utilisation of humour as a tool for criticism. The debate of the two indigenous satirical dramas, *Machonja* and *Nkhuda* in Tanzania generates powerful communication media for promoting social criticism and strengthening peoples' participation in the process of community development.

Theatre for Development is both an artistic event and a planning and decision making process .The community development process involves critical analysis of some complex issues and ideas and its success depends on the participation of every community member.

Indigenous forms of theatre have one major limitation. In most cases, they just raise issues but do not go to the extent of making community members collectively discuss the issues or problems for possible solutions. Their use in contemporary Theatre for Development practice should be geared towards enabling people 'to raise issues, find solutions and spark-off collective action.'[59] In fact there is a need to incorporate some of the contemporary techniques of audience participation that are widely used by Theatre for Development practitioners. For example, freezing a dramatic action at certain crisis moments enables people to have deeper analysis of their reality. In other words, there has to be a reconciliation between what is good and applicable from both the academic approach and the indigenous models of Theatre for Development.

Notes

1 Ministry of Health. Kenya. A guide to effective communication, (A pamphlet by the division of Health Education), p. 1.
2 Nasskau, L *Community Theatre and Cultural Democracy*, (MA dissertation, School of English, University of Leeds, 1986), p. 7.
3 Plastow, J *African Theatre and Politics*. (Amsterdam: Rodopi, 1996), p. 196.
4 Nyoni, F *The Role of Children in the Theatre for Development in Tanzania*. (MA dissertation, School of English, University of Leeds, 1994), p. 6.
5 Kerr, D *African Popular Theatre*. (London: James Currey, 1995), p. 81.
6 Bakari & Materego. *Sanaa kwa Maendeleo*. (Dar es Salaam: Amana Publishers, 1995), p. 81.
7 Mlama, P *Culture and Development: The Popular Theatre Approach in Africa*. (Uppsala: Scandinavian Institute of African studies, 1991), p. 97.
8 Masitha, H *New Directions in Theatre for Development in Lesotho*, (PhD Thesis. University of Leeds, 1995), p. 135.
9 Masitha (1995), p. 136.
10 Loukie Levert & Opiyo Mumma (editors) *Drama and Theatre: Communication in Development*. (Nairobi: Kenya Drama/ Theatre and Education Association, 1995), p. 12.
11 Brecht, B as quoted by Epskamp, Kees in *Theatre in Search of Social Change: The relative significance of different theatrical approaches*. (The Hague:Centre for the study of Education in Developing Countries, 1989), p. 49.
12 *Encyclopaedia of World Drama volume S-Z4*. (New York: McGraw Hill Book Company, 1972), p. 35.
13 Mitchel, L *Staging Pre-modern Drama: A guide to production problems*.(London: Greenwood Press, 1983), p. 128.
14 Kerr (1995), p. 7.
15 Mlama. (1991), p. 97.
16 Lihamba, A . *Politics and Theatre in Tanzania after the Arusha Declaration*. (PhD Thesis School of English, University of Leeds, 1985), p. 11.
17 Hussein, I. As quoted by Plastow, J *African Theatre and Politics*. (Amsterdam: Rodopi, 1996), p. 46.
18 Ngugi wa Thiongo. *Decolonising the Mind*. (London: James Curry, 1986), p. 3.

19 Mlama. (1991), p. 98.

20 Plastow, J *African Theatre and Politics*. (Amsterdam: Rodopi, 1996), p. 71.

21 Mlama. (1991), p. 98

22 Mlama. (1991), p. 106

23 Mlama. (1991), p. 139

24 Mlama. (1991), p. 157

25 Mlama. (1991), p. 203

26 Nyoni. (1994), p. 7

27 Mlama. (1991), p. 127

28 Kerr, D *African Popular Theatre* (London: James Currey, 1995), p. 2.

29 Mlama, P *Culture and Development* (Uppsala: Nordiska Afrikainstitutet, 1991), p. 209

30 Mlama. (1991), p. 63

31 Epskamp, K Learning by Performing Arts. (The Hague: Centre for the study of Education in Developing Countries, 1992), p. 13

32 Lihamba, A The *Performing Arts and Development* in Utafiti Journal vol. vii no. 1 (pages 30-38) (Dar es Salaam: Faculty of Arts and Social Sciences), p. 86

33 Songoyi, E *Commercialisation: Its Impact on Traditional Dances. (B.A* Dissertation. University of Dar Es Salaam, 1983), p. 13

34 Okpewho, I *African Oral Literature. (Bloomington*: Indiana University Press. 1992) p. 277

35 Materego, G& Bakari, J. *Sanaa kwa Maendeleo*. (Dar es Salaam: Amana Publishers, 1995) p. 17&18. Translation mine.

36 Mlama (1991) p. 38

37 Mlama (1991) p. 106

38 Mlama (1991)

39 J. Plastow. *African Theatre and Politics.* (Amsterdam: Rodopi, 1996) p. 193

40 Havnevik, K. J. *Analysis of Conditions, Priorities and Growth in Peasant Agriculture, Rufiji District-Tanzania.* (Bergen. 1987), p. 16

41 Bame, N. K. *Come to Laugh. African Traditional Theatre in Ghana.* (New York: Lilian Berber Press, Inc. 1985), p. 57

42 Mrisho, M. (Former District Cultural Officer for Rufiji.) Discussion held in Bagamoyo in June, 1994.

43 Havnevik, K. J. *The Limits to Development from Above. (Uppsala*: Nordiska Africainstitutet, Sweden. 1993), p. 76-77

44 Kerr, D. *African Popular Theatre.* (London: James Currey. 1995), p. 45

45 Mzee Abdallah is the Leader of the Mbungi group. Discussion held in August 1996 at Bungu village.

46 Mzee Abdallah. (August, 1996)

47 McDowell, D. M. 'Clowning and slapstick in Aristophanes' in Redmond's (editor) *Themes in Drama. (Pages* 1-13), p. 12

48 Lihamba, A. *Politics and Theatre in Tanzania after the Arusha Declaration.* (PhD Thesis, school of English, University of Leeds. 1985), p. 455

49 Ntemo, F.N. 'Some Notes on Ngulu' in *Tanganyika Notes and Records* 45, (1956). 15 - 19 (p. 17).

50 Kabelwa, S. S. (A Zigua elder in Handeni town.) From a discussion held in Handeni in December, 1994.

51 Translation mine.

52 Caplan, P. (editor) *The Cultural Construction of Sexuality. (London*: Routledge, 1987.), p. 115

53 Lihamba, A. 'The Performing Arts and Development'. in *Utafiti Journal vol. vii no. 1*, pp. 30-38. Dar es Salaam (Faculty of Arts and Social Sciences. 1985), p. 37

54 Breitinger, E ,Ed. *Theatre for Development.* (Rossdorf: Tz Verlagsgeseuscheft. 1994), p. 11.

Popular Theatre and Development Communication in West Africa: paradigms, processes and prospects

Bala A. Musa

Introduction

If one agrees with Shakespeare that, 'All the world's a stage; And all the men and women merely players'[1], it stands true that life in West Africa is a highly animated scene in which the daily struggle for survival is the major part played by every character on that stage. The gruesome living condition of most people in Africa, even if exaggerated by the mass media, is a nightmare compared to those of the developed world. Hagher rightly observes that, 'as Africans and West Africans, our survival now is our greatest challenge'[2]. Boafo also paints a vivid picture of the constant survival drama in the region as he observes that:

> Most black African countries have emerged from the struggle for political independence only to find themselves in a seemingly intractable liberation struggle against an inadequate supply of food, water, shelter, and clothing; an ever-increasing population growth rate; low life expectancy, high infant, mortality; and continuous political and economic strife, creating millions of political and economic refugees in Angola, Ethiopia, Mozambique, Somalia, Sudan, the sahel region, and Uganda, among others[3].

Although, the scene being described here is the real life experience of the people, it has often found expression in staged performances that pre-date modern times. There is a unique interplay between life as the art of survival and popular theatre's role in the struggle for a higher quality of life in West Africa. This is underscored by the fact that despite the difficulty of existence in the region, life seems to be a constant celebration for the people. West African culture is full of rituals that celebrate successes and tragedies. Among the various ethnic groups in West Africa, weddings as well as funeral ceremonies are celebrated elaborately for days or even weeks. Planting and harvest seasons, abundant rain and draught, phases of human development from the cradle to the grave are all punctuated by rituals, ceremonies, and festivities. Every event and experience is interpreted in terms of its symbolic cultural context.

As Conteh-Morgan rightly states regarding theatre in franco-phone Africa, 'relations between individuals assume the character of relations between role-players (social personae) and social life becomes an elaborately choreographed play, characterized by play-acting (as in stage drama) rather than by spontaneous and natural interaction'[4]. In West Africa life is a moving drama and drama is a staged reality. When the community performs rituals to purify the land of any individual or communal crimes, though symbolic, they are taken seriously because the future of the community is believed to be at stake. This constitutes the background for analysing the trends, processes and prospects of West African theatre and its role in rural and national development. Part of the concern here is to explore the theoretical map and assumptions that undergird this relationship, and to show how various development communication paradigms have informed the different approaches to West African Theatre for Development.

Changing social, economic and political circumstances within and outside West Africa have also influenced the processes and directions of popular theatre as well as development communication. The complementary and, sometimes, conflicting roles and expectations of parties involved in Theatre for Development has often posed a significant challenge. From Cotonou to Bamako, and from Dakar to Niamey, experience has shown that government officials, community development experts, professional actors and academics embark on development efforts with different agenda. This also compounds the problem of finding the suitable model for integrating and assessing the relationship between popular theatre and development communication. This work seeks to critique the various perspectives, highlight their contributions and address the prospects of popular theatre as a development communication agent.

Concepts and Paradigms of Theatre and Development

The solution proffered to a given problem is often pre-empted by the way the problem is defined. It is often said that a problem is half solved, once it is appropriately diagnosed. Although, the phenomena of popular theatre, development and communication are easy to recognize, they pose a significant challenge when it comes to conceptualizing their essences, functions and relationships. The same is true of most social reality. This chapter uses a historical-critical approach to analyse the theories and practices of communicating development through popular theatre in the West African context.

In the context of this essay, popular theatre refers to staged performances of dance, drama and rituals geared toward the masses of the society as primary audience. Mda distinguishes between literary theatre and popular theatre in the sense that the former is usually the product of a professional playwright, relies on a detailed script, and is performed by talented actors for a passive audience. The latter, on the other hand, is created by the group, using improvised materials with the audience as participants[5]. Mda further identifies three forms of popular theatre namely, the agitprop approach which uses professional performing teams that address local issues, with no participation from the audience. Examples of the agitprop theatre in West Africa include the Ogunde Theatre in Nigeria, the student mobile theatres in Sierra Leone, Ghana and Togo. A second is the participatory theatre approach which is 'produced by and for the people with spectators'[6]. There is grassroots participation but the 'experts' are in control. Community theatres in Burkina Faso, Mali and Benin republic are typical cases.

The third, and most popular among development communication experts is the conscientization approach. This is a format where the people are involved in developing and staging the play. There is maximum collective participation, with all members of the community included in the cast in some form.

Preference for a particular approach to Theatre for Development over another is often a function the prevailing paradigm of development. There are several definitions, conceptualizations and paradigms of development. Contemporary development traditions date back to the efforts by Western powers to integrate Third World nations newly emerging from colonial domination into the global industrial culture[7] . Development in the western model was conceived in terms of modernization. Effort was geared toward transforming the 'underdeveloped' nations of Africa, Asia and Latin America from traditional/agricultural to capitalist/industrialized societies. Europe and North America's transition from rural to urban economies was adopted as the blueprint for growth and development.

Modernization approach, therefore, became the dominant paradigm dictating political, economic and social strategies for Third World development. Rogers identified the fundamental elements of the this paradigm to include an emphasis on economic growth as indexed by a nations gross national product and per capita income; reliance on industrial technology; respect for exogenous innovation and expert initiative; and a blame-the-victim attitude toward less developed societies[8].

From the 1940s to 60s, this paradigm provided the framework for development research and projects in Africa, Asia and Latin America. It had a compatible view of the role of communication in development, which is the linear or transmission model. Development communication in this context reflected the 'macro level' approach where 'problems were identified and solutions offered at the higher levels of the government. Information and other inputs were then channelled down to local communities. Participatory or autonomous development by local communities was considered slow, inefficient, and more often than not, unlikely"[9]. The mass media was the preferred means of communication under this development approach. The flow of information was unidirectional, i.e. from 'expert' sources to 'lay' receivers, with little or no provision for feedback. The view of communication for development imbued the westernization approach. It reflects Shannon-Weaver mathematical model of communication which emphasizes the mechanical process of transmitting message signals, as well as Laswell's system of information flow[10].

Due to its 'big media' bias, theatre, and popular theatre in particular, was not integrated into the development communication mix. Radio, television and newspapers received precedence because policy makers and development practitioners were concerned with reaching the highest number of people within the shortest possible time with their ideas of the good life. In both anglophone and francophone West Africa, much effort was directed toward promoting modern lifestyle, which was narrowly defined to mean western culture. The mass media therefore served as an appropriate tool for cultivating a taste for foreign goods and services.

For decades, the diffusion of innovations theory remained the guiding model for development communication. In those limited contexts where theatre was employed as a means of development communication, the plots centred around the benefits of adopting foreign technology and methods. Plays like Cockcrow at Dawn, which was a leading network show in Nigeria portrayed the rewards of adopted new agricultural technology. The development expert who visited the farmers had ready solutions to hand down to the rural populace. Characters such as 'Mr and Mrs . Bello' who according to Rogers[11] were early adopters were hailed, while the likes of 'Uncle Gaga' who were skeptical 'laggards,' and always insisting on being consulted were vilified as unprogressive[12].

Although the linear communication model is becoming less popular among development communication experts, it has not been completely abandoned. Theatre is rarely used as an organ for development communication within this school of thought. Whenever theatre is employed, it is mostly the agitation and propaganda (agit-prop) approach. More often than not, the intention is to control and manipulate rather than promote dialogue. This exhortational communication style reflects the emphasis on mass mobilization rather than conscientization among West African leaders[13]. Mass mobilization as a medium for development communication suggests that the leadership sets the agenda, owns the project, and dictates the strategy. Communication, or more appropriately, information, is geared toward selling the vision of the ruling elite and recruiting the support of the masses for a set task.

The variations of the dominant paradigm such as the dependency, capitalization and trickle-down approaches, along with the linear information model, have philosophical, cultural and practical appeals to those that favour such strategy over others. Philosophically, it reflects the western, capitalist, and progressive world view that emphasizes control (of human and material variables), certainty (of procedure and results), and closure (of the project through deadlines). Despite the growing popularity of democracy in the sub-region, many political regimes and social institutions in West Africa are essentially authoritarian. From military dictatorships in Nigeria, Gambia and Sierra Leone, to reincarnations of military regimes in civilian garbs in Benin, Ghana, Burkina Faso and Togo, as well as one party, life-time regimes in Gambia, Chad and Mali, the political culture is the same. One that does not encourage dialogue and consultation at the grassroots. Also, it is considered more convenient and less expensive to transmit information to the people in a linear, top-down fashion.

The pitfalls of the modernization approach have been extensively discussed by development communication experts and scholars[14]. To mention but a few, such drawbacks include the absence of feedback, disregard for local initiative, cultural insensitivity, and the perpetuation of dependency among others (Defleur; McQuail, Rogers' *Communication and Development...*, Schramm, Musa, Haule, Eisenstadt, Boafo).

Beltran provides an alternative definition of development that encapsulates this new approach, often seen as the self-reliance paradigm. According to him, national development is a directed and widely participatory process of deep and accelerated socio-political change geared toward producing substantial changes in the economy, the technology, the ecology, and the overall culture of a country, so that the moral and material advancement of the majority of its population can be obtained within conditions of generalized equality, dignity, justice and liberty.[15]

The self-reliance paradigm provides a different perspective for looking at the nature of development, development communication and the role of popular theatre in development. The essential ingredient in this definition, which is also the hallmark of the new paradigm, is that it sees development as 'widely participatory process.' Other elements include the view of development as not just structural or material change, but also social and cultural transformation. This conceptual framework of development has had far reaching implications for development communication in general and popular theatre in particular.

Emphasis on grassroots participation in the development process naturally demands a two-way flow of information. True communication, the sharing or exchange of ideas, occurs in this context. The dialogic model of communication as theorized by Christians[16] as well as the Westely-Maclean model[17] flourishes here. Dialogic communication recognizes the right of both parties in a communication situation to be heard. Both communicators are active speakers and listeners interchangeably. This is the appropriate atmosphere for mutual participation. The participatory approach to development communication requires community or grassroots input in the decisions that affect their welfare. Dialogic communication posits that communicators have an ethical duty to consider every source a receiver, and every receiver a source of information. The Westley-Maclean model suggests that communication is incomplete unless there is feedback.

Servaes (*Communication for development*) notes that participatory development communication model requires a focus on people as moving force, micro-scale (local community) planning and implementation as opposed to national level control. Servaes advocates for a holistic approach that respects the culture as well as the environment, and the sharing of power among the people instead of concentrating it in the hands of the elite. According to this school, 'the participatory model emphasizes on the local community rather than the nation state, on monistic universalism rather than nationalism, on spiritualism rather than secular humanism, on dialogue rather than monologue, and on emancipation rather than alienation.'[18]

Mda calls the relevant popular theatre approach for this development model the participatory method[19]. According to him, the characteristics of participatory popular theatre are that the people are involved in the process of producing and presenting the play. There are actors/actress as well as spectators. However, the community or grassroots people do not control the process. Their involvement and participation is regulated by the experts. In other words, there is both flexibility in terms of improvisation and input from the people; but there is also control by the authorities who try to steer the performance in a pre-determined direction. Also there is closure through post-production evaluation and discussion. This is also called the problem solving model[20].

Participatory Community Development Theatre in West Africa is said to reflect traditional performance styles, be inclusive or participatory in nature, use native languages and use simple plots. Examples of such theatre include the forum theatre the Atelier Theatre Burkinabe (ATB) in Burkina Faso, the Asafo folk theatre in Ghana, the Nyogolon troupes in Mali and the Samariya theatre associations in Niger.[21]

A third, and somewhat more radical, approach to development is the 'culturalist' paradigm.[22] Variously referred to as the democratic model[23], the conscientization model[24], and ecological model[25], this paradigm takes the propositions of the participatory development a step further. It is concerned with the empowerment and emancipation of the people from all forms of dependence. It is distinguished from the other forms in that it focuses on the liberation empowerment of each person in the community. It can be rightly said that while the modernization paradigm emphasizes development at the national scale, and the participatory approach is concerned with the local community, the cultural or eco-development paradigm is targeted at the individual. This paradigm proposes that mental colonization does more to keep the people under bondage than economic and political domination. For the people to be delivered from their oppressed and marginalized position calls for a mental awakening. This is the view is well stated by Harbison in saying that the progress of a nation depends first and foremost on the progress of its people. Unless it develops their spirit and human potentialities, it cannot develop much else - materially, economically, politically, or culturally. The basic problem of most of the underdeveloped countries is not a poverty of natural resources but the underdevelopment of their natural resources.[26]

In other words, mobilization of human resources should precede the mobilization of natural resources. National development is best measured by individual progress or the opportunities thereof. Nerfin also assumes a similar stand in which 'development is seen as a whole, as an integral, cultural process, as the development of every man and woman and the whole and woman.'[27] The doctrine of conscientization from which this development emerges is credited to Latin American educator, author and revolutionary activist Paulo Freire. According to him the greatest enemy of the oppressed is that internalization of the status-quo imposed by their oppressors as the natural state of affairs. Their unquestioning acceptance of their second-class status is what cripples them from any progress and development. Conscientization, the process of awakening and empowering the marginalized segment of the society begins with 'critical and liberating dialogue' by the oppressed.[28]

According to Freire, true freedom or liberation cannot be granted to the people by their oppressors nor won for them by others. Instead they must earn it by their effort. Conscientization calls for a do-it-yourself approach. Former President of Tanzania, Julius Nyerere reinforces the need for a self-reliance approach to development. Nyerere argues that, people cannot be developed; they can only develop themselves. For while it is possible for an outsider to build a man's home, an outsider cannot give the man the pride and self-confidence in himself as a human being. Those things a man has to create in himself by his own actions. He develops himself by what he does; he develops himself by making his own decisions by increasing his understanding of what he is doing, and why; by increasing his own knowledge and ability and by his own full participation - as an equal - in the community he lives in.[29]

As earlier noted, Freire identifies dialogue as the appropriate communication approach. Expounding on the works of Freire, Buber and Ellul, Christians asserts that 'dialogic theory represents a revolutionary alternative which goes to the root and rethinks the problems from ground up and inside out. Genuine dialogue is to our humanness what blood is to the body: When the flow of blood ceases or becomes diseased, the body dies; when dialogue stops, love disappears and hate and resentment are born.'[30] That is an apt description of what has happened to development in West Africa and other Third World regions as a result of the mechanistic, monologic communication approach used in the past three decades by policy makers and development experts.

Some scholars argue that African nations are not developing at all.[31] Such view is borne out of the fact that in most West African countries, indices such as employment rate, literacy rate and life expectancy have continued to reflect a trend of deterioration rather than development. This is because, the structures imposed on these societies based on the modernization approach have only led to unplanned urbanization, inflation and mass unemployment.

There is a theatre-for-conscientization approach compatible with the conscientization model of development. This format employs maximum participation. According to Mda, this kind of theatre involves every member of the community in the production with no spectators. The outcome is not controlled or pre-planned. Most of the set is improvised. Popular theatre for conscientization is still a novelty in West Africa. Although, theatre played a significant role in public conscientization during the struggle for independence, such theatre do not entirely qualify as theatre for conscientization because the majority of the people were rather spectators than participants.

At best, what approximates theatre-for-conscientization is the forum theatre where maximum participation from the members of the community at all levels of the production and presentation are encouraged. It however, requires much effort on the part of facilitators and grass-roots community members to achieve maximum results. Mda rightly notes that it is 'a time-consuming process, which works over a long period.'[32] However, with careful planning and deliberate effort, its potentials can be harnessed for social transformation in West Africa. Ways of attaining this will be discussed later.

Trends and Processes

Theatre in contemporary West Africa is a blend of traditional folk, western classic, urban popular and rural forum approaches. This mosaic also tells the story of the evolution of theatre in the region. Each has arisen from different roots and serves different purposes. As development communication tools, these approaches compliment themselves by making-up for the weaknesses inherent each.

In West Africa, traditional folk theatre has served the function of disseminating information, socialization, education, and entertainment. To some extent, traditional societies have used folk theatre to promote social values. However, its potential for conscientization have not been fully exploited. It is inappropriate to argue, as Mda seems to suggest, that they do not lend themselves as effectively to development communication as other approaches. In reality, theatre- any form of theatre for that matter- is simply a vehicle for communication. The result and kinds of effect achieved from each approach is a function of the philosophy of the users. The same can be said of all the other approaches.

As mentioned earlier, all these forms of theatre interact and shape the industry in some form or another. Distinctions have been made between these modes of theatre based primarily on the production and consumption processes.[33] The potential for mass participation available to community members, either as producers or consumers is used as the criterion for distinguishing between different theatre forms. To understand the roles and potential of each of these theatre forms for development in West Africa, we may examine their relationship using a three-dimensional scale showing audience participation in production, audience participation in consumption and aggregate audience reached (fig. 1). All these factors are essential in assessing social transformation or development. As Beltran's definition stated earlier, development requires a 'deep and widely participatory process of change in various aspects of the community. We find that popular theatre which, in essence, is a hybrid form or middle-ground amalgam of traditional and modern theatre provides the best forum for development communication.

Popular theatres rely on 'local people as performers, use local languages, are performed free of charge in public places, and deal with local problems and situations with which everyone can identify.'[34] Such theatre embraces various forms of performing arts such as drama, singing, dancing and story-telling. It is usually available to and comprehended by most members of the society as a group and as individuals (Leis). Popular theatre constitutes a bridge between folk theatre which belongs entirely to the people but lacks a mobilization agenda and the literary theatre which seeks to exhort from outside without reaching the local population. Literary theatre belongs more to the category of what Etherton calls 'art theatre.'[35] According to him, art theatre underscores the creative process, as opposed to popular theatre which gives priority to the consumption process.

This section of the essay looks at the trends in production and consumption patterns in West African popular theatre and the impact this changes has had on development communication. Significant underlying currents that have shaped these trends include changes in overall popular culture, commerce, technology, politics, aesthetics and intellectualism.

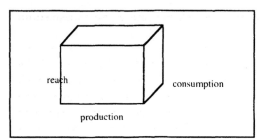

Figure 1. Model interactive plane for factors in development communication theatre.

'Glocal' Tension

I borrow the term 'glocalization,' (which describes the attempt to adapt to the global environment while staying sensitive to local needs as an appropriate label fro the situation I am about to describe). West African popular theatre as a part of the social system, flows in the general direction of the popular culture. That means there is an interwoven relationship between theatre and changes in the culture as a whole. Like any other, West African society is not static but dynamic. The hub of West African culture today is not the pure and unadulterated traditional society. While there are vestiges of undiluted folk culture at the grassroots level, the general landscape reflects a pseudo-modern society that is a confluence of modern western and traditional African culture. This cultural mix finds expression in music, attire, food, religion and communication media, among others. There is a two-way flow of cultural products between rural communities and urban centres. However, urban centres tend to set the pace for popular culture. And urban centres are essentially 'metrotropic' in their orientation. There cultural tastes are biased toward the global metropolies of Europe and North America. Yacouba Konate portrays such image in this observation of the Ivoirien capital: 'Abidjan, pearl of the lagoon, the Manhattan of Black Africa whose influence by the end of the 1970s is not only commercial, economic and political . . . [but] is becoming more and more cultural.'[36]

As one travels across the region, this image is duplicated in almost all urban centres in terms of cultural as well as architectural tastes, depending on each country's colonial history. Other cities such as Cotonou, Lagos, Bamako and Accra are all in the race toward become the cultural stop-gap between the rural communities and Paris, London or Las Vegas. According to Domatob, the trend in Black Africa is one of cultural synchronization, nay imperialism - a situation where North American and European pop culture is fast driving 'black Africa's incredibly rich . . . tradition' into extinction.[37] This trend is attributed to the sophistication of foreign cultural products, colonial legacy, neocolonialism, socialization, technical dependence and international trade. Some of these will be examined in detail later.

Beside neo-colonialism, the creation of a popular culture space that is a blend of different elements of traditional culture along with Western culture is more or less a historical necessity. Since all West African nations are multicultural and multi-ethnic in composition, the urban centres constitute the melting point for various cultural elements. Without this function, each of the cultures will remain in isolation. In other words, there is a negative and a positive side to the marriage between traditional folk culture and western culture as the building blocks of contemporary West African popular culture.

In the same vein, West African theatre vacillates between western literary style drama and African folk theatre. From pre-colonial theatre which was essentially a communal activity with each community member participating as a role player, the pendulum swung to the other extreme of literary drama during and immediately after the colonial era, where educated African artists became thrilled with the new medium as a means of self-expression. West African literary artists perfected the art of communicating to their compatriots through drama. Great playwrights and actors have emerged from the region.

Playwrights and dramatists have tried to advance the collective consciousness by addressing the issues they consider as detrimental to the progress of the society. It is noted that 'Francophone drama is drama of social and political combat, of revolt and not of the lyrical celebration of man's tragic destiny. It believes in the need to awaken the spectator to his condition in an effort to provoke him to action.'38 This sets the tone of the role of literary drama and playwrights in development communication in West Africa. Many see their mission as that of awakening the spectator. This is visible in the themes that appear most frequently in their plays. It is pursued both from the point of historical characters in Charles Nokan's *Abraham Pokou*, Wole Soyinka's *Death and the King's Horseman* and Atta Koffi's *Le Trome d'or*; and in contemporary socio-political themes such as Segun Oyekunle's *Kataka for Sufferhead*.

Literary theatre has played a significant role in drawing attention to the social and political ills of the society. The writers and dramatists are usually the intellectual and educated class who are equipped to interpret and analyse the issues at stake. Their unique positions enable them to draw from local resources such as traditional poetry and oral literature as well as English or French literature in communicating their messages.39 They have served as the voices of the community. A genre of popular theatre that has been very functional in articulating public sentiment is 'protest theatre.' This is the forum where most artists criticize unpopular governments or government policies.

The contribution of literary theatre as a channel for development communication resides in both the form and the content. As a form of communication, its creative packaging makes it possible to address thorny and controversial issues in a less threatening manner. Theatre is able to expose activities and individuals in a way that would be difficult to accomplish otherwise. Through role-playing and characterization, social and political commentaries and criticisms are delivered in a veiled, yet effective, manner. Satires abound in this form of communication. In some way this helps to expand the horizon of freedom of expression, which is essential to the process of development.40

Under colonialism as well as modern dictatorships, theatre serves as an appropriate channel for anti-establishment communication that would not be permitted otherwise. That is not to say that playwrights and theatre artists have escaped with every form of criticism unscathed. Many have been arrested, jailed, and harassed by various authorities that find their works detestable.41 Despite such experiences, the fact remains that they have constantly further pushed the envelope of free speech and social criticism by their works.

Also, literary artists have been able to reach a wider (national and international) with their works than folk artist and folk theatre is able to achieve. Since most West African playwrights produce their works in English or French, they are able to reach a wider audience. In such multi-lingual and multi-cultural national environments, it is very significant that they are able to bridge such communication gaps through these lingua franca.

However, some of these merits of literary theatre and other trends in popular culture also constitute a drawback to development communication. For instance, modern drama's potential for reaching a mass audience likewise alienates a large population of uneducated local folks. Literacy level is still very low in West Africa. It means, therefore, that by catering to the minority literate class, the playwright is unable to effectively reach the local populace. Literary theatre is still an elite phenomenon in West Africa. This only limits its influence as a medium of communication. Since true development requires mass participation from the community, a medium that enjoys a wider reach is certainly most appropriate.

Literary theatre or drama also sacrifices local issues in the effort to appeal to a wide audience. It has been noted earlier that participatory development demands local initiative as well as micro-level planning and execution. Since literary artists write and produce their works with not just the local audience in mind, they must of necessity address larger issues that their diverse audience can relate to. In doing so, they can only pay limited attention to pertinent local issues. Whether this heterogeneous audience is defined geo-politically (regional national or international) or demographically (age, gender, education, income, etc.) it becomes impossible to serve the needs of any particular community. Levels of development differ among regions of a given country, and much more so between countries. In the same way, the issues that need pertinent solution vary according to local situations. Any attempt at defining or solving the problems from a universal perspective would certainly diminish its effectiveness. That can certainly be said of literary theatre in West Africa today.

Etherton has noted that works of African playwrights such Soyinka, Rotimi, Maddy, Nyerere and Kasoma drip with 'transpositions and adaptations' from Shakespeare, Eliot, and Brecht among others.[42] This also has implications for effective communication in the sense that the audience will not be able to identify with the context, content or characters in the play. Although, theatre is mainly role-playing, the closer to real-life situations or personalities the play portrays, the more meaningful it is to the audience. In this regard, forum theatre and folk theatre have and edge over literary theatre as development communication tools.

Commerce

Another trend that has shaped West African theatre is the increasing influence of the commercial sector. The debate over the relationship between art and commerce is not based on a notion of exclusivity or incompatibility. The two have always co-existed in every culture. However, the distinction lies in what stands out as the overriding motive or driving force. Theatre and other arts forms such as music, painting, novels, and sculptures can serve different purposes from both the perspective of the source and the receiver. From the point of the consumer, theatre may serve one or more of the following functions: entertainment, education, information and socialization. To the source, theatre may be a means of communication along the lines identified above, a forum for the expression of talent, and/or a means of living.

The extent to which the business motive or factor dictates or is perceived to dictate an art form is what distinguishes a commercial from a non-commercial art. Here again, as the rest of the culture goes, so goes the performing arts, theatre inclusive. Na'Allah has shown that traditional folk arts was essentially non-commercial in that performers did not place any premium on financial remuneration as the objective for their performance. However, with the increasing monetization of the society, West African theatre has faced the challenge of adapting to a pseudo-capitalist environment. Commercial theatre is one in which the profit motive obviously dictates form and content. Consumers pay some fee to participate in the fare. Based on this analysis, Barber[43] suggests the following criteria for classifying African arts: Those produced and consumed by the people; those consumed but not produced by the people (commercial); Those consumed but not produced by the people (non-commercial); Those produced but not consumed by the people (commercial); Those produced but not consumed by the people (non commercial).

To varying degrees, West African theatre spans this whole spectrum. There are performing groups, troupes and theatre traditions in West Africa that represent each shade. Theatre in pre-colonial West Africa belonged mostly to the first category - produced and consumed by the people. This was either commercial or non-commercial. The performers did expect some financial or material reward but that expectation did not constitute the driving force. They owed no allegiance to any funding agency and were capable of adapting their content to suit the need of the audience. This tradition is fading away as the commercial interest in theatre is becoming the overriding factor. Vestiges of this tradition still exist among concert parties, dancing groups and popular theatre troupes in West African countries like Ghana, Niger, Cote' D'Ivoire, Nigeria, Benin and Togo. The prevalence and role of the various forms has been discussed extensively.[44]

The concern at this point is that the last two decades or so have witnessed an increase in the influence of capital in the arts, including theatre, in West Africa. The entertainment industry has since become big business, particularly in urban centres. It is noted that even traditional folk theatre has come under strong commercial influence. The artists are using their skills to amass great fortunes.[45]

The role of capital in West African theatre as it relates to development communication has been both redemptive and detrimental. Etherton observes correctly in stating that 'the very commercialism, which seemingly gives the group its initial autonomy, eventually undermines its ability to provide the mass urban audience with a continuing and developing analysis of their social conditions from their point of view.'[46]

The commercialization of popular theatre has enabled the performing teams to dedicate their time to the art. They do not have to engage in theatre as a pass-time activity while making a living elsewhere. That is supposed to have translated into greater productivity and better performance by theatre professionals. The flip side of the coin, however, is that its allegiance is no longer to the people. The interest of financiers and wealthy patrons has in many cases overridden the public interest. That is a natural consequences of commercialization. The purpose of development communication is best served when theatre is produced and consumed by the people at little or no cost. Control and accessibility are the key factors here. Maximum participation demands that the people be involved in the process both as producers and consumers. The form of theatre that guarantees participation for the highest number of people in terms of production, consumption and reach is the most functional for development communication. Experience has shown that the profit motive tends to act as dividing line between those who can and those who cannot participate in the fair.

Technology

Technology is used here in a narrow sense to signify the hardware or tools that aid the preparation, packaging and dissemination of communication messages. In the case of theatre, these include stage design, lighting, costumes, and modern mass media such as radio and television.

These 'interposed channels'[47] have their advantages and disadvantages. One advantage is their potential for reaching a wide spread audience. This is essential for national development in may West African countries with large land mass, tortuous geographical terrain, and a widely diversified audience.

The mass media are capable of transcending these barriers and reaching the people simultaneously. Little wonder then, that radio and television drama are very popular in West Africa. The marriage between commerce (advertising) and technology (mass media) is very favourable to both parties. Theatre artists ride on their coat-tails to reach an audience otherwise only imaginable. Policy makers have used this combination as a means of prosecuting social development and political campaigns. Radio and television soap operas and sitcoms feature exhortational themes and prosocial messages designed to promote positive behaviours such as nationalism, healthcare, literacy, and work ethics on the one hand, and to discourage anti-social behaviours like tribalism, corruption and drug trafficking on the other.

While modern technology provides the potentials for reaching a wide audience, the reality remains that television, for instance, has not reached the level of saturation necessary to make it a popular medium. It was reported, at the turn of this decade, that the nearly one-half billion inhabitants of sub-Saharan Africa own only a negligible 3.4% and 0.6% of the world's radio and television receiving sets respectively.[48] If the global economic index is anything to go by, it can be rightly said that this figure has further deteriorated rather than improved. In other words, if policy makers are concerned with reach, the mass media which are still elite phenomena are not effective channels for development communication.

Some governments in the region have tried to bridge the gap by providing community centres for public radio listening and television viewing. However, certain problems still remain. The structures of the modern media pose peculiar challenges to consumers. Trenholm notes that, different media not only call for different levels of technical sophistication, they also require different cognitive skills. . . To understand a TV drama, for example, viewers must be able to decode visual messages; they must accustom themselves to the languages of camera angles, editing, scene composition, and so forth, just as directors must learn to tell a story in visual terms.[49]

Until the mass media becomes easily accessible and consumable by the audience, it can not serve as an effective organ of development communication. If it overcomes the hurdles of reach and consumption, its corporate nature makes it almost impossible for the entire or majority of the community to control or participate in the production process. Because the production process of radio and television drama are capital-intensive, money will continue to dictate the content.

The only mediating factor is that the broadcast media in Nigeria are largely government-owned. Their primary goal has been to serve the state rather than make profit. Public service programs are often aired not because they are popular or profitable but because the authorities consider them relevant for the nation.[50] The draw-backs to this will be discussed later. Suffice it to say that the ineffectiveness of the broadcast media in prosecuting development communication campaigns either through drama, music or other forms is a structural default. As well intentioned as those programs may be, the fact remains that the mass media do not easily lend themselves to popular participation. This applies to all segments of the process. In both radio and television drama, the actors' performance is largely constrained by the technology and the imaginative abilities of the directors and producers. Modern technology may have opened new vistas of creativity that is beyond what is possible on the stage. Manipulations of lighting, space, time and moods are being done in radio and television drama that are difficult to accomplish otherwise. Those also raise new challenges of their own.

The price of these benefits that new communication technology bring to theatre is the loss of autonomy, control and community participation. Unlike folk or forum theatre which are very flexible in their production and presentation process, the format of West African popular theatre on radio and television are predetermined by the medium of communication. In radio drama, for instance, it is not functional to have a large cast. The fewer characters there are in a radio drama production, the easier it is for the audience to understand the play.[51] This is a limitation of the medium. The same applies home videos, film and television. The implication is that these technology favour the creative process. McLuhan's popular line that 'the medium is the message' holds true here in more than one sense. Other than the technical constrain in shaping the message, the medium influences the content and its perception. By their very nature, radio and television empower the producers and directors at the expense of the consumers. Any form of theatre that privileges the few over the many (in both the production and consumption process) is less than ideal for development communication.

Also, the ownership and management philosophy of the broadcast media in West Africa has given them the image of being government propaganda organs. Certainly, the government does interfere with the media, but the phobia that the public has toward the media because of this perceived government control diminishes its effectiveness for development communication.

Politics

The interface between theatre and politics in West Africa is also intriguing. Over the years, politicians and theatre artists have had cordial as well as antagonistic relationships. In principle, politicians and theatre artists are partners in progress in that they each perform roles that are vital to the welfare of the society. A healthy social environment requires the political class as well as the public voice. Ideally, the government exists to protect civil society and provide a conducive atmosphere for social interaction. Theatre serves many communication needs that lubricate the wheel of civil society.

The flavour of modern popular theatre in West Africa is highly tainted by the history of anti-colonial struggles. The bitter experience of colonialism left a sour taste in the mouth of nationalists who used various media, including theatre arts, to confront the system. In both anglo-phone and franco-phone West Africa, budding artists found inspiration in local and national politics. Politics and politicians therefore, became a recurring theme for writers and performers. However, it was a cat and mouse relationship. The theatre was generally critical of government by focusing on abuse of power, corruption and inefficiency. Political authorities on their part were suspicious, if not resentful, of revolutionary theatre. Many artists were censored by the authorities.

The place of theatre in the political process of post-colonial nations of West Africa warrant a closer look. Whereas nationalists of all shades- academics, writers, politicians and entrepreneurs-viewed each other as partners in the liberation struggle, the relationships changed once the initial goals were attained. Politicians expected the artists to use their communication and persuasive abilities in furthering the goals of nation-building. Unfortunately, the definition of nation-building as prescribed by the political class did not synchronize with that of the artists. Political office holders seemed interested in using the various communication organs in promoting their political agenda rather grassroots-oriented development. The existence of costly ultra-modern national theatre in the capital cities and the sponsorship of national theatre troupes are evidences of these governments' commitment to the arts.

Certainly, the political authorities subscribe to the importance of theatre in the process of national development. However, the political culture determines the amount of influence that the arts and other communication media can exert on nation-building. Theatre as a form of speech needs a democratic atmosphere in which to thrive. This is very much lacking in almost all West African countries. Different shades of political dictatorship abound in the region. There is little or no tolerance for dissenting views by those in authority. Freedom of expression, a necessary index of national development, is a scarce commodity in all West African countries. Instead, the leaders seek to control the content of public communication, including theatre arts. The thinking among African leaders is that the regulation of free speech is necessary in view of the numerous problems associated with underdevelopment. The view among power holders is that freedom of expression is a luxury that developing countries cannot afford at this stage of their struggles in building new nations. The implication is that politicians and bureaucrats become intolerant of criticism. Therefore, only theatres that are supported by the government are those considered favourable to the ruling class. This negates the theatre's role in development communication. Public officials tend to perceive the theatre as a medium for political propaganda.[52] In a critique of the use of drama for socio-political mobilization in Nigeria, Obuh shows that such attempts to use the theatre to fulfil the narrow agenda of the ruling elite often fails woefully. Part of the function of theatre as a means of development communication is that it uses humour to express the views and sentiments of the community-both the pleasant and unpleasant aspects.

Government intervention in subsidizing theatre groups and facilities does influence, howbeit in a subtle way, the kind of plays the theatres produce. This also applies to forum and community theatre when the government is seen as an active player on the scene. Based on the framework of production-consumption-reach, subsidized theatre guarantees the highest reach. But it does not guarantee participation in production decisions. Certainly, when the government holds the purse, it also pulls the lever. And experience has shown that political regimes in non-democratic and less developed democracies are not committed to conscientizing or empowering the populace.[53]

It is important to say that theatre artists are not always neutral observers of the political scene. Playwrights and dramatists in West Africa are mostly educated members of the elite. They are generally well-informed and interested in the political goings-on. Their political plays are usually true commentaries on the political situations in their countries. However, these political plays raise questions as to their intentions. West African theatre artists will better serve their society if they perceive their mission as serving the people as well as the government. In other words, they need to provide the two-way dialogue by which the people can speak to the rulers and the rulers can talk to the people. It will amount to a disservice if the artist pays exclusive allegiance to either one party, or worse still, if the artist enters the political arena as a gladiator with a personal political agenda or as the defendant of a particular interest group.

Professionalism

Mention must be also be made of another trend in West African theatre that has had a significant impact on development communication namely, the role of experts or professionals. The trend toward professionalism in both the arts and other sectors of the society has created a challenge of defining the relationship between the various publics of theatre as a mode of development communication. From the foregone, several parties can be identified as having vested interest in Theatre for Development in West Africa. These include the play wrights and dramatist who are mostly intellectuals and/or professional artists; the public or general populace for whom they write or perform; the governments that want to use the theatre to propagate their political agenda as well as regulate what is offered by the theatre; the commercial sector that sees the theatre as a business opportunity; and recently, the Non-Governmental Organizations that want to employ the theatre in promoting specific development campaigns.

The result of this interaction is a growing complexity that makes theatre no-longer the domain of the village fool or the court jester.[54] The audience has grown in sophistication, the writers and actors have sharpened their skills over the years and the stakes have been raised as a result of trends in commerce, politics and international communication. Of significance to development communication is the emergence of professional writers and actors in the region.

Since independence, various schools and colleges have introduced theatre studies. Scholars and students in these programs have worked hard to elevate the quality of their productions. Initially, the move seemed to be toward high art where English and French plays were performed by this intellectuals. Then came the era of local plays that were basically adaptations of Western models, as mentioned earlier. The trend has plateaued with a curious blend of traditional folk theatre and Western literate theatre forming the dominant popular theatre in West Africa.

The current emphasis on alternative media for development communication has brought these groups together in the bid to respond to this need. Departments of theatre have been vanguards of community/forum theatre. This is a positive development in that their training and talents are brought to bear on the community shows. In many West African countries, these artists are willing to learn from the local community. They exchange ideas with the local populace thereby enriching their performance. Non-Governmental Organizations do sponsor College theatre groups to local communities to help organize forum theatres that address subjects relevant to the community.

Even in the rural communities, folk artists are become professional actors, singers and dancers.[55] They are no longer loafers 'living at the edge of social life.'[56] Many are successful artists who make their living, a good one for that matter, from their acting careers. The various forms of theatre in West Africa have developed to a level that makes them to command attention, respect an followership.

Inherent in this scenario is the problem of finding the right balance between the orientations and concerns of the various groups that are committed to Theatre for Development. In a situation like this, there are bound to be differences in perception and expectation. For instance, academics tend to be ideological in their approach to problems. This world view is bound to frustrate bureaucrats, business folks and the local community who may be more interested in a quick fix to the problem. Non-Governmental Organizations that sponsor forum theatres tend to have short-term focus on specific needs and projects that have to be addressed and the results quantified. The same applies to the roving theatre groups, be they students or other professional performing troupes. They do not have the time to carry out extensive ethnographic studies prior to the production, neither do they have the ability to follow-up on the after-math of the production. This situation may not serve the local community effectively.

Financial gain is an attendant element of professionalism. As stated before, this liberates as well as binds the artist. With financial autonomy, the theatre artist is able to commit more to the career. Artists can be more proficient and prolific if they do not face financial difficulties. However, the goal of financial success does work against the community service agenda that is so vital to development communication. Once money becomes the concern of any development project, the emphasis shifts from effectiveness to efficiency. While it is good to properly manage the resources, the need to conserve resources may lead to sacrificing vital aspects of development communication projects.

More importantly, professionalism privileges the expert over the lay person. Many at times the experts forget their mission. They may think of perfecting their skills as the primary concern of the moment. This will rob the recipients of the goal of the project. In short, reliance on experts and professionals has the danger of marginalizing the community. Unless the professional is good at facilitating and moving the people along, tensions will arise. While the local community may be seeking to participate, the professional may feel undermined. In West Africa, the effort is being made to arrive at an appropriate working relationship.

By professionalizing the theatre in West Africa, the practitioners hope to improve the quality of their productions. It is rational to expect better performance from trained artists. Critics of West African theatre agree that the standard of performance of the artists has continued to improve. However, in striving to earn the respect and recognition of the society, some writers and actors seem to equate professionalism with elitism, high-tech and higher pay. These are not bad in themselves. But when they are pursued at the expense of community service theatre, they become detrimental to the cause of development. In assessing the overall impact of this trend, we return to our fundamental premise by asking how has professional theatre helped in promoting development communication in terms of conscientization, participation and access to cultural empowerment by the average person in society?

Prospects and suggestions

On the whole, one can predict better days ahead for the theatre industry in many West African countries. That does not automatically imply greater prospects for the role of the theatre in development communication. If this line of argument did not appear obvious from the preceding analysis, it needs to be restated: that the fortunes of theatre arts in West Africa are not synonymous with the role of theatre in development. Whereas the former is a function of the transformations in the national and international social, political and economic arena, the latter depends on the vision and philosophy of the artists and development experts.

The author's faith in the continual growth of modern theatre in West Africa is based on the recent trend in the direction of better training, public awareness and demand for quality (art) products, the pressure to excel in view of foreign external competition, and the global prospect of political democratization. These developments have potential prospects for growth in theatre arts as well as the entertainment and communication industry in particular. Does this also mean better days ahead for development communication theatre. Not necessarily so.

As seen from the preceding discourse, the political, economic and social trends that have influenced West African theatre are underlain with both positive and negative consequences for development communication. If development communication is to receive the appropriate treatment in the agenda of West African theatre it cannot come by accident or omission. All the parties concerned have to make a deliberate effort toward placing it on the stage. This is because Theatre for Development (conscientization) is not the natural preference of commercial sponsors gunning for profit, politicians seeking cheap publicity or artists wanting national and international recognition.

Before making any suggestions regarding the best approach for the preservation and promotion of development communication in theatre, it is appropriate to acknowledge positive developments presently occurring in this direction. Two groups that have championed the cause of Theatre for Development in West Africa are the Universities/Colleges and Non-Governmental Organizations. Their forum and community theatre approaches are still the closest they have gotten toward popular participation and mass conscientization. With proper funding, these projects hold promise of significant contribution toward community education for development. Although it is externally initiated, the visiting teams try to bond with the local community by encouraging their maximum participation. This affords the populace the opportunity to play active parts in deciding the process and outcome of the performances.

As far as popular theatre goes - both on stage and in the media- the growing influence of capital, technology, western cultural imperialism and the privatization of the mass media should be of genuine concern to development communication experts and agencies. This is because the underlying interest of the institutions that are promoting these changes sometimes conflicts with the new paradigms of social development. The profit motive, the massification mentality and the efficiency approach are at variance with the cultural paradigm of development.

The reality is that these trends cannot and need not be arrested. There are some positive elements in them. The only challenge is that inherent in these trends is the seed of the kind of progress that is antithetical to holistic development. The future of development communication in West African theatre lies in a pro-active approach that responds to the changes with a set agenda. Without a well articulated philosophy of development communication theatre, other competing purposes will take precedence over development concerns. Freire's conscientization and cultural empowerment approach has been identified as a starting point for this philosophy. The individual and the local community need to focus of planning and performance.

The appropriate view of development will ultimately lead to a relevant communication model that suits the need for participation, interaction and multiple exchange. It is therefore suggested that the triadic model of communication is most appropriate.[57] This is most suitable for development communication theatre in that it is dialogic, participatory and transactional at the same time. That is the highest level at which optimum participation in production, consumption and reach of Theatre for Development can be attained. According to Woodward, 'triadic communication as participation moves thinking even more decisively away from a transmission model.'[58] The three ingredients of the triadic communication model that makes it a suitable alternative are (a) the symbolic material/material environment in which communicative action occurs (*the theatre or related medium*), (b) the process, motivations, and satisfactions that underlie or characterize communication (*placing premium on development goal over profit, style or professionalism; or making the art functional*), and (c) the products that develop out of it (*events that empower the people*).[59] (italicized parentheses mine). The event of theatre should be the message. The more people that can be involved in the event the more effective is the performance as a medium of development communication.

Also, keeping up with the changes in the environment and for the purpose of deriving maximum benefits from them calls for prioritizing of values. Until now, Theatre for Development has been portrayed as non-profitable, too instructional and unpopular. This perception, rightly so or not, has led artists to not give it much attention. Those artists who participate in it seem to do so out of a sense of duty rather than a personal choice. There is the need to bridge the gap between success in the acting career and public service. This can be done if the artists are willing to sacrifice some fame and fortune in order to serve the public interest. At the same time the government and private institutions that are committed to development programmes should seek ways of making Theatre for Development reasonably lucrative and popular.

Presently, priority career goals for West African artists seem to be fortune, fame and fun. And since development communication theatre does not offer much of these, few are attracted to it. One would therefore suggest that all interested parties work at closing this gap. Development communication theatre can be made attractive and financially rewarding if the organizations that sponsor other forms or theatre are willing to support it. This also has to be done in a way that its autonomy is not sacrificed.

Academic institutions and Non-Governmental Organizations can promote artists' interest in development communication theatre by instituting awards for writers, actors and social workers who have contributed significantly to Theatre for Development. These and other strategies will provide some motivation to the experts.

Theatre for Development which has been rightly described as 'infortainment' (Brown) calls for a delicate balance between education and entertainment. Whenever it tilts too heavily to either directions, the purpose is defeated. Playwrights, actors and facilitators should endeavour to make Theatre for Development popular and functional. This can be achieved by using culturally relevant symbols and drawing from local experiences. The needs of the local audience should take precedence over the needs of the global market.

The problem of creating harmony between the numerous parties engaged in such projects can be solved if the interest of the audience is given priority of place. In the present atmosphere where various academics, bureaucrats, artists and corporate organizations all have stakes in the performances and presentations, their is every tendency for clashes of interest. The best way to resolve such is for each party to be committed to doing whatever is in the best interest of the people for whom the development effort is intended.

The potentials for participatory development communication in the social, economic and political trends that affecting West African theatre are enormous. But like other natural resources that abound in the region, they have to mined and harnessed to serve the desired purposes. Where this is left undone the weeds of banal entertainment and ideologically barren consumer taste will continue to clutter the landscape thereby hindering the process of development.

Notes

1   William Shakespeare, *As You Like It* in *The Complete Works of William Shakespeare* ,

2   I. Harry Hagher, 'African Literature in Search of Policy: The Case of West African Drama and Theatre'. In E.N. Emenyonu & C.E. Nnolim (ed.), *Literature and Languages Studies in West Africa*, Ibadan: Kraft Books Ltd, 1994, p. 141.

3   S.T. Kwame Boafo, 'Communication Technology and Dependent Development in sub-Saharan Africa'. In Gerald Sussman and John A. Lent (ed.), *Transnational Communications: Writing the Third World*, Newbury Park: Sage Pub, 1991, p. 103-104.

4   John Conteh-Morgan, *Theatre and Drama in Francophone Africa*, Cambridge: Cambridge University Press, 1994, p. 9-10.

5   Zakes Mda, *When People Play People*, Johannesburg: Witwatersrand University Press, 1993, p. 47.

6   Ibid. p. 50.

7   Srinivas Melkote, *Communication for Development in the Third World: Theory and Practice*, Newbury Park: Sage Publications, 1991, p. 37.

8   Everett Rogers, *Diffusion of Innovations*, New York: Free Press, 1962, p. 57.

9   S. Melkote, op. cit., p. 57.

10 Em Griffin, *A First Look at Communication Theory*, (3rd Ed) New York: McGraw-Hill Co. Inc, 1997, p. 22-23.

11 cf. Everett Rogers, *Diffusin of Innovation*. op. cit.

12 cf. Ebele Ume-Nwagbo, "Cockcrow at Dawn': a Nigerian Experiment with Television Drama in Development Communication'. In *Gazette*, 37 (1986), pp. 155-167. See also, William J Brwon, 'The Use of Entertainment Television Programs for Promoting Prosocial Messages'. In *Howard Journal of Communications*, 3.3-4 (1992): pp. 253-266.

13 Alubo; Uche and Musa. See Bala A Musa, 'Effective Communication as a Tool in Mobilizing Rural and Urban Communities'. In Davis S.M. Koroma (ed.), *Community Participation and Rural Development in Nigeria*, Maiduguri: University of Maiduguri, 1991, pp. 44-60.

14 The literature on new perspectives has grown significantly in the last two decades and could be examined in other contexts.

15 Beltran, Luis Ramiro. 'Rural Development and Social Communication: Relationships and Strategies.' *Communication Strategies for Rural Development*. New York: Cornell University, 1974. 11 -27.

16 Christians, Clifford G. 'Dialogic Communication Theory and Cultural Studies.' *Studies in Symbolic Interaction*, 9 (1988): 3-31.

17 McQuail, Denis. *Mass Communication Theory*. London: Sage, 1983.

18 Servaes, Jan. 'Communication for Development in a Global Perspective'. IAMCR Conference, Sydney, 18-22 August, 1996. pp. 1-19

19 Mda. p. 50.

20 Morrison, Joy F. 'Communication Healthcare Through Forum Theatre: Egalitarian Information Exchange in Burkina Faso.' *Gazette*, 52 (1993), 109-121.

21 Conteh-Morgan, p. 81; Morrison, 'Feminist Theatre in Africa: Will it Play in Ouagadougou?' *Howard Journal of Communications*, 5.3(1995), 245-253.

22 West, Harry G. and Jo Ellen Fair. Development Communication and Popular Resistance in Africa: An Examination of the Struggle over Tradition and Modernity through Media. *African Studies Review*, 36 (1993), 91 - 115.

23 Beltran, *The Quest for Democracy*. p. 47.

24 Mda., p. 44-45.

25 Servaes, *Toward a New Perspective*. p. 67.

26 Harbison, Frederick. 'Education for Development,' *Scientific American* 209.3 (1963): 140.

27 Nerfin, M. *Another Development: Approaches and Strategies*. Ed. Uppsala: Dag Hammerskjold Foundation, 1977. p. 11.

28 Freire, Paulo. *Pedagogy of the Oppressed*. Trans. Myra Bergman Ramos. New York: Seabury Press, 1970.

29 Ibid. p. 60.

30 Christians. p. 18.

31 Opubor, Alfred. Mass Communication and Modern Development in Nigeria. Ed. Onuora Nwuneli. *Mass Communication in Nigeria: A Book of Readings*. Enugu: Fourth Dimension Pub., 1985. 154- 171.

32 Mda. p. 184.

33 Baber, Karin. 'Popular Arts in Africa.' *African Studies Review*, 30 (1987), 1 - 78. Etherton, Michael._*The Development of African Drama*. New York: African Publishing Co., 1982. Leis, Raul Alberto. 'The Popular and Development in Latin America.' *Educational Broadcasting International*, 12.1 (1979).

34 Mda. p. 46.

35 Etherton, op. cit., p. 190.

36 Land, F. Mitchell. 'Reggae, Resistance and the State: Television and Popular Music in the Cote D'Ivoire. *Critical Studies in Mass Communication*, 12.4 (1995), 438-454. p. 438.

37 Domatob, Jerry Komia. Black Africa's Cultural Synchronization Through Pop Music.' *Mass Communication in Africa: A Book of Readings*. Ed. Alkali, Mohammed N. et al. Enugu: Delta, 1988. 74 -83. p. 74.

38 Conteh-Morgan. p. 27, emphasis added.

39 Riley, Marie. Indigenous Resources in a Ghanaian Town: Potential for Health Education. *Howard Journal of Communications*, 4.3 (1993), 249-264.

40 Nyerere, Julius K. *Freedom and Development*. New York: Oxford University Press, 1973. Musa Bala A. 'Trends in Popular Culture and Freedom of Expression in West Africa.' Freedom of Speech Division, Speech Communication Association Convention, San Antonio, 20 Nov. 1995.

41 Etherton, *The Dilemma of the Popular Playwright*. p. 26.

42 Etherton. op. cit., pp. 102-142.

43 Barber. op. cit.

44 Karin Barber's classic article on Popular Arts in Africa details the state of each of this art forms in Africa today.

45 Na'Allah, Abdul Rasheed. 'Oral Tradition, Islamic Culture, and Topicality in the Songs of Mamman Shata Katsina and Omoekee Amoa Ilorin.' *Canadian Journal of African Studies*, 28 (1994), 500 - 515. Ogede, Ode. S. 'Songs from the Edge of Power: Interpreting Some Political Polemic of the Igede Etuh (Proverbs) Poet Ode Igbang.' *African Affairs*, 93, (1994) 219 - 231; and Etherton. op. cit.

46 Etherton. op. cit., 323.

47 Trenholm, Sarah. *Thinking Through Communication*. Boston: Allyn and Bacon, 1995. p. 279.

48 UNESCO. *Statistical Year Book*. Paris, 1989

49 Trenholm. p. 279. See also Birringer, Johannes. *Theatre, Theory, Postmodernism*. Bloomington and Indianapolis: Indiana University Press, 1991.

50 Musa, Bala A, Uses and Abuses of Development Media Theory in Sub-Saharan Africa: Critique of a Quasi Prescriptive/ Descriptive Theory. *Ecquid Novi*, 18.1 (1997, in press).

51 Umukoro, Matthew M. 'Radio Drama in the Nigerian Theatrical Scene: Promise and performance.' *Theatre and Politics in Nigeria*. Ed. Jide Malomo and Saint Gbilekaa. Ibadan: Caltop Pub., 1993. p 130.

52 Epskamp, Kees P. and Jaap R. Swart. popular Theatre and the Media: The Empowerment of Culture in Development Communication. *Gazette*, 48 (1991). 177-192. Hochheimer, John L. 'Organizing Democratic Radio: Issues in Praxis.' *Media Culture and Society*, 15(1993), 473-486

53 Epskamp. Swart and Morisson. op. cit.

54 Conteh-Morgan. p. 102.

55 Na'Allah and Ogede. op. cit.

56 Conteh-Morgan. p. 102.

57 Woodward, Wayne. 'Triadic Communication as Transactional participation.' *Critical Studies in Mass Communication*, 13 (1996), 155-174.

58 Ibid. p. 165.

59 Italicized parentheses mine.

Werewere Liking and the Development of Ritual Theatre in Cameroon: towards a new feminine theatre for Africa

Valerie Orlando

African drama, in much the same manner as literature, immediately following the end of colonialism, rarely expressed the needs and concerns of women. As in the case of politics, women found themselves virtually effaced, or at best beholders of minor roles, in the often militant and nationalist rhetorics of post-colonial literature and drama. It was clear that all over Africa the spoken and written word of the educated, political and intellectual *intelligentsia* of Africa would be dominated by masculine protocol. Postcolonial themes in the late 1960s early 1970s of West Africa, in particular, both in works of literature and drama, were masculine in nature reflecting the 'new man persona' Frantz Fanon had cultivated a decade previously in his anti-colonial theoretical text, *The Wretched of the Earth*[1]

The 'new man' of Africa within the postcolonial nationalist framework was a psychosexual phenomenon which, after years of oppression under colonialism, was freed both physically and psychologically to attain, 'full manhood or *wholeness* through revolutionary solidarity and the violent overcoming and expulsion of the colonizer'[2]. The affirmation of a collective revolutionary masculine ideal effaced individualism and the assertion of any feminine presence. As Fanon states in his text the ideal of the singular 'I' had no place in the unification of the population to fight *en masse* in favor of the African decolonization movement. Fanon's focus is on what the black man as a race feels in a position of subservience within both sexual and social boundaries; individual subjectivity has no place. Homi K. Bhabha maintains that Fanon's denial of individual subjectivity was pure intention and meant to collectivize the social struggle of black humanity; a sort of 'united we conquer, divided we fall' kind of reasoning. The extremity of this colonial alienation of the person - this end of the 'idea' of the individual - produces a restless urgency in Fanon's search for a conceptual form appropriate to the social antagonism of the colonial relation.[3]

There is no doubt that the militant rhetoric of Fanon and the general social struggle of whole peoples against colonialism within Africa would influence the thematic structures in Francophone drama. While critically acclaimed and heralded as solidifying the foundation for postcolonial African drama in Francophone Africa and the West Indies, early dramatists such as Bernard Dadié, Cheik Ndao, Jean Pliya, Guillaume Oyono-Mbia and Aimé Césaire left little place in theme or role for the voice of women. Historical themes (*Le roi Christophe* by Césaire) or epic folklore tales where masculine heros such as Chaka of the Zulu nation (both the 1956 version, *Chaka*, by Léopold Sénghor and later Tchicaya U'Tamsi's *Le Zulu* written in 1977) re-enacted or satired the great kings and warriors of past history.[4] These epic themes were told in French and have been studied in schools and universities, thus attaining the status of canonical texts.[5] However, their fame in the West is largely due to the colonial imposition of traditional Western staging and technique, which left little room to move out of a French framework[6].

More traditional African productions performed as *Kote-tlon* drama, re-developed more actively after colonial rule in Senegal and Cameroon, also left little room for new feminine roles. While serving the people as a viable outlet for social criticism, it has also been criticized for being, 'conservative and patriarchal in its social vision and [for preaching] a rigid adherence to normative behavior patters and values, especially for women, who are forever depicted as fickle, adulterous and therefore potentially disruptive of the social disorder.'[7] Thus, in the late 1970s women were still left without voice and unaccounted for in the wings of dramatic productions in West Africa. It is from this wasteland of feminine artistic deprivation that Werewere Liking has emerged.

Werewere Liking and her postmodern agenda: 'We now get the histories of the unsung many and the much sung few'

Sheer lack of women directors, playwrights, dramatists and actresses has contributed to Francophone postcolonial Africa's gender gap and to the hinderance of feminine voice in the theatrical arena. While the militant, postcolonial messages of much of the literary/dramatic milieu immediately following the decolonization process of the 1970s (in most cases) in Francophone Africa was warranted in many respects, continuation of these themes seems outdated at best. The vestiges of colonialism have left their marks on Africa, this is a fact upon which we can all agree. However, as V.Y. Mudimbe has stated in his pivotal work, *The Invention of Africa*, a new African *gnosis* - a body of knowledge about/on or 'episteme' defining Africa - must be cultivated for the world. This new 'episteme imposes itself, different and opposed to its own history and prehistory' allowing new African discourses to take root and multiply.[8]

In our postmodern era of the 1990s, where old meets new, and genders criss-cross with ethnic, religious and cultural differences, the dramatist of Africa also has come face to face with the question, How and where do I negotiate old encultred French styles of drama which have been used very affectively with my own traditional forms to cultivate a third space 'in-between' wherein I can negotiate these modern questions? How can I promote a new dramatic arena where all stories are told or, as Linda Hutcheon states, promote a new narrative where 'we now get the histories (in the plural) of the losers as well as the winners, of the regional (and colonial) as well as the centrists, of the unsung many as well as the much sung few, and I might add, of women as well as men.'[9]

Werewere Liking [10] born on May 1, 1950 in the town of Bonde Bassaland (Cameroon) has fought an uphill battle both because of her gender and her 'un-orthodox' dramatic style to tackle the aforementioned postmodern questions. Virtually alone as one of the few female dramatists of Cameroon,[11] she has created a viable means - the stage - through which women may voice their roles and carve out their place in the postcolonial world. While giving voice to women, her drama also 'distinguishes itself by its powerful inspiration from tradition.'[12] Her style is truly the old meeting the new played out in the form of popular theatre which promotes dialogic, multicultural, gender and ethnic diversity where everyone may meet, as she explains, 'at last to begin a dialogue.'[13]

Through old styles of ritual theatre, dating back to an epic before colonial times, Liking seeks to not only re-discover an almost lost medium, but also to expose new young generations who have no schooling in the arts or drama. In an interview with Christine Pillot in 1990, Liking draws attention to her goal of reducing the gap between the new younger generation in Cameroon and Senegal and tradition: 'The problem of ritual theatre is, exactly that. We want to target young people, who have no training in technique, theatre [and] who don't know anything [because they] haven't had the time to have training'.[19]

By creating a popular ritual based theatre for old and young generations, Werewere Liking's larger agenda is exposed to a wide range of spectators. Her message is threefold, 1) to revitalize pre-colonial/Non-Western African forms of theatre, 2) to blend these forms with modern day gender issues, giving women voice both in cultural and social matters, and 3) to bring theatre to the people, thus tearing down the elitist barriers which were drawn both because of a deep seated Western dramatic tradition and the use of French, a language which many rural people do not know.

In order to effectively consider the work of Werewere Liking I have divided this chapter into three succinct parts. Part I considers the new agendas of contemporary Francophone theatre and how Liking's work has enhanced and enriched an original body of theatrical work in the last twenty years. Part II offers a critical feminist reading of her two plays, *The Power of Um* and *A New Earth* and how these works negotiate through ritual the clash between modernity and tradition. Part III provides an overview of the new trends launched by Liking for a new future of Francophone feminine drama.

African theatre of Cameroon: New agendas in traditional rituals

As stated above, from the time of independence to 1970, Cameroon like its fellow West African Francophone neighbors produced theatrical works which were politically engaged, militant and for the most part very masculine:

> [In 1953 in Cameroon]....the national Cameroonian discourse, the anti-colonial discourse, advocated notably
> by the Union of the Populations of Cameroon [was] aimed at independence. Literary and national discourse
> developed at the same time wholly as a male affaire, for evident historical reasons.[15]

In the early 1950s Ivory Coast dramatists such as Amon d'Aby, Bernard Dadié and Koffi Gadeau, while experimenting in new venues, continued to review the same themes of colonial conquest and historic figures which reflected the old French vestiges of the William Ponty School 'where pieces were acted out, for example, in French but the folkloric songs could be in an African language...at this time, the theatre was conditioned... there was no opportunity for exploiting other things in life.'[16]

It was into these two dramatic traditions; the masculine and the French, that Werewere Liking was born. Both in style and in theme, she has sought new inroads to dramatic production away from the 'conditioned' theatre cultivated with the aid of the French school. Like her colleague, Cameroonian novelist Calixthe Beyala, Liking has adopted a style 'which reminds one more of the magical realism of South-American authors than the typical realism of Cameroonian literature.'[17] These women have, therefore, created a new path away from their male predecessors to employ new techniques and innovations which have transformed the literary and dramatic arena of Cameroon and, indeed, West Africa.

Reviewing the Ponty tradition

In the case of the Ivory Coast, as in Cameroon, it was not until the independence movements (as early as the 1940s) that theatre became a vehicle of militancy; one which was both politically engaged and ideological. Certainly militancy is noted in plays such as *La Mort de Chaka* and *Les Malheurs de Tchakô*. In addition to militancy, social criticism is evoked in works such as *Monsieur Thogo-Gnini* and *Trois prétendants, un mari*[18]

However these militant nationalist trends, which as previously stated favored the heros of the male educated French speaking elite of newly formed African intellectual circles, founded their origins in the old entrenched French dramatist school, L'École William Ponty. The School was first founded as l'École Normale W. Ponty in 1913 in Saint-Louis, Senegal and later moved to Gorée and then to Sébikotane, Senegal in 1938.[19] Its mission was to train the native upper classes of French speaking Africa: Togo, Cameroon, Côte d'Ivoire and Senegal. The most promising students of Africa arrived to confront 'a relatively difficult and coveted entrance exam' in order to gain access to the prestigious school .[20] In 1933 in an effort to revitalize colonial education in Africa, the inspector general of schools decided to instill in his students a taste for 'folkloric research.'[21] The 'devoirs de vacances' (vacation homework) for the student was to do research on costumes and customs of his native region, and document it in the form of a report. This often elaborate information was then recorded. Folkloric research instigated among many a taste for ethnology and regional studies.[22] These studies were later encouraged to take on the form of oral reports.

It was with the same precision, and scholastic aptitude, that students were encouraged to research traditional material in order to write and act in 'native plays performed in French'[23] However plays were closely monitored by instructors to insure theatrical productions would align themselves 'the closest to European taste.'[24] The French dramatic straight-jacket left little room for deviation. From this time on, although African themes were encouraged, the W.Ponty school appealed to only the elite French speaking slices of the African population.

In the late 1940s early 50s, *négritude* and the anti-colonial struggle led many Ponty trained dramatists to leave the school and forge out on their own. Keita Fodéba, breaking with the Ponty tradition in *l'Aube africaine*, takes to heart Fanon's militant dialogue in *The Wretched of the Earth* to offer spectators a work which 'breaks totally with the William Ponty tradition' plunging into a world of lived reality and actual events. [25]

By 1960 the vestiges of the William Ponty School had been effaced from the dramatic repertoire of the Ivory Coast. After this date, dramatists were trained more in university drama courses which after independence had become more accessible to larger numbers of the population. Great names in African theatre made their mark at this time; 'The theatre of Césaire dominated this period, along with that of Badian, Bernard Dadié, Soyinka and all the Nigerian theatre which was so rich and so African in theme and technique.' [26]

Secular and historic drama: influences on Werewere Liking

In the wake of the Ponty, and later *négritude* traditions, was born a postcolonial revitalized interest in historic, ritual and secular performance based theatre in Francophone Africa. However, as John Conteh-Morgan explains in his extensive book on Francophone drama, *Theatre and Drama in Francophone Africa*, in actuality both secular and ritual theatre had always existed, they had simply been little recognized during the colonial period. As early as 1916 the French administrator to the Ivory Coast, Delafosse, remarked:

> I heard griots recite stories in which their heroes were made to speak; stories which in their hands came alive in theatrical scenes with several characters played by a single narrator.[27]

Today dramatists such as Werewere Liking continue to delve into the beauty of these dramatic genres by mixing the techniques of the old oral narrative tradition of secular theatre with that of ritual performance. In both *The Power of Um* and *A New Earth*, Liking blends the role of the griot (storyteller) and his 'tale' with an intricate ritual performance to form a net of interlaced genres.[28]

A further secular genre which has influenced Liking is the traditional *Kotéba* performance.[29] Comprised of three sequences: 'an opening ballet, a prologue and a succession of short plays' the kotéba offers spectators dance, music and drama.[30] However, as stated previously, the kotéba and its off-shoot *Kote-tlon* drama is considered conservative and often short sighted in its vision. Although usually offering commentary which is socially critical, it also reveres traditional patriarchal themes which tend to offer little outlet for modernizing the role of women.[31] Both the griot technique and the kotéba performance tend to adhere to a Western mode of staging and general style of production. Therefore, Liking as well as others (Zadi Zaourou and Senouvo Zinsou) have sought to draw on the kotéba but extend its socio-cultural dimension to touch upon modern themes which appeal to all classes and issues involving race, gender and the revision of history.

One example is modernized techniques of staging. In order to make their drama more accessible to audiences, these dramatists have sought to integrate the spectator through direct participation.[32] Thus the concept of dramatic space and distance between audience and actors is, consequently, reworked offering new modes through which to view modern issues, while engaging in a direct collective dialogue. These 'dialogues' encompass a wide range of topics extending from questions of health and healing to politics and social welfare.

Ki-Yi M'bock Theatre

In an interview[33] Liking explains that *Ki-Yi M'bock* in Bassa means Ki-Yi 'ultimate knowledge' and M'bock 'arranged universe'. Established in 1985, Ki-Yi M'bock is a theatre born from her research during the 1970s on traditional rituals, death and healing ceremonies, and initiation rites.[34] It is theatre which strives to 'respect both the rules of traditional african theatre and those of today' while using 'traditional sources which are interrogated and readapted for problems which are no longer the same.'[35]

Liking's theatre troupe is Pan-African she states in an interview; 'We are very panafrican here. There are many nationalities, that's what makes our richness.'[36] This also adds to the multiculturalism of her performances and their wide-spread appeal across Francophone Africa.[37] She not only incorporates traditional themes and language (in both *The Power of Um* and *A New Earth*, Liking has incorporated some words in her native Bassa language) but also uses various props and techniques from a wide variety of sources. One such source are the marionettes from Mali which the actors of the Ki-Yi theatre have sought to 'integrate in a new original manner into present day theatre.'[38]

Using diverse sources demonstrates Liking's efforts to synthesize a common ground for all theatres of French speaking West Africa in order to create a new unanimous voice - culturally and socially enriched. In this effort to create a theatre by the people and for the people, Liking and the members of the Ki-Yi M'bock troupe have sought untraditional methods with which to train their actors. One such method which she calls 'girophène' is a technique which 'irrigates the brain by turning it on itself.'[39] Liking explains that girophène causes the encephalic liquid to hydrate certain parts of the brain which 'are not usually very well irrigated and puts them in movement.'[40] Therefore 'if you fixate on your thoughts at that moment, you might not forget as easily. This method is a memorization technique which is widely used in Africa.'[41].

Ki-Yi also draws on other traditional African techniques in the areas of gymnastics for body mastery; KI-YI, Liking insists is 'to work concretely at a new and typically African method of training for the actor.'[42] It is through the Ki-Yi M'bock group that Liking has been able to not only touch the people with her ritual performance theatre, but also prove to the world and to Africa that an African *gnosis* - a vast body of knowledge - does exist. This gnosis promotes an artistic message which she explains shows that 'African artists can be professionals on African soil and be represented internationally.'[43]

A new venue towards a feminist African gnosis?: *The Power of Um* and *A New Earth*

The pan-Africanism which Liking professes in her work reaches beyond Africentric movements to embrace a global message which promotes a plurality of African cultures. However it is the position of women, often explored in her Ki-Yi theatre, which has set the troupe apart from more traditional forms of dramatic productions. It is here, within the larger global postmodern arena, where not only African themes are played out, but also human ones as well touching upon the most intimate questions which arise between man and woman.

In her works[44], particularly *The Power of Um* and *A New Earth*, 'Liking subverts the woman's traditional position...women impose their views in a way that makes them hammer out society's destiny.'[45] Giving power to women through voice, visibility on the stage, and acting in untraditional 'non-passive' roles, all contribute to create a new negotiating space for women; one in which they now can call into question traditional socio-cultural parts they have been obliged to play. Such feminine liberty on the stage as participating *subjectivizing bodies* allows women to 'discover that sense of freedom and of being alive as people. When tradition acts as a barrier to this then such a tradition ought to be discouraged in the interest of theatre.' Placed in terms of current feminist literary theory, Liking *multiply* organizes[46] her works so that they not only address the needs of women, but also larger social issues linked to 'being woman' within African tradition. Liking makes her mark along with other non-Western women who write and contribute to the world's literary production with the goal to 'de-exoticize the non-West, indicating the centrality of their concerns to the self-understanding of people everywhere.'[47]

This goal, or dramatic project as in Liking's case, promotes not only a feminist objective, but a humanist one as well. Once this self-understanding has been achieved women are free to establish new inroads toward the refabrication of their own identity outside the borders of male preconceived notions of how they 'ought' to be. For this reason, performance theatre has become important for a larger feminist project in Africa. The bulk of the 'communicative interaction' promoted in Liking's plays is reserved for her strong feminine characters. Depicting women as going against tradition, or questioning the lot they have been given in life, allows for the development of new paths towards original concepts of feminine identity. Liking has moved feminine space outside into the public view in order to dialogue on traditional stereotypes women have had to bear in more conventional theatre and in the home. By having women play strong roles, the dramatist shifts traditional male space, (which has always been characterized by everything 'outside': social, professional, economic and intellectual), over to women. Women, in turn, leave their traditional passive spheres of 'interiority' where all is emotional, sexual and domestic.[48] Redrawing gender space while cultivating this self-understanding of Africa and what it means to be African first and woman second, Werewere Liking builds a bridge between the ancient past and the modern future. She attests that this must be done because 'the ancient african arts affirmed themselves, that is they had something very strong, which could be transmitted. We tell ourselves that our contemporary art must attain the status of ancient art. That means that we must try to live in a true manner, without copying models.'[49]

It is, through this 'going back to,' 'seeking out,' and 're-identifying with' the ancient, while drawing new insight into the modern feminine, that Werewere Liking most formidably writes a new role for the African feminine character.

In *The Power of Um*, Liking brings to light the entrapment an ancient widowhood ritual causes her heroine, Ngond Libii Ntep Iliga, and how this enslavement does not coincide with what should be the modern consciousness of Africa: 'Ngond Libii is subjected to gender and class oppression. She is subdued by the phallocratic system which is the cornerstone of traditional society.'[50] Soo, heroine of *A New Earth*, also fights against the traditional phallocentricism of her tribe. 'Soo picks up the key that opens new doors'[51] as she forces positive change in the community, 'the structures have collapsed' she states.[52] This collapse metaphorically leaves room to build a new modern understanding of gender and of relationships between men and women.

Strong feminine roles in Liking's dramatic productions have also carried over into her prose. One of her later works, *Elle sera de jaspe et de corail*[53] with a subtitle *Journal d'un misovire*, (journal of a man hater), also delves into the realm of 'womanhood' and the difficulty a woman has when all venues are dominated by men in society. It is a blend of prose, theatre and poetry which offer a 'discourse on society, values and the future of Africa...a journal which she dedicates to the new generations which will make up Africa in the twenty-first century.'[54]

In *Elle sera de jaspe et de corail* the principal narratrice tries to write a journal but can never write more than eight pages because each time she begins she is interrupted by the dialogue of two men and their discourse on the problems of Africa.[55] The word 'misovire,' subtitle of the text, is made up by Liking to represent the predicament of a woman caught not exactly in the throws of misogyny, but nevertheless, between the diatribe of what Liking refers to as 'a surrounding of larvae, [men] solely preoccupied with their woes and their genitalia and incapable of aspiring higher than their heads, incapable of inspiring in her the grand feelings which grow...Thus she becomes *misovire*.'[56]

Collapsing phallocentric structure in The Power of Um

Although her troupe promotes pan-Africanism, Werewere Liking, curiously, has often been criticized for writing ritual theatre which only appeals to the Bassa people because it inherently draws on only their customs as Conteh-Morgan, citing Anne-Claire Jaccard, suggests: 'Werewere Liking's research is too complex and rooted in the Bassa cultural universe to appeal to a public of non-initiates.'[57] Often her plays have been faulted for being too esoteric and ritualized within a world of symbolism and 'gestures, costumes and sounds and of the repetition of songs, dances and movements' which are not universal among all African tribes.[58] Yet Conteh-Morgan points out that her work marks a 'departure from anything yet produced in Francophone Africa. . .[even though] it has been described as 'provocative, impertinent and obscure'[59] And, although the rituals are perhaps indigenous to the Bassa people, her underlying message is universal: women in the modern world must be given a chance to change their place and role in culture and society.

Her plays often have no 'plot' *per se* and are mainly vehicles of communicative language. Drama rooted in Bassa rituals of healing, initiation, and death provides the foundation for her work. Dealing openly with these themes allows Liking to force her audience and participants 'to overcome their traumatic experience, as successful ritual ceremonies allegedly do: to 'heal' and restore them.'[60] Thus, the ritual performance becomes a sort of collective catharsis where audience and actors cleanse themselves in order to see more clearly; to open themselves to change.

The Power of Um, based on a ritual for the dead that is still performed in Bassaland today, is adapted by Liking to promote a double message. The dramatist seeks in her story of the death/widowhood ritual to bring to light not only the unfairness of certain ceremonies which disfavor women in Bassa culture, but also to condemn the mediocrity and hypocrisy of African governments which have often manipulated the people of Africa since the end of colonialism. However, the idea and practice of 'ritual' as Liking uses it, may be viewed in two different ways; first, in its negative form of a widowhood ritual which is old fashioned and oppressive for women, and secondly as a collective play of reconciliation where both actors and spectators reflect upon their actions in life; as Asanga points out, 'Liking's drama ...is essentially concerned with laying bare untamed passions and survival instincts in the community'[61] The Ritual play as developed by Liking has three phases: 1) the crisis, 2) the accusation and 3) the confession/purification[62]. The end-result of the process leading from the crisis to the confession through the accusation is the purgation of the disruptive forces in the whole society. Hence the purification and restoration of peace and harmony that generally ensue at the end of these rituals.[63]

The word 'Um' in the title of Liking's 1979 play, 'refers to the second most important deity in the Bassa pantheon.'[64] As the goddess of fertility, purity and peace, she is believed to provide for her people rejuvenation and to ward off both individual and communal bad luck. Um is the most revered daughter of the water spirit. She is also the goddess of dance, music and theatre.[65] The Um cult is one of the most popular among the Bassa people because it generally is open to young people and women '....some of its rites, particularly the fertility and healing rites, were accessible to women and even to children, though they could not become members of the cult.[66]

Crisis, accusation and confession: 3 phases in The Power of Um

The Power of Um (1979) begins with Ngond Libii Ntep Iliga (literally, the slave woman of Ntep Iliga) singing a funeral song to bury her late husband, Ntep Iliga, whose remains are unburied as of yet. Her desperation is not over the death of her husband, but over the spent life she has wasted by his side:

> In desperation, I extend my vibrant eyes, I extend myself...I extend my syncopated voice, I extend myself...I extend my clasped hands towards this dead eye, the lantern that no longer shines for me in this time of crisis....(28)

Since according to Bassa tradition death is never accidental, but always due to someone else, the communal question is raised of who committed the crime and caused the death of Ntep Iliga. Ngond Libii shows little remorse over her husband's death remembering him as 'dirt...He does not deserve to be mourned' (30). She then shocks the spectators who have gathered to pay homage to the man they remember as 'a lion' by stating that she is responsible for his death:

> I could tell you the story of Ntep if it were not a story to make someone with an empty stomach throw up. I have killed no-one else, I have killed my husband, not that of another woman, I killed my own husband! And if Ntep had nine lives like the one that he has just lived, I would kill him nine times. Bury him, he is already fouling the air. Bury him, and have wine to drink. A dirty story; how does one tell you the story of Ntep? (31)

However, her confession seems to go unnoticed as the collective body shouts: 'It is the fault of the West'(31-32). The blame is thus shifted to a collective outlet; one which is exterior and over which they have no control. The collectivization of the condemnation alludes to the tribe's larger concern of seeking to blame 'something' for the social ills they are facing. Thus Ngond Libii's husband's death is but a catalyst for a larger soliciting of justice. This justice is sought from the *outside*; from history and from current post-colonial socio-cultural strife. Ngond Libii tries to draw attention to her individual plight and the degraded life she lived while her husband was alive.

> My father provided me with the most varied and richest herd of cattle and with the most practical trousseau. Ntep gave out my cattle and destroyed my furniture. Moreover, he exploited my health and myself, and I was not aware of anything. I preached love where force was needed. He convinced me of that. (36)

However, this lament does not obtain her any sympathy from the crowd. As if to reign them back in and force them to take stock of the situation, she turns on them, accusing them of her husband's death:

> Murderers! Vampires! It is you who have killed him. You imprisoned him in a carcass which he dragged about throughout his life to protect you and your blasted tribe, your wretched traditions, your monstrous customs, all manner of things whose understanding you lost a long time ago because of laziness and meanness...Yes, meanness! That's all that inspires you at present...You have wronged us, you have killed and eaten him; only a carcass is lying there and it still attracts you, that is why you don't want to bury him; you are hungry and you want more to eat...Murderers, vampires, no! Bury him! I pray you, bury him, I will give you what to eat. You will be feted...(39)

The give-and-take of social blame and the 'stock-taking' of the entire tribe pivot back and forth between the woman and the crowd. The collective body matches her accusation with their own views and their own woes of self degradation and lack of traditional values which eventually overshadow the death of Ntep and the need to find the murderer as they realize their own lowly plight in life. Subsequently, one voice in the crowd ends the banter and brings everyone together with cultural questions that affect everyone present:

> Only he who has seen nothing likes to recount the story of his life. How will I tell such a thing to my father in the other world?: 'We don't even know how to perform a ritual anymore!' What are we witnessing today? Is it a ritual for the dead? Is it a mourning rite performed on the ninth day, or is it a memorial? What is all this muddle? (39)

This collective confession marks a pivotal instance in the play. It is here, through the cathartic element of Ngond Libii's accusation and the death of Ntep, where the Crowd realizes that they must mend their ways of decadence and self betrayal. There must be found a way to recapture old traditions while still advancing in modern times. They realize that it is Ngond Libii who has pointed this out, and therefore, she is finally acknowledged for her ideas and clear vision, as a second voice from the Crowd exclaims:

> It is nobody's fault if you are not creative; did you hear what the woman said? It is necessary to create...Seek to give meaning yourself to expressions offered to you. Consider this new ritual aesthetics: repetition which shocks and compels one to react, incantations which awaken superior forces, cyclical progression which liberates one from time and space, the gesture which rekindles long-forgotten wisdom and revitalizes language...And then, what a performance, Listen to the choruses...Narrators, narrate! That's good! One finds in it what one wants, tell your story! One finds in it what one wants, that is good! (39-40)

The self criticism of the crowd continues until the children of Ngond Libii interject their views in support of their mother's words against the community. They act as mediators who strive to negotiate the identity of the defunct father between their mother's hatred for him and the crowd's idolization of his heroic deeds. The first daughter cries, 'He is not dead, my father shall not die...he is alive in the ambitions which he abandoned, and alive also in your weaknesses which he embraced. He is not dead, my father shall not die; why would I cry?' (43). Such mediation may be viewed as, again, the search to negotiate the ancient traditional rites of the past with the modern ideals of the present. There is a sort of cleansing, of putting into place, so that the community can all understand and recapture their dignity in order to be alerted to the new demands placed upon them.

The last part of the confessional 'setting things right phase' comes with the resuscitation of Ntep Iliga himself. As he rises back from the dead he is endowed with a new clarity of vision. It is he who finally tells the audience his own views on both his individual murder and the general cancerous state of the community:

> Gosh...What a story! who could have believed it? See how they refused to bury me...All that for what? All of them say the opposite of what they think...The very one who poisoned me gets up and says:' he was among the 27 celebrities of his father, the source of pride for the whole tribe..' and HE killed me! ....And my wife..my word! She has gone mad. She couldn't stand it anymore and so she killed me in her dream. And my poor eldest son who wants to outlive the tyrants, when he is the king of tyrants. Rogue! (47)
>
> . . . Politics has never served the people. . . . The people think that politics means the quest for power. And power has never served any objective other than to enslave the people. But with time, the people will understand that, for power to be effective, however slightly, it must remain upright, apprehensive, alert...only such apprehension can force it to let some crumbs fall down to the people. Any firmly established power becomes a monarchy and . . . 'Inch Allah!'. The people will understand that and..but enough said. A dead man must stay in his bed, mustn't he? They will end up burying me, I hope. . . . An honest corpse must know how to decompose. (47)

He returns to his bed. There is a certain resolution, or cleansing between Ntep and the crowd, however Ngod Libii still very much needs to be heard. As Conteh-Morgan points out in his reading of the play, she 'does not revolt only in the name of women. For the very ancestral traditions whose shackles have kept her prisoner are also responsible, in her view, for ruining many a man, including her husband.'[67] In her last long monologue she reviews the roles both she and her husband have had to play because of the social barriers which hemmed them in:

Let the waters of my anguish flow...Yes, it is important for me to understand that man is weak, to recognize that he is wicked to others and sincere to me, and forgive him for sleeping with my girl-friends on my bed because he deserves comfort and a warrior's rest. I must be a partner in the struggle against opposing ideas, I must fight against sleep and hunger; I am an ascetic woman, one who feeds on hope; I must fight against loneliness so that he should have company, I am a cerebral woman who knows how to occupy herself; I must fight and especially understand and forgive...'You understand, don't you...certainly, you understand, no?...' No! Forgiveness has the overtones of imprisonment and understanding has the sense of surrender. Woe betide the one who loses his head! Forgiveness has the taste of cold ashes and it has no hole in which to deposit pollen, no!...I don't wish to understand anything anymore, the cold, the loneliness, no! I don't want to understand anybody anymore, O mother!...(52)

The cathartic release of Ngond Libii's monologue is also an invocation for all women who have been left widowed, betrayed and lonely by men. It is meant to force both actors in the play and spectators to review their own views on the position of women in society. However, Ngod Libii refuses to be a martyr, 'I am especially not an understanding woman..' (52), she simply demands to be heard and to be reckoned with on a social level. Her appeal, at first to change the lot of women, is transformed into one of a broader social level. She seeks an active role in the making of collective harmony and well-being. Ngond Libbii becomes the necessary catalyst and positive power which will turn the collectivity around and, therefore, save her society. Empowered with a clarity of vision she uses her strength to mediate between the crowd and their despair over their own mediocrity and hypocrisy. In her last few lines, Ngond Libii appeals to the community to change for the benefit of all:

What is the weather like for a lonely soul frozen by fear, the core of your heart splintered in a thousand pieces of sacrificed dignity, all ready and good for the undertaker...a piece from a friend betrayed...a piece from a wife deceived...a piece from a daughter sold...a piece from a brother slandered...all in crumbs of dirt...and no bits of love to the point of losing one's honor. What is the weather like in the cold? (58)

As a result of Ngond Libii's appeal, the community repairs itself 'We shall pour palm-oil on the dying fire, And from the ashes will spark new light' (58). Even Ntep Iliga, rising from the dead, pardons his assassin in order to reinstall peace within the community: 'May there be peace...' (59), 'May energy and power descend upon us' (60).

Even though she inserts women in strong roles in order to make her audience re-view the larger feminine place in tradition and society, seeking to promote what she calls 'la voix féminine' of her work, she does not wish to marginalize men:

When I write, I do not feel that I'm either man or woman. I suppose that there are different ways to see, that there exists a feminine sensibility and a masculine sensibility which are not expressed in the same forms.[68]

Liking's objective is rather to appeal to the universal, it is truly to create a new African gnosis where both men and women will, she states, 'interrogate new forms [and] search in other directions' within the arena of literature.[69]

A New Earth

A New Earth (1980), Liking's dramatic work also based on Bassa ritual, touches upon some common themes of *The Power of Um*. Soo, whose name also means 'passionate female militant' and 'exaggeration' in Bassa, acts as the conscience of a group who has lost its way morally, traditionally and culturally due to corruption and inertia.[10]

The play's sub-theme is based on the legend of *Koba and Kwan*, brothers who are ancient legendary heros in Bassa culture. They were responsible for first leading the Bassa people to their new homeland in Cameroon. Koba and Kwan are linked to a secondary legend, brought out by Liking, known as the 'myth of Ngog Lituba.' Ngog Lituba is a place of calamity for the Bassa people, situated in the Sanaga Maritime region of Cameroon, but avoided at all costs by the Bassa[11]. It was from here that Koba and Kwan led the people to safety. Ngog Lituba is thought to have perhaps once been a Garden of Eden from which men were chased away because of their lack of love for their wives, or if they forgot to pay homage to the gods.[12] In any case, Ngog Lituba became a site to avoid.

Another important legend is that of Ngue, a principal god in Bassa cosmology. He is the god of power, justice and authority and appeared to a woman called Soo whose name also represents 'first woman in Bassa culture.'[13] Ngue's head is shaped like a ram, upon seeing it, Soo became frightened and fled to tell her people. The tribe returned to see the apparition itself. However, the men, upon seeing the power the god represented, chased the women of the tribe away in order to gain all the knowledge for themselves. The men later established the Ngue cult which was responsible for wielding judicial power, 'enforcing high moral values [and] thus combining political, judicial, and religious authority both at the individual and the community levels.'[14]

Liking takes these legends and subverts them to question the all male authority set up by the Ngue. Her objective is to demonstrate how this authoritative system has not only oppressed women in Bassa society, but also has been responsible for corruption, waste, poverty and general inertia within the tribe.

The play is divided into three parts: the 'first,' 'second' and 'third movement'. As a musical score, the 'first movement' introduces the audience to the rhythms of the play which will set the tone and carry through the second and third movements to the play's end. In the same manner as *The Power of Um*, Liking divides her dramatic work into the three phases: crisis, accusation and purification.

Soo is the first to accuse. The object of her accusation is Nguimbus, her husband who is also the village intellectual. She chastises him for his lack of conviction, action, drive and willingness to speak up in the name of change. Nguimbus claims that the time is not ripe for change, while Soo responds by saying that waiting and inertia have been responsible for the downfall of their people. This demise has been brought on by colonialism, poverty, and a lack of cohesion within the tribe:

> Wait till we are soiled right down to the soul...until the uncircumcised people desecrate all our secret places...You are waiting...And our brothers are dying in exile...Women are losing their dignity...Children are being uprooted. The country is being partitioned and sold out in silence...What else are you waiting for? (65)

Nguimbus, replies:

Just think of the blood shed unnecessarily...The country has suffered too much... The people are tired of losing even though they are right! All the heroes are dead and buried...Let's play the game like everyone else...Nothing lasts forever...(65)

The first movement concludes with Soo, exasperated by his impotence, exclaiming, 'No! I don't want to rot! And I shall not be the prisoner about to be hanged' (66). She runs off leaving Nguimbus shocked and waiting by the side of the road.

In the Second Movement Liking physically shows the products of corruption and poverty of a tribe in modern times. Her stage is a garbage dump made from 'the ruins of the village where are strewn, here and there: rickety seats, leaking saucepans, old calabashes, rusty guns, a whip...palm-fronds, a large key..'(66). The one emblem of curiosity is Ngue, 'The Old Ram Mask' placed on top of a pile of rubbish.

What ensues in the second movement of the play is a collective body of accusations between characters which represent different pluralities of the society: People who speaks in a universal tone for the tribe, Chief a corrupt and fallen leader, Cop the military underling manipulated by the Chief, and Nguimbus and Soo who act as revealers of the Truth.

Through these metaphorical personae, Liking draws the attention of her audience to the modern predicament of the independent African state. It is a global message which exposes the lack of many African governments to a commitment of democratic and just processes. It is equally the accusatory summary of the overwhelming legacy of colonialism that will mark Africa forever unless change is made. The Chief who 'now depends on [his] gun in order to maintain the balance of his shaky throne' (68) exclaims, 'I am a martyr' (68). The Cop responds, 'But you are the chief: you have the throne, that compensates....And what about me? All my life, I wear boots and white gloves, in all seasons, to serve this ungrateful people...'(68). Their bland complaints are a parable for the military inept discourse that has ruled post-colonial Africa for more than twenty years.

The character, People, accuses the leaders of tearing the tribe apart by their diminished judicial and moral values: 'Bandits, prostitutes that's still us. They are our armed hands. They are our strategists. Do you presume to protect us against ourselves? As for poverty...' (69). Soo and Nguimbus also step in to add their accusations:

Nguimbus: 'These are our ruins. You have ruined us! These represent the failure of our hopes. You have desecrated us, plundered us. You've killed us!' (70)

Soo: 'Waiting in one's loin-cloth for the petrification, putrefaction, until one is dead flat and finished.' (70)

The intensity of the accusations increases until the Wise Man and the Child enter. It is the Child who finds the mask of Ngue and picks it up. The Child and the Mask become the centering force which turns the play around. They act as catalysts for a new vision. The Mask is viewed as a link to the past which will, through understanding of lost tradition, provide a means to cope with the future:

Wise Man: 'You reflect back to Man his image twice enlarged,
And Man is ashamed...,
The consciousness of his shame is his hell on earth,
And Man kills his god.
And Man without god dies,

When the reflection on water dies...' (72)

His words freeze all characters on the stage. It is here where the 'taking stock' and purification, so widely used by Liking, take root. People exclaims, 'We must build a new village!' (73). But, as Soo remarks, this rebuilding must take place carefully so as to not reinstall the same corrupt practices they all know too well, 'not to transfer unwholesome things to the new village' (74). The key to a new beginning lies in rediscovering the past, as Ngue the Mask (which now possesses a voice) points out:

> I am the sum total of the past and the present
> Your experience and that of the ancestors
> I cannot be worse than yesterday
> And I must become better than today.
> In order that there should be more light. (77)

The ancient story of Koba and Kwan is interjected, as Liking allows her characters to discover their new earth. The whole tribe walks towards the east, representative of a new dawn and a new beginning. As in the legend of Koba and Kwan, Soo and the others begin their journey. People reiterates the story:

> Courage, I am picking you up as did Koba and Kwan:
> They crossed the White River on a 'Likogui' leaf.
> They paddled, they swam.
> And they arrived at The Hollow Rock
> On the threshold of a new earth (81)

The Child concludes the Second Movement with the words, 'And unity shall reign!' (86).

The Third Movement is the dawn of a new beginning. Its peacefulness begins with 'early morning, The place is a clearing on the slope of a mountain, The birds are squealing, Nature is singing, All the characters are seated in a circle' (86). As in the legend of Koba and Kwan, the people have brought with them only precious objects which will help them rebuild their new lives. Werewere Liking's important message in the concluding scene of her piece is the necessity of a unity of the people; 'And unity shall reign! Unity shall reign! There shall be unity!' (87). Within this unity there is equality between men and women and the restoration of peace and harmony within the community. As in *The Power of Um*, the ideal of continuity through remembrance of legend and tradition in addition to recognition of present modern conflicts which will continue to manifest and threaten communal harmony are Liking's principal messages at the end of the piece.

Werewere Liking uses her feminine characters, Soo and Ngond Libii, to propose not only a new, more emancipated and modern view for women, but also to pay tribute to the oral stories and traditions for which they have been responsible for generations. It is the women who have forced the community to look at itself, to take stock, and to remember the traditions of their tribe. It is these same traditions which will be handed down as a means through which other themes may pass leading to the more modern and untraditional. Liking attests here in an interview with David Ndachi Tagne in 1989 the importance of the communication of traditions in her work:

> We are inspired by mechanisms and techniques of the communication of traditional rituals. My theatre and

my literary works rely on this same source. But, oral literature only influences the form of these works, which generally, relies on other genres at the same time. The thematic, alone, is more modern and current."

As Liking asserts through her revitalization of the ritual performance, it is primarily women who have provided the link between that which is traditional and should be revered, and that which is contemporary and should be embraced in order to benefit all of the community. In terms of theatrical production, a review of women's place and roles is also necessary because since the dawn of the postcolonial era, women's contribution has rarely been remarked:

> The texts of Liking…invite us to a new reflection on the situation of postcolonial Africa and underline the fact that we must henceforth count on the voice of those who have been absent since the first nationalist struggles."

Language: French and Bassa

Werewere Liking had very little formal schooling. While most girls her age where being exposed to Western culture through the vestiges of the French educational system in Cameroon, a hold over from colonial times, Liking was learning the traditional lore of her Bassa culture. It was only much later in life when she taught herself to read and write in the foreign language." Her later friendship and professional work with Marie-José Hourantier, a French woman with an acute interest in African, and particularly Bassa traditions, cultures and folklore, also was of benefit to Liking's development in French. There was a mutual exchange of information between the two women from 1977 onward. Hourantier was able to gain from Liking a significant amount of Bassa cultural knowledge, whereas Liking improved her level of French education immensely with the aid of Hourantier. In 1979 both women moved to Côte d'Ivoire in order to pursue their careers: Hourantier taught drama at the Institut de Littérature et d'Esthétique Négro-Africaines at the University of Abidjan and Liking developed the Atelier de Recherche en Esthétiques Théâtrales Négro-Africaines"⁸ through which she stage her earlier plays."⁹ It is this mutual sharing of two cultures, languages and perspectives which adds to the multiculturality of Liking's work.

In both of the works cited earlier, Liking has retained words and songs in the original Bassa language in the published versions of *The Power of Um* and *A New Earth*. In *The Power of Um* the crowd, which is also the chorus, sings traditional Bassa tunes accompanied by music and dance. 'Me Ngond Libii Ntep Iliga, me nnol inlô wem Ntep' which means 'I, the slave girl of Ntep Iliga, I have killed my husband Ntep Iliga' (60) is a traditional Bassa song which Liking incorporates periodically throughout the duration of the play. In *A New Earth*, Soo shouts 'Heyoom for life!' (66). 'Heyoom' and 'Heeyoo' are traditional victory cries in Bassa which, loosely translated, mean 'Hurrah' in English (*New Earth* 89). Although the plays are written predominately in French, the periodic interjection of the Bassa traditional words and music reminds readers and French audiences that Liking owes no allegiance to one nationality. This melange of words and music demonstrates Liking's commitment to her individual style which is beyond the constraints of any one tradition. Her theatre is truly that of the 'dream, trance and spirit-possession techniques, of an intricate symbolism of gestures' all of which make her dramatic production original.⁸⁰

The Future of Francophone African Drama: Beyond the 'Post-colonial'

It is clear that Werewere Liking's ritual performance theatre is leading Francophone african theatre, as one columnist put it, 'out of the doldrums'[81]. Her use of ritual performance, which involves both participants and actors and brings theatre to people from the poorest areas of Cameroon and Senegal to the elite upper classes, stands alone in innovation.

In addition to her unusual dramatic style and the untraditional views of socio/cultural themes she shares with her audiences (the role of women in and outside the community and her political criticism), Liking seeks to bring to the dramatic world the beauty of what she describes as both the spirituality and the 'physical plenitude' of life that are inherent in every culture. Each person must go back and discover his/her roots, traditions and rituals. In this respect, her plays are universal and multicultural because they require a certain will, as she states, 'to see differently'[82]. Siga Asanga writes about Liking: 'She is like a radio which brings to a village waves from all over the world' (23).

It is this will to see differently which contributes to the gnosis of the African, not postcolonial, but postmodern world. Liking and her contemporaries are seeking out new modes of expression; ones which incorporate, as stated previously, both the old and the new of indigenous culture and history. In pursuit of this new expression Liking's dramatic project forces us to acknowledge that perhaps it is time to review the word 'postcolonial' itself. The hinderance of 'postcoloniality' and the cultivation of militant male discourse in the years immediately following independence in Africa for women have been obvious, but the implications of the term 'post-colonial' extend further. Anne McClintock in her article, *The Angel of Progress: Pitfalls of the Term 'Post-Colonialism'* suggests that, although many of the influences of the colonial power have been erased from literary production by contemporary indigenous authors, intellectuals and scholars, Western insistence on the use of the term 'postcolonial' to define their work needlessly places these authors in a 'hybrid state.' This split state suggests that the West retains a 'reluctance to surrender the privilege of seeing the world in terms of a singular and ahistorical abstraction'; that of the colonizer's.[83] Are we therefore forever going to categorize literary production from the non-Western formerly colonized world as 'post-colonial'? In the case of Cameroon and the other countries of West Africa where independence has now been in effect for almost thirty years, insistence of this 'postcolonial' state[84] seems somewhat ludicrous.

Use of the term 'postcolonial' has continued to cultivate the idea of the indigenous formerly colonized people's (of Africa and elsewhere) reliance on colonial motifs and influence of 'foreign' languages: English and French.[85] This reliance has carried through from nineteenth and early twentieth century views of European travelers/colonists to and in Africa who placed the African in certain time frames that, V.Y. Mudimbe states, 'localize African cultures as 'beings-in-themselves' inherently incapable of living as 'beings-for-themselves.'"[86] Time has overcome the legacy of the prepositional ahistorical ideal the 'post' evokes. The African author has now emerged into a new era and identity promoting a gnosis of literary production which reflects the historical past, the present and new aspirations for the future.

Werewere Liking takes us away from this hybrid, postcolonial state, beyond to a new view which promotes a new African historical practice. She seeks to question the legacy of both colonial and postcolonial history which have hindered the development of Africans 'being-for-themselves' in favor of creating a new African gnosis which in terms of Mudimbe's text will redraw the lines of historical and cultural time. Her going back into tradition and ritual practices to the timeless representations of her people have given Liking 'the voice of vision of her time' which is one that shows the African at a crossroads of 'social, moral, cultural and political impasse.'[87] Such a vision has led Africans, as Siga Asanga suggests, 'to recreate their gods' and to realize that 'they cannot achieve their collective destiny if they keep on merely copying foreign models and values'[88]

Going beyond the European episteme of nineteenth and twentieth century static colonial time will reshape the destiny of Africa and help heal the open wounds of colonial oppression and postcolonial corruption allowing for 'real salvation [which] will only come through the integration of all the elements that have helped shape Africa's destiny...among these, the traditional elements [which] are by far the most important.'[89] Through art and theatre, Liking attests, a 'divine spark' will be found in human beings. It is this spark she says which will guard the people of Africa from total corruption and lead it to rebirth:

> ..this divine spark which is in human beings, cannot submit to total corruption. Even if we have the impression at a certain moment that everything is corrupt. It is not because the diamond is covered in mud that the diamond becomes mud. I am not worried, I am sorry sometimes to live in this period where we have not attained the hour of shinning in the sun...by ourselves. I think that work is underway. A birth is preparing to be born. And we, all that we are trying to do is to bring to our little stone this rebirth.[90]

It is this divine spark in her theatre which is reshaping African notions on feminine participation in the socio-cultural and political arenas of Africa. Werewere Liking's calling into question the terms of postcoloniality and her contribution to a new African gnosis will take African theatre and artistic contributions from a multiplicity of areas into the twenty-first century with strength and grace.

Notes

1   Frantz Fanon, *The Wretched of the Earth*, (New York. Grove P, 1963). Trans. C. Farrington. *Les Damnés de la Terre*, (Paris, Maspero, 1961).

2   Kristin Ross, *Fast Cars, Clean Bodies: Decolonizing and the Reordering of French Culture*, (Cambridge, MIT Press, 1995). p. 159.

3   Homi K. Bhabha, *The Location of Culture*, (New York: Routledge, 1994). p. 41.

4   John Conteh-Morgan, *Theatre and Drama in Francophone Africa*. (Cambridge: Cambridge UP, 1994), p. 174-175.

5   Ibid., p. 2

6   John Conteh-Morgan writes in *Theatre and Drama in Francophone Africa* that since the early 1970s Francophone drama 'has emerged as one of the fastest-growing areas in African literature, with a significant corpus of published plays that today stands at more than 300. And this does not include the several hundreds, in countries like Burkina Faso, or literally thousands, in places like Cameroon, that exist only in manuscript form but are regularly staged to live and enthusiastic audiences' (2).

7   Conteh-Morgan, p.39.

8   Mudimbe, V.Y. *The Invention of Africa: Gnosis, Philosophy, and the Order of Knowledge*. (Bloomington: Indiana UP, 1988). p. 25

9   Hutcheon, Linda. *The Politics of Postmodernism*. (NY: Routledge, 1989). p. 66.

10 Liking took her name from her husband from whom she was separated in 1978. The name 'Werewere' in her native Bassa language means 'velvet.' A term, the translators of her two most popular plays, *The Power of Um* and *A New Earth*, state 'was meant to reflect her mother-in-law's perception of her as a soft, young bride of 16" (Asanga, et al., 7).

11 John Conteh-Morgan writes 'Whereas Francophone Africa can boast important female writers in the novelists Mariama Bâ, Aminata Sow-Fall (Senegal) and Calixthe Béyala (Cameroon) and in the Ivorian poets Véronique Tadjo and Yanella Boni, it has produced only one female dramatist of stature, the Cameroonian Werewere Liking' (211). There are two other women who have occasionally written for the stage in Francophone milieus: Josephine Bongo (*Obali*) and Rabiatou Njoya (*La dernière aimée, Toute la rente y passe* and *Ange Noir, Ange Blanc*) (CM 211).

12 Asanga, Siga et al. *Introduction to African Ritual Theatre: The Power of Um and A New Earth.* Trans. J. N. Dingome et al. (San Francisco: International Scholars Publications, 1996): pp. 7-24.

13 Makehle, Caya. 'Elle sera de jaspe et de corail,' in Notre Librairie Vol. 79 (1985: p.43.

14 Pillot, Christine. 'Le 'Vivre vrai' de Werewere Liking,' in Notre Librairie Vol. 102 July-August (1990): pp.. 54-58. All translations from French to English are my own.

15 Briere, Eloise. 'Problématique de la parole: le cas des Camerounaises,' in Esprit Créateur Vol. 33 No.2, 1993: p. 95.

16 Kotchy, B. *'Discours inaugural,'* in the *Actes du Colloque sur le théâtre négro-africain,* April 15-29 (Paris: Présence Africaine, 1970): p. 49.

17 Brière. p. 96.

18 Kotchy. p. 49.

19 Traore, Bakary. *'Le théâtre africain de l'École William Ponty,'* in *Actes du Colloque sur le théâtre négro-africain,* April 15-29 (Paris: Présence Africaine, 1970): pp. 37-50

20 Ibid.

21 Ibid.

22 Traore. op. cit. p. 40.

23 Ibid.

24 Ibid.

25 Kotchy. op. cit. p. 47.

26 Traore. op. cit. p. 49-50.

27 Cohn-Morgan, p. 36, citing Delafosse.

28 This topic will be more fully discussed in the narrative analyses of these two plays in part two of this chapter.

29 'Kotéba' literally means 'traditional performance.'

30 Contch-Morgan. p. 38.

31 Ibid. p. 39.

32 Ibid. p. 46.

33 See the interview with Christine Pillot *'Le 'Vivre vrai' de Werewere Liking,'* in *Notre Librairie* Vol 102. July-Aug. 1990: 54-58.

34 Liking created her 'villa Kiyi' in Abidjan, Côte d'Ivoire, as a center for artists with diverse talents and as a cultural center which would offer plays, expositions and meals in an atmosphere of creativity (see David Ndachi Tagne's article, *'Werewere Liking: Créatrice, prolifique et novatrice,'* Notre Librairie, Vol 99 Oct-Dec 1989: 194-196).

35 Houedanou, Lucian. *'Le théâtre rituel,'* in *Afrique nouvelle* Vol. 1803 January 25-31 (1984): p. 12.

36 Pillot. op. cit., p. 54.

37 The members of the Ki-Yi M'bock theatre have widely traveled and performed across Côte d'Ivoire, Cameroon, Mali and Senegal.

38 Ibid.

39 Pillot. op. cit. p. 54.

40 Ibid. p. 55

41 Ibid.

42 Ibid. p. 57.

43 Ndachi-Tagne, David. *'Werewere Liking: Créatrice, prolifique et novatrice,'* in *Notre Librairie* Vol. 99 Oct-Dec. (1989): p. 196.

44 Liking, Werewere. *African Ritual Theatre: The Power of Um and A New Earth.* Trans. J. N. Dingome et al. (San Francisco: International Scholars Publications, 1996). Original titles: *La Puissance de Um* (Abidjan: CEDA, 1979); *Une Nouvelle Terre: Rituel d'investiture d'un nouveau village* (Dakar: Les Nouvelles Editions Africaines, 1980).

45 Asanga. op. cit., p. 20.

46 See Françoise Lionnet's *Postcolonial Representations: Women, Literature and Identity,* page 5.

47 Lionnet, Françoise. *Postcolonial Representations: Women, Literature, Identity.* (Ithaca: Cornell UP, 1995). p. 5.

48 See Gayatri Spivak's work, *In Other Worlds,* p. 103

49 Pillot. op. cit., p. 58.

50 Sanga. op. cit., p. 20.

51 Ibid.

52 *New Earth*. p.78.

53 *Elle sera de jaspe et de corail*. (L'Harmattan, 1983).

54 Brière. p. 96.

55 Ibid.

56 Magnier, Bernard. 'A la rencontre de Werewere Liking.' in *Notre Librairie* Vol. 79 (1985): p. 18.

57 Conteh-Morgan. op. cit., p. 212.

58 Ibid.

59 Ibid.

60 Ibid. p. 213.

61 Asanga. op.cit., p. 14.

62 Ibid. p. 12.

63 Ibid. p. 13.

64 Ibid. p. 10.

65 Asanga notes further that: 'When the Um ritual is performed, the goddess is believed to descend only after the priest, the initiates and the whole village, amid profuse song and dance, have repeatedly appealed to her in the following terms: 'A Um log ni! Um a nlôl isi maa' which literally means 'O, Goddess Um we appeal to you, do come upon us! The abode of Um is below the rock in the riverbed.' It is noteworthy that this chant which clearly points to the aquatic origin of the goddess, is taken almost word for word in the closing scene of *The Power of Um* (11).

66 Asanga. op. cit., p. 10.

67 Conteh-Morgan. op. cit., p.

68 Magnier. op.cit., p. 19.

69 Ibid. p. 20

70 Asanga. op. cit., p. 12.

71 Ibid. p. 11.

72 Ibid. p. 12.

73 Ibid.

74 Ibid.

75 Ndachi-Tagne. op.cit., p. 195.

76 Brière. op. cit., p. 105

77 Conteh-Morgan. op. cit., p. 211.

78 The atelier was co-developed with Hourantier whose help 'was favorable to the promotion of African traditional drama, most of which was experimental' (Asanga 8). It was through the atelier that Liking was able to stage several of plays in experimental performances before they were actually published.

79 Asanga. p. 8

80 Conteh-Morgan. p. 212.

81 Kimalando. B.R. 'In Search of a New Aesthetic Theatre: Liking Werewere,' in *Afrika Verlas* Vol. 20 No. 5 (1979): pp. 25-26.

82 Magnier. p. 19.

83 McClintock, Anne. 'The Angel of Progress: Pitfalls of the Term 'Post-colonialism,' in *Colonial Discourse and Post-colonial Theory: A Reader*. Eds. Patrick William and Laura Chrisman. (New York: Columbia UP, 1994: pp. 291-304.

84 The idea of the 'postcolonial state' not only carries through literature but also politically. We can easily consider current European and American socio-economic policies concerning Africa in order to find examples of the destruction this reliance on colonial ties has caused many African states.

85 However Liking and many of her contemporaries are writing more and more in their native languages, or mixing both French, for example, and Bassa.

86 Mudimbe, V.Y. *The Invention of Africa: Gnosis, Philosophy, and the Order of Knowledge*. (Bloomington: Indiana UP, 1988).

87 Asanga. op. cit., p. 24.

88 Ibid.

89 Ibid.

90 Pillot. op. cit., p. 58.

Women Playwrights and Performers respond to the project of development

Laura Box

The relationship of women to cultural, political, or societal development is ambiguous. Since women, in recent history, have seldom been agents in social or political policy-making, development has often happened around them, or through them. The trope of woman-as-cultural-vessel positions women to contain culture, rather than to define it. Women artists, particularly women who perform in public in cultures where this activity has traditionally been forbidden or constrained, seize agency and participate in the project of development obliquely . They often serve to question the direction a given developmental project (such as a post-revolutionary government) has taken. Like a grain of sand in the proverbial oyster, they irritate in productive ways.

In North Africa, formerly colonized by the French, this irritating productivity holds tremendous risks for women. These range in severity from being ostracized to being killed, especially in Algeria, where a bloody conversation is being conducted on and through the bodies of women and other social outsiders. It is not surprising, therefore, that plays by North African women are somewhat difficult to find. The texts that do exist, however, have tremendous literary, historical and sociological value because they are written from destabilizing positions on the borders of culture. Women tend to write from the outside, looking in.

In spite of the risks, a growing number of women are writing and performing plays, screenplays and performance texts in francophone North Africa. Except for Algerian writer Assia Djebar, virtually all of them are unfamiliar to speakers of English: Fatima Gallaire, Fadila Assous, Myriam Ben and Nacéra Bouabdallah of Algeria; and in Morocco, Farida Benlyazid, Leila Houari and Fatima Chebchoub. Of these, only works by Gallaire, Djebar, Assous and Benlyazid are available for the present work. Obviously, more study of this group is needed before a comprehensive treatise on North African francophone women dramatists can be produced. Nevertheless, the texts are vital to the understanding of the practice of performance by women in North Africa, the treatment of which is usually limited to ethnographic studies of more traditional forms. It is precisely in the uneasy mix of western and traditional performance forms, and in the unstable field of post-colonial francophonie, that feminine dis-ease regarding the direction of post-colonial 'development' in North Africa can be expressed.

It is needlessly essentializing to suggest that women in North Africa have a single view of how their societies should conduct themselves. North African women have a heritage of plurality. They are Arab and Amazigh [Berber]; Muslim, Christian, Jewish and irreligious; traditional and 'progressive;' rich and poor; urban and rural. They speak Tamazight, Arabic and a host of European languages. They live both inside the region and out of it. Some inside wish to leave, and some outside wish to return. One of the few things they all have in common is that their identities are overlapping, and in flux. Because their modes of self-identification and self-expression are so complex, this study can only begin to imagine what North African women artists envision for the future development of their cultures. The works discussed here suggest a desire for inclusion in the decision making processes of governmental programs, an end to the brutalization of women by conflicting patriarchal systems, economic independence, and the legitimization of a body of feminine literary, oral and performance production which is centuries old.

Patrice Pavis defines culture as a 'signifying system...thanks to which a society or a group understands itself in its relationship to the world.'[1] Two cultures create a dialogue in which the lines of communication are based, as with language, on agreed-upon constructions of Otherness. In what would seem to be a paradox, the more acrimonious the dialogue, the more need there is for an agreed-upon Other, a third party who becomes the landscape upon which the battle is conducted.

The construction of the female body as a cultural landscape/repository/artifact/ object is not unique to North Africa's dialogue with Europe, and lately the United States. Rather, it is the constructed, unchanging feminine principle which pre-figures and enables the project of culture itself. In order for North Africa to be constructed by Western imaginations as an unchanging, feminized Other, a background against which the dynamic project of Western progress is carried out, 'woman,' in North Africa and elsewhere, must signify the immobile principle which permits the masculine-principle of the Self to move and to 'develop.'

This contestedness of the female body resides in its function as a territory which may be controlled by competing masculine agents, in this case the coloniser and the colonized. As such, it is permitted no agency of its own. A woman attempting agency is subversive because she, by definition, disrupts the project of culture. In francophone North Africa (although again, not uniquely) this disruption is regarded as a harbinger of chaos (*fitna*), and is associated not only with gender but also with sexuality. As a body-object, a woman cannot be separated from her sexual 'nature', which must perform itself in strictly controlled ways in order not to invoke fitna. The mark of 'difference' between the West and North Africa lies not in the necessitated control of women's bodies, but in the form that the control takes.[2]

Performance strategies are a powerful coping mechanism. Women who have a particular set of restraints placed on their images and persons may respond by manipulating these images to their advantage, or to lessen seemingly inevitable disadvantages. They may also refuse the imposition altogether, making the project of controlling them less satisfactory for the agents of power. In order to better understand how this is done, and to apply this analysis to contemporary dramaturgy in North Africa, it is useful to first examine selected women's performance models in response to the projects of colonialism and revolution in Algeria.

Malek Alloula's *The Colonial Harem*[3] is a pictorial introduction to the notion of the colonized female body as a contested landscape. The volume consists of two elements: facsimiles of pornographic picture postcards manufactured for French consumption during the French occupation of Algeria, and Alloula's explication of them. Post-colonial studies have made much of the fact that, by selecting the postcards and arranging them in a certain order, Alloula has manufactured a product for further pornographic consumption. The images, framed by scholarly inquiry, still coerce the (now almost certainly deceased) colonized female subjects. Alloula's text has been criticized as 're-eroticising,'[4] and his agenda is certainly suspect. Continuing, and academically sanctioned, publication of the photographs perpetuates the colonizing gaze that created them. Yet they continue to be useful in providing a clear, visceral paradigm for the inscription of gender performance on a living body. They also point to the ways the subjects themselves have manipulated the image.

It is important to remember that the women pictured in the Alloula collection were *actors* - they helped to create the fantasy that was being packaged for French consumption. They were agents of the image, one which was degrading to Algerian women, but which also protected private lives from the prying eye of the colonizers' cameras. If the original aim of the postcards was to penetrate the 'harem' - a colonialist fantasy of Algerian private life - it ultimately failed. The relationship of the postcards' subjects to the viewer is that of prostitute to customer. The subject is commodified, but the subject also has at least partial control over the commodity. Since the 'scenes and types' portrayed have little or no relation to reality, it can be argued that they are cheap theatrical tricks, and that their consumers are dupes. To paint the subjects as victims robs them of the agency they obviously had.

The women in the Alloula photographs were paid for posing; their images were not stolen from them. Marc Garanger's infamous government identification photographs, published by him in 1982 and 1983, and re-published with intervening text in a photo-essay on colonialism by Carole Naggar, are another case entirely.[5] These pictures, taken some time in the early 1960s, are portraits of Algerian women, unveiled publicly and by force for what was possibly the first time in their adult lives. Many of the women are probably still alive today. As in Alloula's presentation, the aim of Naggar's article is scholarly, but this time the image is indeed stolen. Naggar correctly calls the forced unveiling and image-taking a double rape.[6] She does not, however, problematize the re-publication of the image that proliferates the act of violence. Alloula and Garanger[7] have created a dilemma for scholars who choose Algerian women as their subjects. There is unconscious ethnocentrism in the following comment about Garanger's subjects from Naggar's essay: 'Pushed from behind, they enter the twentieth century in its most frightening aspect: they are identified so they can be controlled, supervised, repressed.'[8] While this demonstrates sympathy for the survivors of photographic rape, it also presumes that they were living in some timeless, featureless, unevolved place until the moment they were photographed and denies their participation, however involuntary, in the event itself.

The subjects of the Garanger photographs refuse the project of objectification altogether. As agents, they turn the power of the image back upon itself and mutely testify against their oppressors. Their refusal de-legitimates any further use of the image, including the present one, and de-stabilizes the image as a tool for analysis. As such, the image alienates, in the Brechtian sense,[9] forcing the spectator to continually question her motive for looking.

As the Algerian war for Independence progressed, women were drawn into the struggle in various ways. Their participation crossed socio-economic lines, involving women from both the rural and urban-bourgeois classes. In the cities, their work took on a performance aspect: the veil became a manipulatable costume, and the trope of the powerless Algerian native woman so cherished by the colonizer became an effective disguise for women carrying supplies under their veils and bombs in their handbags. Some donned the veil for the first time in their lives, while others, selected for their 'European' features, were able to pass, unveiled, for French nationals while carrying out clandestine operations.[10] These women and their rural counterparts, using such performance strategies, exercised tremendous control in the course of their lives, and those of their male comrades, during the war. When the war ended, Algeria became a textbook for the ways in which nationalist revolutions all over the world have failed to live up to women's expectations. Women were touted as heroines of the liberation in Algeria, but the new nationalism required them to return to their pre-revolutionary roles as keepers of the home. They were most useful to the nation as the preservers of a re-invented, and increasingly monolithic, culture. Some of them supported the idea that women must bear this burden for the greater good of the new Algerian nation. Others rebelled. The post-war stories of the 'Djamilas', revolutionary women fighters who were jailed, tortured and raped by the French during Algeria's war for Independence, reflect this internal conflict. In 1971, Jamila Burahyd, one such Algerian national heroine, expressed the view that the nation must come first:

> The young women of Algeria don't have time to discuss the problems of sex right now. We are still in a struggle to make our new country work, to rebuild the destroyed family, to preserve our identity as a nation. In the future, perhaps, we will arrive at a kind of life where men and women relate on a more friendly, equal, and open basis. I hope so.[11]

Burahyd planted bombs for the FLN during the Battle of Algiers. She describes herself in the same interview as a mother of three, and ordinary woman who lives a simple life. She feels that her contribution to the nation must be as an exemplar of family values: 'the role of heroes is not finished at the end of the battle. It's the way they behave in ordinary life, their day-to-day actions, that is important, for this will influence others. Their lives must be based on ideals.'[12] Burahyd seems to approach the delicate negotiation of her roles as revolutionary icon and ordinary woman from a position of strength. One wonders if the same can be said of Djamila Boupacha.

Boupacha[13] was tortured and raped by the paras while being held in prison for her revolutionary activities. Released in 1962 by the Evian Accords, she moved into the Paris home of her lawyer, Gisèle Halimi, a Tunisian Jew. She told Halimi that she did not want to return to Algeria because of her fear that the 'brothers' of the National Liberation Front (FLN) would force her to assume a traditionally feminine role and lifestyle. The FLN contacted Halimi through her colleagues, lawyers who belonged to the FLN themselves, and demanded the return of Boupacha. They threatened to use force, and Boupacha went into hiding in Paris. Halimi was then approached by the 'Comité Intermouvement Auprès des Évacuées' (CIMADE), a Protestant organization involved in assisting evacuees, to set up a meeting with Boupacha. Boupacha agreed, and was kidnapped by the FLN from CIMADE offices, locked up, and shipped back to Algiers. In spite of her unremitting work defending the Algerian freedom-fighters, Halimi was denounced by the FLN. Years later, Halimi encountered Boupacha in Algiers. She was married to a maquisard, and was working as a secretary at the Algerian Ministry of Employment. Remarkably, the French feminist/existentialist philosopher Simone de Beauvoir sided with the FLN in this 'affair', demonstrating a decidedly unfeminist disregard for the wishes of Boupacha herself.[14]

What can be determined from this story is the extent to which the new nationalism of Algeria relied upon the manipulation and control of the images and persons of its national heroines. It also evinces the willingness of movements, both nationalist and feminist, to ignore the agency of the female individual for the purported good of the cause. This is why women performers and playwrights have begun to represent themselves through their art, often in isolation, without a direct connection to a political movement. They have become performing and writing bodies on their own behalf, negotiating the margins of language and culture on their own terms.

The study of colonialism and its relationship to the production of performance is indebted to the work of Helen Gilbert and Joanne Tompkins, who have identified a number of the strategies that are used by colonized and formerly colonized artists to destabilize hegemony and disrupt the canon of the colonizer. Although plays by North African artists are absent from their work, many of the trends that they have distinguished do fit the performances and texts by the women in this study.[15] Foremost among these are distinct uses of the body in time and space: traditional (pre-colonial) dance and music forms within the theatre format, politicized use of the physical space and costuming, non-linear temporal narratives; uses of language: storytelling techniques, pluri-lingual text and intertextuality, counter-hegemonic readings of history; and, finally, uses of distinctly indigenous ritual. There are also clear examples of the (formerly) colonized 'writing back' - sending their re-presentations of the imperial hegemony back into its gaze.

In order to consider the (formerly) colonized woman as a performing body in theatrical space, one must first examine the notion of 'theatre' as it is distinct from that of 'performance.' Many human activities have been identified as performance: dance, music, religious rituals, courtship practices, sporting events, political campaigns, conversations, revolutions and even the production of an individuated personality can all be justified as performative behaviour. Theatre is a kind of performance, the rules of which vary from culture to culture and from place to place. It differs from other performances in its manner of selecting the visions to be presented, in the conventions by which it is governed, and most importantly, in its distribution of power. In the European tradition, theatrical endeavours are most often hierarchical, and actors are usually at the bottom of the hierarchy. Hence, as performing bodies, they risk much, but have little real power in the business of re-presentation. The aim of agency is not achieved unless the vision being enacted is that of the performer herself.

Why does a performing body perform? What compels a human being to abandon the relative anonymity of a limited social sphere and step into the privileged, contested and liminal space of the theatre? And once the body becomes, notoriously, a performing body, why is it then at once both revered and suspect?

The business of theatrical endeavour is that of re-presentation. An actor does not step into the theatrical space (any space which is set apart and designated for theatrical work) in order to simply act as herself. She does so in order to present a selected, heightened vision of self: her vision or someone else's, someone else's self or her own. This envisioned selfhood, this carefully selected, crafted characterization, is launched into the theatrical space, where it lives a brief life of brilliant intensity. During this life, it is variously at odds or in harmony with other such visions and re-presentations: those of the other actors occupying the space, the director, the playwright or poet, the designers - any of whom may be the actor herself. What makes the work of the actor-performer different from that of all the other above-mentioned theatre-workers is that it is the actor's body which is exposed to the gaze of the audience, the actor's self which may be conflated with the envisioned self of the character, and the actor's mind which is (often, not always) erroneously identified as the originating site of the vision itself. In order to be an actor, the performing body must de-acculturate itself, acquiring the new 'body techniques' of the culture of actors: 'a repertoire of signs, attitudes, 'authenticity effects'.'[16] Thus, the performing body adapts itself to the project of re-producing culture.

The performing female body is suspect because of its power. In turn, social suspicion robs it of power. The entire paradox revolves on an axis stretched between shame and desire. As we have seen, both the colonizer and the colonized in North Africa have found the need to tame the performing female body. When the French arrived in Algeria, they encountered the Nailiyat, a group of women entertainers from the region of Ouled Nail whose social organization permitted them great personal freedom. They were at liberty to choose their sexual partners, but they were not prostitutes in the western sense of the term. The dances for which they were renowned were exquisitely refined, characterized by complex hand gestures. The French turned the Nailiyat into prostitutes, forcing them to dance in scanty clothing.[17] The art of the Nailiyat has ceased to exist, because it could no longer operate on its own terms. The Nailiyat were especially vulnerable to degradation by the French; as women performing within their own agenda, they were potential agents of chaos for both sides of the colonial power struggle, and had to be controlled.

The presence of traditional dance in the texts of North African women reclaims the performances of women like the Nailiyat. In Fatima Gallaire's *You Have Come Back* [*Ah, vous êtes venues ... là où il y a quelques tombes*][18] a chorus of middle-aged Algerian village women dance for each other in bursts of joy when their childhood friend comes home from Paris. By staging within her play a performance by women for women, she recalls for the viewer the fact that many of the most important modes of women's performance in North Africa take place in front of an all female audience. Not only is dance a way of 'illustrating - and countering - the territorial aspects of western imperialism,'[19] but it re-establishes female space in defiance of masculine encroachment. When that same space is violated by patriarchal authority and male-authored murder at the end of the play, the memory of the dance resonates in the mind of the spectator, placed in juxtaposition with what follows.

Fadila Assous, in her one-woman play entitled *Wounded Smile*[20], uses dance and song as signifying systems which play ironically on the tropes of nationalism and traditional Algerian culture. In one particularly humorous moment, the protagonist recalls being ordered to dance at a post-independence women's conference by a male government official who exhorts the assembled women to remain the bastions of family honour: 'Dear women! Dear mothers - Dear sisters - Dear wives! Be women!' It is obvious that it has not occurred to him to think of women in any other context. He finishes his rant by reminding the women to have many children, mind their kitchens, and, if they have extra time, to make carpets - and to dance ebulliently in celebration of the government that gives them these dicta. The elaborate sound-design for Assous' production of the piece employs several military marches which draw the audience's attention to the ways in which the project of nationalism has had a deleterious effect on the lives of two particular women, the protagonist and her friend, Yasmine. Assous portrays the protagonist, Yasmine, and the government official in lightening-quick character shifts which are facilitated by the changes in music. Contrasting with the recorded martial themes, Assous sings snatches of song in Algerian Arabic, presenting to her francophone spectators a counterpoint which is potentially linguistically impenetrable, at once a trope of culture and a sign for the self-identifying process of the protagonist herself. Assous' fragments of dance and song alienate, '...draw[ing] attention to the constructedness of all dramatic representation.'[21]

In *Au loin, les caroubiers* [*In the Distance, the Carob Trees*],[22] Gallaire employs live music in a different way. The nostalgic songs of Enrico, a young Constantinian Jewish musician, are played against a text of increasing post-independence Franco-Algerian tensions, as French and Algerian characters attempt to resurrect a friendship that endured the war. They are foiled by the sinister secrets of the colonial past. Again, the text is in French, the lyrics are in Algerian Arabic. The themes of *Au loin* are betrayal and loss; the choice of a doubly marginalized character, both Algerian and Jew, to deliver the nostalgic strain is appropriate. The musical message in Assia Djebar's *Rouge l'aube* [*Red the Dawn*],[23] the oldest of the texts under consideration, is less oblique. Co-authored by Walid Carn and published in 1960 in French, it was staged in Arabic for the First Pan-African Cultural Festival in 1969. Carn did the scenic adaptation for that production, with which Djebar took exception.[24] In a manner reminiscent of the Irish revolutionary plays of Brendan Behan, the final act stages two parallel prison scenes: first, in the women's prison and then in the men's, where an execution is about to take place. None of the prisoners know who will be chosen to die. In defiance of the ignominy of an anonymous death, and the cat-and-mouse torture of the random selection process, the male prisoners sing 'the song of the condemned': *'Je suis prêt, je suis prêt / La nuque rasée le coeur en paix / Je n'ai pas plus de souvenier que je n'ai d'avenir.…* [I am ready, I am ready / My neck shaved, my heart at peace / I no longer remember that I have no future…].'[25] The men's voices are joined, invisibly, by the women's as they reject the primacy of the guillotine, suggesting prophetically that the red dawn will ultimately be coloured by the blood of the French as well as their own.

One other use of specifically North African vocal production deserves mention here as a semiotic code for the presence of women. Ululation, a signal for joy or approval, marks the presence of women at a male circumcision rite in Gallaire's *La fête virile* [*The Manly Rite*].[26] Unseen, presumably hidden in the women's apartments of a large traditional Algerian rural home, the women comment upon the progress of the rite by giving or withholding their '*youyou*'s, circumventing the stricture against female intervention in a masculine rite of passage. It is a feminine interpolation into masculinised space. Similarly, in *Au loin*, the Algerian matriarch marks the return of her adopted French son and his Constantinian Jewish friend into her home: the ululation signals her approbation and her reclamation of Chris and Enrico as sons and members of her household.[27] In both cases, the cries mark the male child as the territory and product of the (m) Other.

Walls mark feminized space in North Africa; the interior space of the home has traditionally been the appropriate place for women. When they move outside of the walls, they are transgressing into masculinised space: dangerous territory, where they can be seen by men who are not members of their family. At first glance, women's dramatic literature in North Africa, as well imagery in the visual arts, seems overwhelmingly concerned with interior spaces. Of the five Gallaire plays discussed here, only *La fête virile* has any exterior scenes at all. Women do move in and out of the interior spaces, but only when they are in some way disturbing the roles prescribed for them, and in only one case is a woman actually seen outside. She is Sedka, in *La fête virile*, the lover of Pierre, the European stranger who will seek ritual circumcision from her village elders in order marry her. She appears briefly at the beginning of the play in a tryst with Pierre, out-of-doors and obviously out-of-bounds.

Gallaire's two one-act memory plays, *Rimm, la gazelle* [*Rimm, the Gazelle*] and *Témoignage contre un homme stérile* [*Madame Bertin's Testimony*][28], take place in claustrophobically small places: a Paris apartment and a room in a French home for the aged. *Rimm*'s one-sided dialogue with her dead mother is laden with references to stuffed corridors and overflowing rooms in her ancestral home, peopled by squabbling female mourners attending her mother's funeral the previous year. Madame Bertin is surrounded by the flotsam of her past, massive pieces of furniture which have been brought to the old-age home from the house that she and her spouse have been forced by time to abandon. In You Have Come Back, the interior space is bigger. A courtyard accommodates a large chorus of middle-aged women in the first act; the same cast doubles as a chorus of elder women in Act II. Nevertheless, the first-act dances and the murders at the end of the play strain the capacity of the space to contain them. The effect in all of these works is of walls straining to hold in check the unruly female body.

A complementary discourse which represents feminized interior space as protective, rather than constraining, is found in Farida Benlyazid's screenplay *The Gate of Heaven is Open*[29]. This text concerns the founding if a *zawiyya*, or Islamic house of refuge for women in distress, and the re-awakening of Muslim faith in its founder, Nadia. The *zawiyya* is an inviolate space which must be respected, even by patriarchs, although this particular institution is threatened by a legal challenge from Nadia's expatriated brother, who wants to sell his share of the inherited building which houses it. This piece upsets the notion that all bourgeois Moroccan women can and should remain indoors: Nadia may lose her home, and the respectability and safety it represents, when it suits the economic interests of a male relative. In addition to the women who have sought respite from domestic violence in the shelter, there is Fatima, a physics professor who locks *herself* in at night because the competing demands of a professional life in a traditional milieu have left her a little mad. Like the battered child who becomes self-destructive in order to save her parents the trouble of abusing her, Fatima locks her door to prevent herself from escaping entirely the strictures of patriarchy.

Although women in interior spaces dominate this study, there are some notable exceptions to the rule. *Rouge, l'aube* shuttles between public and domestic spaces as diverse as the *souk* [market-place], a private home, a battlefield, and the prison of the final act. Women move out of the home and onto the battlefield, they undergo hardship and violence and they finish their movement encaged in the prison. Men begin in the ambiguous space of the *souk*, traverse the battlefield, and complete their journey trapped and feminized between the prison walls. Djebar and Carn thus manipulate the theatrical space to draw powerful parallels between colonialism and the repression of women. The *souk* serves this Algerian play as a carnivalesque field of permission; a no-man's land where things are not as they seem. People and events change their shape; performances within the performance are staged. This is the home of the blind Poet, a Tiresian raconteur whose intertextual commentary on the action functions as unheeded prophesy. In addition to providing 'ritual catharsis and/or community renewal,' North African market-place oratory, like Carnival staged in formal Caribbean theatre, 'positions itself deliberately and self-reflexively as art, even if Eurocentric modes of thinking would deny it that status.'[30]

Fadila Assous takes the uses of ambiguous space a step further. *Wounded Smile* employs both an undefined unit set and a non-linear temporal narrative which allow the actor to move fluidly from character to character through space, time and even gender. Evoking both a slaughterhouse and a trash-midden, the expressionist setting is comprised of a double arch fashioned of blade-like panels. Assous moves through the arches in such a way that the playing space is an interior at one moment, an exterior the next. In the centre of the space, there is a trash heap, where the widowed protagonist painfully excavates the 'dolours of her life.' A ruined stool becomes a lost child, a rickety chair is a podium. The heap at centre-stage forces Assous into a pattern of circumnavigation, an inward spiral which becomes tighter as she plunders the heap for her story's details. Her liminal space is not a narrow margin, or a carnival, but the yawning chasm of no-*woman's* land. Assous' character is not constrained precisely because she is refuse on the trash heap, a being without worth to her society who has absolutely nothing left to lose: '*Femme libre. Femme rebelle. Je refuse de mourir.*' ['Free woman. Rebel woman. I refuse to die.'][31]

Costumes operate as yet another signifying system in these texts, one which intersects with the binary of public and private space in the discourse of the veil. Assous' character unveils herself at the beginning of *Wounded Smile*; at the end she uncovers her hair as well, simultaneously signifying freedom, exposure and derangement. Rimm spends the entire duration of her monologue packing her mother's *gandoura* robes, which occupy the space of the absent mother the way a kimono can evoke the presence of a character in a Japanese noh play. Costumes may also delineate a site of permission, as with ritualized cross-dressing. There are two transvestite characters in Gallaire's plays: the clown-dwarf in *La fête virile* and Madame Bertin herself. In both cases, drag permits these male characters to say the unspeakable, the vulgar, the obscene. By assuming feminine dress, they take on the magical ability of the uncontrolled female body to transgress, while the phallic power they still possess protects them from harmful consequences.

The pluri-lingual terrain of North Africa is slippery to navigate, but it offers women unprecedented opportunities for new self-presentations. Auto-translation, the tool of the pluri-langue, allows the writer to evade the project of culture: 'We cannot simply translate a linguistic text into another; rather we confront and communicate heterogeneous cultures and situations of enunciation that are separated in space and time.'[32]

Current linguistic tensions in North Africa have created a set of competing discourses in which languages jostle for position. Writing and speaking in North Africa have become complicated projects. Both Morocco and Algeria were bi-lingual prior to the arrival of the French. The invasion of North Africa by the Arabs imposed Arabic on the indigenous people of the region, Imazighen [sing. Amazigh], or Berbers. Moreover, Imazighen speak a group of languages with varying degrees of mutual intelligibility.[33]

In Morocco, the Arabic that is spoken differs from literary Classical Arabic because of its proximity to Amazigh languages, yet, due to Arab-identified nationalism, the official national language is Classical Arabic.[34] To make matters more complex, the French imposed their language as the mode of instruction in all of the schools in their North African colonies. It is not surprising that bilingualism has become a signifier for liminality, and that literacy is a primary marker for class. The Amazigh language is now undergoing a renaissance which disturbs the notion of francophone North Africa as an Arabic-speaking region, and French, the language of the former colonizer, is still functioning as the language of instruction in institutions of higher education in Morocco, Algeria and Tunisia. Moreover, the act of privileging of literature over oral cultural production is being questioned due to the emerging consciousness of the Imazighen.

North African writers, particularly Algerians, who choose to write in French are sometimes rejected by their compatriots for not promoting nationalism in their writing. Some experience guilt for distancing themselves from the 'mother tongue,' but find that they can say things in French that cannot be articulated in Arabic or Amazigh. This linguistic rift causes what Jean Déjeux calls 'wounded writing.'[35] Abdelkebir Khatibi articulated it thus:

> Bi-langue? My luck, my own individual abyss and my lovely amnesiac energy. An energy that I don't experience as a deficiency, curiously enough. Rather, it's my third ear. Had I experienced some kind of breakdown, I liked to think I would have grown up in the dissociation peculiar to any unique language. That's why I admire the gravity of the blind man's gestures and the desperate impossible love the deaf man has for language.[36]

The concept of *l'écriture féminine* [writing the body], promulgated by the French feminists, can be carried to new levels when applied to North Africa. Not only do North African woman playwrights write the body - that is to say write from the location of the female corpus - but they write a body, one which will represent them to the public. These playwrights are beginning to create 'bodies' of words in order to enter the contested (and liminal) space of theatrical imagination on their own behalf. Theatrical space is a battle of re-presentations, each one vying to be taken for truth. Just as a woman actor uses her body in order to construct a presentation of self, the woman writer uses words. The difference is that the woman actor may not have agency, whereas the woman writer attains not only agency, but metaphorical, if not literal, social mobility.

Like the walls of the *zawiyya*, the 'body of words' has a protective function as well. It deprives the spectator of his gaze. A performing body is subjected to scrutiny; that is part of its function. A body of words, by virtue of its agency, subverts and re-directs the gaze. If deftly done, this manoeuvre may even force the spectator to be self-reflexive. The (formerly) colonized writer also has the advantage of surprise when working in the (former) colonizer's terrain. The colonizer/spectator does not expect the terrain to be contested, nor does he expect to lose the contest. Just as some women have re-veiled in order to move more freely in hostile, masculine, public space, North African woman writers have launched their word-bodies into theatrical space in order to have a stronger, and protected, voice in their society.

Gallaire and Assous write in French with occasional interpolations in Algerian Arabic. Gallaire and MacDougall provided a glossary of Arabic terms for *You Have Come Back* when it was published in the United States.[37] Benlyazid's *The Gate of Heaven* was written in French, but filmed in Moroccan Arabic.[38] *Rouge l'aube* was performed in Arabic and published in French.[39] The playwrights' choices of language have depended on the target audience, as well as political and biographical factors and the availability of publication resources in North Africa and France. Auto-translation, with various degrees of permeability, has become a valuable tool for these artists, both to bring the complexities of the *pluri-langue* into sharp relief, and to reach the widest possible audience.

Another feature of the North African playwright's textual tool kit is the rich heritage of oral transmission of stories and poems, particularly among women. In the Moroccan Rif, for example, among the *tarifit* speaking people of Aith Waryaghar and Ibuqquyen, teenage women express themselves through the institutionalized creation and performance of poetry. Young women of marriageable age dance before a male public[40] at weddings, performing rhyming couplets [*izri*, pl. *izran*] of their own devising.[41] These women, who have been learning to compose poetry from the age of six,[42] form the bride's party [*dhiwzirin*]. They enter the performance space in groups of four, dance a shuffling unison dance, recite the *izran* individually, and finish with an undulating dance designed to showcase their sexuality.[43] The *izran* function as a way for the composers to ridicule aspects of village society, to counteract spells which have been cast at them, to appease or provoke rivals, to chide faithless lovers, and to display their charms to prospective husbands. This *izri* was designed to discourage an unwanted suitor: 'A thsib- banah-tasebnath: astsah ho fades/ Jemah zucar-inik. Nish d shik udentes [I am going to wash my headscarf; I shall hang it on the fades bush./ Take your sugar away. You and I aren't good together.]' A prospective groom brings sugar to a woman's father to open the negotiations for a marriage contract. The headscarf is the one she will wear to her wedding; the *fades* bush is used to make soap. Using metaphors for purification, the composer publicly rejects her suitor. Since she will not be present at the marriage negotiation, this is her one opportunity to make her wishes known.[44]

By presenting counter-hegemonic personal histories, as well as alternative accounts of national history such as *Rouge l'aube* and *Au loin*, the playwright herself functions as storyteller, reclaiming and giving voice to the forgotten, the overlooked, and the disappeared. Gallaire's Rimm, Assous' protagonist, Djebar's Poet and even Madame Bertin are relatives of the Rifi poet, and a host of other storytellers and poets in North African history and literature. The raconteur is a feature of African plays of the sub-continent as well, in places as diverse as Nigeria and South Africa.[45] 'Telling stories on stage,' assert Gilbert and Tompkins, 'is an economical way in which to initiate theatre, since it relies on imagination, recitation, [and] improvisation... .'[46] Storytelling subverts the colonial modes of marking time, space and memory on stage and restores oral transmission to its rightful place in societies where widespread literacy among women is a recent phenomenon. Recollections, like those of Rimm and Madame Bertin, interrogate the production of memory, while non-linear narratives, like that of Assous' protagonist, juxtapose memories and events in ways which startle and inform.

The Poet, on the other hand, provides a through line, however surreal, to the epic panorama of *Rouge l'aube*. Although he is grave and wise, he is a shape-shifter like his satirical cousin, Puff-of-Smoke, in Kateb Yacine's *La poudre d'intelligence* [*Intelligence Powder*]. A blind man who sees the future more clearly than his sighted Guide, he comments upon the action of the play meta-theatrically as he moves through it: '*Après une aube triste vient un soir de tristesse...mais je ne crie jamais a cette agonie: cesse.* [After a sad dawn comes a night of sadness... but I never cry to this agony: cease.]'[47] Only when his voice is silenced by death do the young people awaiting torture and execution give voice to their revolt in song. He presents different faces to various people in the play through his intertextual performances; the spectator alone sees them all. To the marketplace men he sings the classical poetry of Ibn al Faridh, switching to mildly erotic love poetry in order to beguile French soldiers. Finally, in open defiance, he speaks the poetry of the revolution and is martyred. Like any good orator, he manipulates his recitations to give his on-stage listeners what they want (or need) to hear.[48]

> The rituals that occur in the plays of North African women have their roots in two continents. Neither universalizing gestures nor gratuitous exoticising colour, they create a place apart, a playing field for difference: When traditional performance elements are incorporated into a contemporary play, they affect the play's content, structure, and style, and consequently, its overall meaning/effect. This process, which usually involves a departure from realism, stretches colonial definitions of theatre to assert the validity (and the vitality) of other modes of representation.[49]

Ritual addresses the large questions, pushing at the boundaries of space/time, and provides a vehicle for healing and transfiguration within the theatrical event.

Staged representations of ritual must here be distinguished from ritualized theatrical moments. Both occur in North African drama, and both have roots in non-theatrical rituals which occur among members of North African societies, either at home or in the diaspora, and in western rituals the playwrights have observed through the process of their nations having been colonized. These often intersect, particularly in the plays of Fatima Gallaire. *La fête virile*, a farcical rendering of an Algerian male circumcision rite, goes to great lengths to compare the circumcision practices of North Africa and Europe, playing on the ignorance that members of each society have about the other. Pierre, a European adult, is seeking a traditional-style circumcision in order to marry Sedka, a woman of the village. For him, the rite becomes a fetish, more than just a means to an end. As he bumbles his way sincerely through the village, he tropes the well-meaning 'colonist who refuses' of Albert Memmi, the one who wants to lose his status as ugly westerner and 'go native.'[50] He also provokes a mirroring response in the village's ritual circumciser or Tahhar, who finds his uncircumcised state fascinating. Yet, even within the format of a farce, Gallaire honours his rite of passage; the event itself is never farcalized. To the contrary, it heals a grudge held between two families of a rural village and permits the acceptance of the transfigured foreigner into their midst.

The importance of ritualized cross-dressing as a space for permission to speak the unspeakable in Gallaire's plays has already been mentioned. Drag characters, as well as dwarves, madwomen, slaves, and men who are sterile or impotent like Madame Bertin, function as bridges between binary categories, sites of ambiguity where reconciliation between opposing categories is facilitated. In *You*

Have Come Back, all of the characters of this kind are killed and reconciliation is rejected. It is this consequence which defines the play as a tragedy.

You Have Come Back places in parallel a staged ritual and a ritualized moment. The dances of the first act, specifically those which result in trance, prefigure the ritualized murders which occur in the second act. The murders are a twisted purification rite, a perversion of the Eid sacrifice, and they are carried out by old women. Old women's magical power, which is considered sinister and threatening to Islam,[51] is harnessed to the patriarchal project of cleansing the village of a female heretic, one who has married outside of her faith. In *Rimm, la Gazelle*, on the other hand, death is a beneficent thing, reuniting extended family, lovers, and a mother and daughter who were constrained from communicating freely in life. The ritual funeral in *Rimm* is lovingly described, rather than shown, but the transfigurations it creates are nonetheless palpable: not a sacrifice, but a sea-change.

The rituals of violence and death alluded to in *Rouge l'aube* are western creations: aggression against non-combatants, the colonial trail without due process, and the guillotine. Staging martyrdom is a powerful political message, but it holds certain perils, as do all universalizing nationalist projects, for women. Women do not die in *Rouge l'aube*, they watch men die. In this sense the play serves as a hegemonic, rather than a counter-hegemonic, discourse. Women did indeed die in the Algerian war for independence, but they do not appear here. Instead, they are positioned once again as vessels of culture in danger of being violated by the colonizer: they are raped. The staging of rape is difficult; unless the 'emblematisation' of the victim is somehow undermined, it may reify the trauma to the subject, in much the same way as the dissemination of the Garanger photographs perpetuates the rape event.[52] The painful rituals in *Rouge l'aube* are not countered by rituals for healing and change; as a prophetic artifact of the war years, the piece foretells the violence in 1990s Algeria. By wielding the tools of the master, the firebrands of the Algerian revolution have broken their own house and sent their artists into exile. It is as much to the neo-imperialist excesses of post-colonial development as to the past and continued cruelties of the former colonizer that North African women playwrights are addressing their 'writings back.'

Using a panoply of strategies both contemporary and traditional, women are writing plays which speak to the very issues which North Africa must face if it is to survive its present circumstances. The plays are underrepresented in anthologies and theoretical texts, and almost non-existent (the work of translators Jill MacDougall and Miriam Cooke excepted) in English translation. There are westward-directed messages in the texts wherein the formerly colonizing societies of Europe and the United States may learn to regard themselves differently, if only they have the eyes to see.

The texts contained in this study suggest the beginnings of a radical future vision for North Africa, one which takes women into account as agents, rather than vehicles, of culture. Their authors call for the safety, economic independence, enfranchisement, and legitimization of women. They are both evidence of, and a demand for, personhood. They are also a warning: the societies of North Africa and the world at large cannot continue to develop while ignoring the needs of half their citizenry.

Placing their bodies of words at the service of the madwomen who excavate the trash-middens of culture and shuttle back and forth between opposing camps, the women playwrights of North Africa bring to mind Hélène Cixous tribute to Clarice Lispector:

> She had the two courages: that of going to the sources, - to the foreign sources of the self. That of returning, to herself, almost without self, without denying the going.[53]

Notes

1 Patrice Pavis, *Theatre at the Crossroads of Culture*, trans. Loren Kruger (London: Routledge, 1992), 8-9.

2 Perhaps the most widely disseminated discourse on the subject of North African/Western difference is that of the veil. The veil has been a visible marker of the unavailability of North African women to the Western colonizer, and the West's response has been to co-opt the discourse of Western feminism, criticizing the treatment of women in North Africa to justify foreign occupation. Some men (and women) in North Africa and other parts of the Near and Middle East have responded to this aggression by defending as traditional practices such as the veil, the harem, and polygamy. Leila Ahmed points out that the veil and the corset both serve to control women's bodies, and Halim Barakat quotes Khalida Sa'id who observes that whether a woman is encouraged to wear the veil or a mini-skirt, it is nevertheless her body which is being objectified and controlled. Mernissi adds an additional insight: in a depressed economy, the veil serves as a 'division of labor,' discouraging women from replacing men in the job market. See Fatima Mernissi, *Beyond the Veil: Male-Female Dynamics in Modern Muslim Society* (Bloomington: University of Indiana Press, 1987), vii.; Leila Ahmed, *Women and Gender in Islam* (New Haven: Yale University Press, 1992), 244; Halim Barakat, 'The Arab Family and the Challenge of Social Transformation.' In Elizabeth Warnoch Fernea, ed., *Women and the Family in the Middle East: New Voices of Change* (Austin: University of Texas Press, 1985), 35; and Fatima Mernissi, *Islam and Democracy: Fear of the Modern World*, trans. Mary Jo Lakeland (Reading, M.A.: Addison Wesley Publishing Company, 1992), 165.

3 Malek Alloula, *The Colonial Harem*, trans. Myrna Godzich and Wlad Godzich (Minneapolis: University of Minnesota Press, 1986). 126.

4 Marnia Lazreg, *The Eloquence of Silence: Algerian Women in Question* (New York: Routledge, 1994), 191.

5 Carole Naggar, 'The Unveiled: Algerian Women, 1960,' *Aperture* 119 (Summer 1990): 2-11.

6 Ibid., 4.

7 For an more complete discussion of the photographic collections of Marc Garanger and Malek Alloula, see: Winifred Woodhull, *Transfigurations of the Maghreb: Feminism, Decolonization and Literatures* (Minneapolis: University of Minnesota Press, 1993), 42-46.

8 Naggar, 8.

9 As is often the case with border studies, existing theoretical frameworks are too narrow for the task of literary and political analysis. Employing Brechtian theory, one could argue that female agency in performance is inherently alienating and revolutionary. A female body performing its own story has a *verfremdungseffect* that Brecht never intended. Being Other, its presence, and its demonstrated will, are in and of themselves distancing. Augusto Boal has suggested that the empathy Brecht's texts create is a kind of politicized emotion which does not coerce the passive spectator, as in the Aristotelian model. However, there may be another explanation as to why Brecht's plays are not perfect examples of his theory. As recent scholarship has suggested, many of the strong female characters attributed to Brecht may not have been his creations, but those of his uncredited female collaborators. The fact of hidden female authorship would go a long way to explain why so-called Brechtian female characters resist alienation in favour of a politicized empathy which is neither coercive nor completely distancing. When it comes to women, our best theoretical model for analysing twentieth century revolutionary drama has a serious flaw. See: Augusto Boal, *Theatre of the Oppressed* (New York: Theatre Communications Group, 1985) 102-103, and John Fuegi, *Brecht and Company: Sex Politics and the Making of the Modern Drama* (New York: Grove Press, 1994), 261.

10 Lazreg, *Eloquence*, 121-123, and Gillo Pontecorvo, dir., *The Battle of Algiers* VHS videorecording, Stella Productions (New York: Axon Video Co., c1988).

11 Jamila Buhrayd, interviewed by Walid 'Awad, in *Middle Eastern Women Speak*, ed. Elizabeth Warnock Fernea and Basima Qattan Bezirgan (Austin: University of Texas Press, 1977), 261.

12 Ibid. 262.

13 See Simone de Beauvoir & Gisele Halimi, *Djamila Boupacha* (Paris: Editons Gallimard, 1962). Trans. Peter Green, *Djamila Boupacha, The story of the torture of a young Algerian girl which shocked liberal French opinion.* (Andre Deutsch and Weidenfeld and Nicolson Ltd. 1962).

14 Gisèle Halimi, *Milk for the Orange Tree*, trans. Dorothy Blair (London: Quartet Books, 1990) 297-301.

15 Gilbert and Tompkins' work focuses primarily on anglophone post-colonial societies which were or are part of the British Commonwealth. Helen Gilbert and Joanne Tompkins, *Post-Colonial Drama: Theory, Practice, Politics* (London: Routledge, 1996).

16 Pavis, 9-10.

17 Lazreg, *Eloquence*, 29-33.

18 Fatima Gallaire-Bourega, 'You Have Come Back,' trans. Jill MacDougal, in *Plays by Women: an International Anthology*, Volume Two, ed. Catherine Temerson and Françoise Kourilsky (New York: Ubu Repertory Theater Productions, 1988). A different version of this play has been published in France under the title *Princesses* (Paris: Édition des quatrevents, 1988)

19 Gilbert and Tompkins, 239.

20 Fadila Assous, *Wounded Smile* (unpublished video-recording), produced by Kamal Salhi, Cited with the kind permission of K. Salhi and F. Assous. Play written by Omar Fermouche, translated to French by Fadila Assous. Reference here is made to the performance at the London Royal Court, 23 & 24 June 1995, Directed by Ahcene Assous.

21 Gilbert and Tompkins, 239.

22 Fatima Gallaire, *'Au loin, les caroubiers' suivi de 'Rimm, la gazelle'* (Paris: Éditions des quatrevents, 1993).

23 Assia Djebar and Walid Carn, *Rouge l'aube* (Algiers: SNED, 1969).

24 Jean Déjeux, *Assia Djebar: romanciere algèrienne, cineaste arabe*, (Sherbrook: Quebec, 1984), 11

25 Djebar and Carn, 91.

26 Fatima Gallaire, *La fête virile* (Paris: Éditions des quatre-vents, 1992).

27 Gallaire, *Au loin*, 19.

28 Fatima Gallaire, 'Madame Bertin's Testimony,' trans. Jill MacDougall, in *Monologues: Plays From Martinique, France, Algeria, Quebec* (New York: Ubu Repertory Theater Publications, 1995; and *'Témoignage contre un homme stérile,' L'avant scène théâtre* 815 (Oct. 1987): 38-56.

29 Farida Benlyazid, 'The Gate of Heaven is Open' ['Bab al-Sama Maftuh'], trans. Miriam Cooke, in Margot Badran and Miriam Cooke, *Opening the Gates: A Century of Arab Feminist Writing* (Bloomington: Indiana University Press, 1990), 297-303.

30 Gilbert and Tompkins, 88.

31 Assous's performance. See K. Salhi videorecording, London production.

32 Pavis, 136.

33 Abdelâhi Bentahila, *Language Attitudes Among Arab-French Bilinguals in Morocco* (Clevedon, UK: Multilingual Matters Ltd., 1983), 1.

34 Ibid., 3.

35 Jean Déjeux, 'Francophone Literature in the Maghreb: the Problem and the Possibility,' *Research in African Literatures* 23.2 (Summer 1992): 8-11.

36 Abdelkebir Khatibi, *Love in Two Languages*, trans. Richard Howard (Minneapolis: University of Minnesota Press, 1990), 5.

37 Gallaire, *You Have Come Back*, 221.

38 Benlyazid, 297.

39 Déjeux, 11.

40 Roger Joseph and Terri Brint Joseph, *The Rose and the Thorn* (Tucson: University of Arizona Press, 1987), 48. See also Terri Brint Joseph, 'Poetry as a Strategy of Power: the Case of Riffian Berber Women,' in Vévé A. Clark, Ruth-Ellen B. Joeres and Madelon Sprengnether, *Revising the Word and the World: Essays in Feminist Literary Criticism* (Chicago: University of Chicago Press, 1993).

41 Ibid., 87.

42 Ibid., 90.

43 Ibid., 68-70.

44 Ibid., 92-96.

45 For satirical uses of the raconteur in Algerian and Nigerian drama, respectively, see Kateb Yacine, *Intelligence Powder [Poudre d'intelligence]*, trans. Stephen J. Vogel (New York: Ubu Repertory Theater Publications, 1985 [1959]), and Wole Soyinka, *The Jero Plays* (London, Eyre Methuen, 1973).

46 Gilbert and Tompkins, 126.

47 Djebar and Carn, 33.

48 It is interesting to note that marketplace oratory is becoming a popular performance form for women in some parts of North Africa. For an account of female marketplace orators in Morocco, see Deborah A. Kapchan, 'Moroccan Female Performers Defining the Social Body,' *Journal of American Folklore* 107 (Winter 1994): 82-105, and *Gender on the Market* (Philadelphia: University of Pennsylvania Press, 1996).

49 Gilbert and Tompkins, 54.

50 Albert Memmi, *The Colonizer and the Colonized*, (Boston: Beacon Press, 1965) 19-44.

51 For occult practices in Algeria see Lazreg, 178. For Morocco, see Susan Schaefer Davis, *Patience and Power: Women's Lives in a Moroccan Village* (Rochester, VT: Schenkman, 1987), 114-118 and Melissa L. Davies, prod./dir., *Some Women of Marrakech*, VHS videorecording, 52 min. (London : Granada Television International, 1977).

52 Gilbert and Tompkins, 213.

53 Hélène Cixous, *The Hélène Cixous Reader*, ed. Susan Sellers (New York: Routledge, 1994), 91.